INVISIBLE IMMIGRANTS

INVISIBLE IMMIGRANTS

The English in Canada since 1945

MARILYN BARBER *and* MURRAY WATSON

University of Manitoba Press

University of Manitoba Press
Winnipeg, Manitoba
Canada R3T 2M5
uofmpress.ca

Printed in Canada
Text printed on chlorine-free, 100% post-consumer recycled paper

19 18 17 16 15   1 2 3 4 5

Cover design: David Drummond
Interior design: Jess Koroscil

Library and Archives Canada Cataloguing in Publication

Barber, Marilyn, author
Invisible immigrants : the English in Canada since 1945 / Marilyn
Barber and Murray Watson.

(Studies in immigration and culture ; 12)
Includes bibliographical references and index.
Issued in print and electronic formats.
ISBN 978-0-88755-777-4 (pbk.)
ISBN 978-0-88755-500-8 (PDF e-book)
ISBN 978-0-88755-498-8 (epub)

1. English—Canada—History—20th century. 2. Immigrants—
Canada—History—20th century. 3. Oral history—Canada.
I. Watson, Murray, 1947–, author II. Title. III. Series: Studies in
immigration and culture

FC106.B7B37 2015   971'.00421   C2014-907487-5
                                              C2014-907488-3

The University of Manitoba Press gratefully acknowledges the financial support
for its publication program provided by the Government of Canada through the Canada
Book Fund, the Canada Council for the Arts, the Manitoba Department
of Culture, Heritage, Tourism, the Manitoba Arts Council,
and the Manitoba Book Publishing Tax Credit.

FSC
www.fsc.org
MIX
Paper from
responsible sources
FSC® C016245

For Betty (Watson) Davidson, who became a
landed immigrant at age seventy and, sadly,
died during the writing of this book, at the age of
eighty-three, in White Rock, British Columbia;

And for John Wesley Barber, whose ancestors
emigrated from England to Canada in the 1830s;

And for all the English immigrants who kindly
agreed to be interviewed for this book.

CONTENTS

LIST OF ILLUSTRATIONS

Figures

Tables

Photographs

INTRODUCTION

Canada is a place where you can see your dreams come true.[1]

It was a very difficult time in England and there was still rationing in many things, right up until the 1950s. And we just got tired of it. And then [we took] this visit to Canada and the United States, land of milk and honey [laughs] … then we decided it was time we got out. And that's what we did.[2]

While much has been written about Canada's many immigrant communities, the English are conspicuous by their comparative absence in the pages of Canadian history. In particular, apart from war brides, English immigrants who came to Canada after World War II have tended to be invisible. This book seeks to address this notable void by exploring the memories and experiences of English immigrants who formed part of the last major movement from England to Canada between the end of World War II and the mid-1970s.

Immigration has been a central element in the making of modern Canada. In the three decades after World War II, over 4,000,000 immigrants, including those from England, landed in Canada,[3] and in all but eight years between 1945 and 1975 the English formed the largest national group of immigrants.

Traditionally, migration histories were written from a "top down" perspective, relying on government reports, passenger lists, agency records, and other documents that leave paper trails in official records. Bruce Elliott observed that these documents "all too often highlight what the government wanted to happen rather than what really did happen."[4] To find out what really did happen one needs access to the reminiscences and experiences of the migrants themselves. Oral testimonies, such as those revealed and analyzed in this book, provide an excellent source. The recorded life stories generate rich content, providing a level of detail about the personal experience of migration often missing from most documentary sources. As migration scholars Colin Pooley and Ian Whyte observed, conducting studies of immigration without being able to interview the migrants is "like doing a difficult jigsaw in the dark."[5] Oral testimonies, however, can be problematic. For example, how reliable are interviewees' memories, and to what degree does the interviewer's approach influence what the interviewee says? We discuss, below, the steps we took to capitalize on the strengths and overcome the limitations of the life history approach to oral history.

Our recorded life stories are intensely private, often funny, and occasionally heartbreaking. Many of the English-born immigrant interviewees talk frankly about their fears, expectations, and family separation anxieties. Others refer mainly to their public lives revealing insights into how individuals and families integrated into local communities and the Canadian way of life. Some accounts are positive, others negative; some are sad, others happy; some are success stories, others are not. They reveal memories about hardship, first impressions, culture shock, heartbreak, love, family, illness, death, ambition, work, patriotism, and much more.

We start by examining, in Chapters 1 and 2, conditions in England and in Canada from the years immediately after World War II to the mid-1970s. Did the political, social, and economic climate encourage migration? What did Canada have to offer, and how did it compare with other countries that attracted English emigrants? People left England at different stages of their lives and from different backgrounds. They were children and adults, male and female, singles and families, working class and middle class. They gave various and often distinctly personal reasons for taking the life-changing step of coming to Canada. We will explore their motivations in depth, along with the way conditions and events in contemporary England and Canada influenced their decisions. For instance, in the years immediately following the war, an atmosphere of gloom and the harsh realities of austerity led over half a million English people to apply to emigrate to the Dominions or elsewhere. Indeed, so many people left England that no less a figure than Sir Winston Churchill appealed to those considering emigration to "stay here and fight it out."[6] Ten years later the economic climate was much rosier, and the English prime minister, Harold Macmillan, famously proclaimed, "Most of our people have never had it so good."[7] In spite of improvements in the economy, however, emigration continued apace and English newspapers were full of stories about the resulting "brain drain."[8] Significant English emigration to Canada persisted from the late 1940s to the mid 1970s,[9] effectively drying up toward the end of the twentieth century. The propensity to emigrate was encouraged by the competitive promotional activities of three Dominion governments: Australia, New Zealand, and Canada. We will explore the degree to which such recruitment influenced emigrants, and why Canada was the interviewees' destination of choice, rather than Australia or New Zealand, which offered more attractive financial incentives. We will also explore why English immigration then dried up toward the end of the twentieth century.

Becoming an emigrant, leaving loved ones behind, and venturing into the unknown, is a life-changing event and, for most, an extraordinarily bold and brave step to take. In Chapter 3 we look at the preparations for departure, the sadness of farewells, and the experience of the journey across the Atlantic. For some this was the adventure of a lifetime; for others seasickness and the perils of early passenger air travel proved daunting. Our interviewees were among the last group of emigrants to sail to a new land and the first to fly, initially in unpressurized, propeller-driven aircraft and later in passenger jets. These changing modes of transport had a revolutionary impact upon the migration experience.

Chapter 4 deals with the immigrants' adjustment to life in Canada—from first impressions after arriving, to settling in, building, and developing a new life. For some, adaptation happened quite quickly, while for others, it took much longer. Initial experiences were instrumental in shaping how the new arrivals consciously and unconsciously developed personal strategies for assimilation and acculturation. These processes were strikingly different, varying with age, gender, social class, and family structure or marital status. White, English-born immigrants in the postwar era seldom stood out as visibly different from Canadians; the minute they opened their mouths, however, their accents set them apart. A number of our interviewees who settled in the Montreal area felt unexpectedly isolated in francophone Quebec. They found themselves in the midst of a powerful resurgence of nationalism that became known as the "Quiet Revolution" in the 1960s. Analysis in this and other chapters provides rare insights into English-born immigrants' reactions to Canada's anglophone-francophone divide. Chapter 4 also includes an assessment of the importance of sensory perception, noting the impact of Canadian sights, sounds, tastes, and smells.

Two of the more common reasons many English wanted to come to Canada were to obtain a better job and to improve earnings. Most migrants believed they would achieve a higher standard of living. Chapter 5 explores how immigrants found work and what difficulties they overcame. Throughout, we continually assess the role played by employment in integration into Canadian society. The work patterns reflected the socioeconomic backgrounds of these postwar English migrants. While some interviewees pumped gas or worked in retail sales, most were professionals, including teachers, nurses, civil servants, and engineers. Among this number were a handful of interviewees who succeeded as entrepreneurs. The chapter traces the ups and downs of the interviewees' employment histories through to retirement and beyond. It also incorporates some intriguing reminiscences of a helicopter pilot in the Arctic and a couple who were pressured by the Royal Canadian Mounted Police to spy on Soviet diplomats.

Closely related to employment are home, family, and community life. These topics are explored in Chapter 6. Setting up home was important for families with young children; we trace how, often from impecunious beginnings, many of the interviewees strove to achieve their dreams. We also examine the different living arrangements and social lives experienced by single migrants. For many, especially families with children, suburban living and involvement in voluntary and community work were important aspects of participation in Canadian society. We also look at the role of English/British ethnic associations, as well as the role of religion. One of the consequences of emigration is that extended families and friends are left behind. For earlier generations of immigrants, separation meant the likelihood of seeing each other again was remote and communication infrequent. The introduction of passenger jets, improvements in telecommunications, and in the latter years of the twentieth century, the introduction of the Internet, e-mail, video-conferencing, and social networking radically changed the way families stayed in touch. A revolution has occurred in immigrant family dynamics.

Finally, we turn to questions of national identity—a perennially problematic and contested concept. Applying tools developed by leading identity scholars, we explore how our interviewees perceive their identities. Do they come to see themselves as Canadian? If so, what does being Canadian mean? Are they English? Are they British? Are they a combination of two or all three national identities? Or are they something completely different? In the decades following World War II, Canadian governments actively sought to change and enhance the nature of Canadian civic consciousness. One of our interviewees landed in Halifax on 1 January 1947, the day when Canadian citizenship was introduced. Hitherto, national identity in anglophone Canada had been aligned with British heritage. Most commentators would probably agree that in less than fifty years, Canadians shifted to adopt a new stance, one of belonging to a multicultural civic nation without ethnic peculiarities. These fundamental changes introduce a fascinating complexity for our analysis.

The strengths and limitations of oral history

Our approach throughout this book is to allow the voices of the interviewee migrants to be heard and to make their memories central to our analysis. While each testimony describes uniquely personal and individual experiences, there is significant overlap among the testimonies. Analysis of the testimonies identifies multiple themes, often interrelated and always rich in complexity and occasional contradiction. Our interviewees' life stories certainly conform to Michel Foucault's observation that, "the world as we know it is a tangled profusion of events."[10] It is the job of the historian to untangle confusion and to attempt to make sense of events. That is the principal aim of this book, using the actual words of the participants as the primary source. As Jim Hammerton and Al Thomson, respected oral historians and authors of *Ten pound Poms*, observed, "personal testimony enlivens the presentation of history where the stories of so-called ordinary people make history more engaging and accessible for the general reader."[11]

Assessing the benefits of oral history, Stephen Caunce wrote that "every family and every place has a history of its own, and one that can contribute detailed knowledge to the study of wider themes."[12] But what is oral history? According to Paul Thompson, modern oral history begins with recording the spoken testimonies of individuals or groups that are the subject of study. The testimonies collected become a source for historical interpretation and analysis.[13] And, as with all sources, these testimonies, preferably in audio rather than written (transcript) form, need to be subjected to rigorous scrutiny. Oral history presents a unique set of challenges to the researcher, but in a number of respects it also provides distinct advantages over conventional documentary sources, especially in studies of migration. Many professional historians, however, have been—and some remain—highly critical and skeptical toward it. In summarizing the main thrust of these criticisms, Thomson, Frisch, and Hamilton noted "that memory was unreliable as a historical source because it was distorted by physical deterioration and nostalgia in old age, by personal bias of both interviewer and interviewee, and by the influence of collective and retrospective versions of the past."[14] Clearly some of these criticisms are valid, especially concerning the reliability of memory and the potential for distortion arising from nostalgia and hindsight. While the veracity of oral testimonies can be checked by seeking internal consistency and external corroboration, our understanding of how memory works is, sadly, imperfect. Memory is a field that is now receiving considerable attention but still needs further theoretical and empirical investigation. The work of cognitive psychologists and other scientists tends to be focussed on issues like amnesia, child development, and the veracity of evidence in legal cases. For oral historians memory is also a subject of analysis and research; for them, what is remembered and how it is remembered, rather than what actually happened, are significant in understanding people's lives. As eminent oral historians Steven High and Alessandro Portelli consistently argued, this is the strength of orality "from below."[15] "Oral sources tell us not just what people did, but what they wanted to do, what they believed they were doing, and what they now think that they did."[16] Additionally, Penny Summerfield argued that oral history is a dialogue between the present and the past, the personal and the public, and memory and culture.[17]

The application of sociological and anthropological techniques related to interviewing and interpretation has made oral history much more robust. We adopted the life story approach, starting with an open-ended question. For example, "Noel, may I start by asking you your life story and what brought you to Canada?" Using an approach developed by German sociologist Gabrielle Rosenthal,[18] we deliberately allowed the contributor to set his or her own agenda and ensured that the themes raised were spontaneous, and free from the interviewer's bias. In the majority of cases the interviewees were happy to talk, without interruption other than nonverbal encouragement, for up to three-quarters of an hour. The second phase was for the interviewer to draw out details of what had been said and clarify issues raised. One common request was to identify when events had occurred. An important goal at this phase, and later in the interview, was to avoid the use of leading questions. The purpose was to minimize the possibility of colouring the response. The relationship between the interviewee and interviewer permits the oral historian to pin down the evidence in a way that he or she cannot do with written sources. The third stage in the interview was to explore omissions, identify themes that had not been raised but that had been raised in other interviews, and challenge what the contributor had said. This stage not only helped us verify the accuracy of the testimony, but also helped us clarify and contextualize complex issues, interdependencies, and relationships.

The main body of the interviews used in this book were conducted by Marilyn Barber, Murray Watson, and two groups of graduate students at Carleton University. In conducting our interviews we were sensitive to the risks of bias or variation in content arising from interpersonal relationships between interviewer and interviewee. Would testimony content be influenced by differences in age, gender, class, and nationality? Our interviewers represented three different groups: a female Canadian academic, a male British academic (both of whom were a similar age to the interviewees), and a much younger group of male and female students who were Canadian nationals, except for one English female and one German male. Overall, the tenor, structure, and duration of the testimonies were much the same. We did notice, however, that the interviewees, who were mostly elderly or in late middle age, tended to provide more detail about England or circumstances they considered would be unfamiliar to their younger interviewers. Otherwise, differences in age, gender, and nationality appeared to make little difference with this research.

We also had access to interviews conducted six or seven years earlier by A.J. (Jim) Hammerton. Jim is an English-born, Canadian-educated academic. He later moved to La Trobe University in Australia where he co-authored *Ten pound Poms: Australia's Invisible Immigrants* about postwar British migrants. Use of an additional source of interviews helped us to create a more robust and well-rounded sample. Jim also employed a different interviewing technique, in which he used a questionnaire. This approach meant that the interviews were more consistent, with each interviewee addressing the same questions and topics at a similar stage of the interview. As a result the testimonies were significantly easier to analyze, but the approach tended to restrict the interviewee from exploring other themes and issues that he or she considered relevant. That was a relative weakness of Hammerton's approach because, as Paul Thompson argued, interviewees frequently surprise, with "nuggets of information...wholly new perspectives, evidence and also interpretations, from previously ill-represented standpoints."[19] Nuggets of information certainly emerged from our interviewees.

A word about the testimonies, and some qualifications

When people record their life stories orally they do so in a completely different manner than when they write them. For example, most people tend not to speak in complete sentences. Additionally, some testimonies are littered with personal interjections like "you know," "um," and "er." This can make them tedious to read so we adopted a degree of standardization to prevent the reader from being unduly distracted by different styles and ways of speaking. Transcription and editing involved translating the spoken word into grammatical forms commonly expected from the written word. To improve readability, we inserted words naturally omitted in speech and enclosed them in square brackets. We also used square brackets to indicate pauses or expressions of emotion like laughter. We used ellipses (…) where we omitted testimony that was repetitive or irrelevant. Great care was taken to avoid misinterpreting what the interviewee actually meant. For example, if an interviewee was asked if he or she thought something was a good idea and answered "yes," when transcribed into text this would appear thus:

Q. Do you think this is a good idea?
A. Yes.

From reading this text you would take the answer to mean affirmative. But, upon listening to the recording you would hear the interviewee saying "yes" in a hesitant, dubious tone. Perhaps the answer meant "maybe" or even "no"! Transcripts sometimes are open to varying, even contradictory interpretations.

Pseudonyms have been used to protect the privacy of the immigrants whose testimonies we recorded and are quoting in this book. The only exceptions are where the individuals are recognized public figures such as novelist Peter Robinson and journalist Noel Taylor. Pseudonyms have also been given to people mentioned in the testimony extracts. Again the only exceptions are public figures such as Pierre Trudeau, Morley Safer, and Robertson Davies. We have not cited in endnotes details of the interviews we and graduate students at Carleton University carried out. Interviews conducted by other researchers, however, are fully cited.

As Chapters 1 and 7 show, it is more difficult than it first appears to be clear about what we mean by *English* emigrants or immigrants. In the interest of clarity, our definition of *English*, when referring to migrants, means born in England. We have deliberately excluded war brides, the majority of whom were English-born, from our study. There is already an extensive literature about war brides. The Canadian Citizenship Act of 1947 officially recognized them as Canadians, although some experienced problems because of incorrect form-filling.

A final caveat: the majority of the testimonies in this book were from immigrants who remained in Canada. It is estimated that around a third of English immigrants to Canada returned to England or moved to another country. Therefore, caution needs to be applied when drawing conclusions about the immigrant experience. It would be reasonable to conclude that for many returning migrants the Canadian immigration experience may have been somewhat different.

Chapter 1

MIGRATION AND SOCIETY IN THE POSTWAR YEARS

Migration research "is a little like doing a difficult jigsaw in the dark."[1]

Two years after the end of World War II, Winston Churchill broadcast a heartfelt appeal on the *BBC Home Service*. He warned that emigrants were threatening postwar recovery:

> More than half a million of our people have applied to emigrate
> to Canada, South Africa, Australia, New Zealand, and several
> hundred thousands more want to go to the United States or
> South America. These must be among our most lively and
> active citizens in the prime of life who wish to go to some
> place where they can make the best of themselves and their
> children.... I say to those that wish to leave our country, "Stay
> here and fight it out." If we work together with brains and
> courage, as we did in days not long ago, we can make our
> country fit for all our people. Do not desert the old land.[2]

This was a battle Churchill was destined to lose and his feelings were made palpably clear when he described emigrants as "rats leaving a sinking ship."[3] A few years later, however, Churchill had totally changed his views. During his 1952 visit to Canada, he said, "A magnificent future awaits [immigrants] in Canada."[4] What made Churchill change his mind, and why was emigration such an important social phenomenon in England in the years after the war?

Figure 1 | **ENGLISH-BORN IMMIGRANT
ARRIVALS 1946–1970**

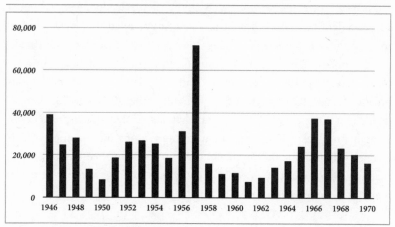

Source: *Canada Year Books (1946–1971)*

Figure 2 | **PERCENTAGE OF ENGLISH-BORN IMMIGRANTS
AGAINST ALL OTHER ARRIVING IMMIGRANTS**

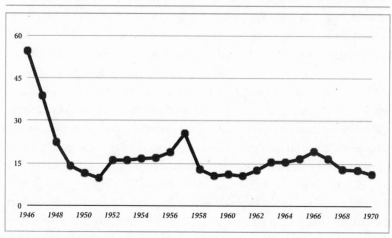

Source: *Canada Year Books (1946–1971)*

The war and its aftermath was a period of social, political, and economic disruption. With peace came euphoria and hope for a better future. When war ended, Sue Jones, who emigrated to Canada in 1955, was a young mother with two children and an absent husband, Gordon, who had spent six years fighting in Burma and elsewhere. She recalled VE (Victory in Europe) Day: the happiness of walking down the Mall to Buckingham Palace, and the police allowing her to climb on the statues. In England, however, this general air of intense excitement and happiness was short-lived. In his broadcast, Churchill recognized the difficulties the country faced, but suggested that it was a sense of anticlimax that had created a widespread desire to emigrate. Was this the case or were the reasons more complex? This chapter will examine the social, cultural, political, and economic contexts that may help explain why people migrated in such large numbers and why many chose to leave England for Canada.

Numbers and migration theories

A natural place to start is with the numbers. How many people emigrated? Where did they go, and when? This exercise should be relatively easy, but there are complications arising from the different ways the data were collected, and many of the available sources of data fail to make the distinction between migrants from England and migrants from the United Kingdom. Toward the end of the twentieth century, some sources do not differentiate between migrants from the United Kingdom and migrants from the European Union. Furthermore, some official statistics refer to immigrants' country of birth, while others do not; statistics documenting arrivals from England would include immigrants born in Scotland, Ireland, and elsewhere, while still other data would report immigrants' ethnicity, which is not always the same as their country of birth. Statistical methodology could be applied to work round these limitations, but caution always needs to be taken when considering statistics referring to *British* or *United Kingdom* immigrants; these terms do not mean *English*. Because England accounts for the bulk of the British population it is reasonable to assume that where British or U.K. is the designation, the majority will be English. A further potential complication is the meaning of the term *English*. (See Chapter 7 on national identity.) For our study and interviews, we define English migrants as people born in England, or in a handful of exceptions, born outside England because of the family's temporary absence from the homeland.[5]

In the twenty-five years after the war, over half a million English-born people emigrated to Canada. Figure 1 shows the number of English-born immigrants landing in Canada annually between 1946 and 1970. In absolute terms the largest numbers arrived in the years immediately after the war, 1957, and the years of financial crises under Harold Wilson's government in the late 1960s. The year after the Suez crisis, 1957, witnessed an exceptional number of arrivals. Several of our interviewees mentioned the impact of Suez; one, Alan Thoms, said, "I came to Canada in 1957 because of the Suez crisis." A young journalist, Noel Taylor, whose emigration story appears in the next chapter, observed that Suez certainly acted as a stimulus for others even though it did not affect his own decision to come to Canada.

Figure 2 shows the proportion of English-born immigrants compared with arriving immigrants of other nationalities. In all but four years between 1945 and 1961, the English were the largest group of arriving immigrants in Canada. The proportion of English-born immigrants measured against immigrants from all other countries witnessed a decline from a postwar high of slightly more than half to around one in nine in 1970. Numbers of English-born immigrants declined in absolute and proportional terms from the 1970s on. By the late 1970s, published figures show that numbers of British immigrants fell to around 15,000 a year, or around 12 percent of all immigrants; between 1983 and 1990 the average fell to about 6,000 a year, representing less than 5 percent of all immigrants; and by 1991 only 4,600 U.K. immigrants, or around 2 percent of the total, arrived in Canada.[6] Historically, the postwar period was the last era of significant immigration from England. Earlier, between 1900 and 1920, 1,356,665 immigrants from Great Britain, or 40 percent of all immigrants, landed in Canada; between 1921 and 1940, with most of the arrivals coming before the Great Crash and Depression years of the 1930s, the numbers were 547,097 or 39.4 percent of all immigrants.[7] From 1946 to 1970 English-born immigrants numbered 597,057 or 17 percent of all immigrants.

Ontario was, by far, the most popular destination for these immigrants. Next in popularity was British Columbia, followed closely by Quebec because of the employment opportunities offered in Montreal. Alberta attracted more English immigrants from the 1960s as a result of the development of the oil industry. Coincidentally, Quebec became less attractive in the 1960s; we shall examine some of the reasons in later chapters.

Migration is a significant social phenomenon that has attracted considerable attention from scholars from a wide range of disciplines, as well as from public policymakers in many different countries. Even though twentieth-century English emigration to Canada has not been a specific focus of much study, how can the work of migration theorists help us understand why so many English migrants crossed the Atlantic and settled in Canada after World War II? Ever since the pioneering work of Ernest Ravenstein[8] in the nineteenth century, migration scholars have developed theories to explain migratory flows, processes, outcomes, and impacts. Recent literature contains an abundance of theories, models, and frameworks seeking to explain migration. However one looks at theory, it is an extremely complex and controversial field.[9] Taking into account the complex and multidisciplinary nature of the study of migration, it is useful to examine briefly how theory can help us explain and understand the motivations and experiences of postwar English immigrants in Canada.

There are a number of theoretical frameworks to explain migration.[10] Some frameworks are essentially quantitative and related to economic theory, while others are almost entirely qualitative. Howe and Jackson, in their survey of theoretical approaches, distinguish explanations in terms of push and pull factors:

> Push factors, which create migration pressure within a sending
> culture and region, range from poverty and unemployment
> (labour migrants) to political turmoil (refugees). Pull factors
> are generated by the attractiveness of the receiving country and
> give a direction to migration flows. The neoclassical framework,
> since it derives from a supply and demand analysis of economic
> and demand conditions in both sending and receiving countries,
> encompasses both push and pull factors in equal measure. Other
> frameworks tend to lean in practice more to one or the other.[11]

Many historical studies of migration tend toward the push and pull model. For example, Tom Devine suggested that one of the critical features in mid-nineteenth-century Irish emigration was the combination of push factors from Ireland as a result of the potato famine and pull factors created by employment opportunities in the chosen destinations of Scotland, England, and North America.[12] Bruce Elliott, in his study of nineteenth-century

English immigrants to Upper Canada, concluded they came for "economic reasons: [in the main for] land."[13] But he went beyond the push and pull model, pointing out the influence of chain migration where "most of the migrants came from the north of England, a part of the country with extant trans-Atlantic migratory connections."[14] Elliott's analysis highlights the role of family and social networks. In addition, Elliott and other migration scholars have found geographical factors and transportation networks to be important in explaining patterns of migration. One might observe that push/pull are overly simplistic explanations of a complex process, possibly reflecting the quality and nature of the available source data. With richer sources, like oral history life-story testimonies, a more complex picture often emerges, as was certainly the case in three recent studies of twentieth-century English migration that employed oral history as their prime source.[15] These studies demonstrated that reasons for migration were infinitely more complicated than just push and pull factors. We shall see in the forthcoming chapters whether migrational motivation and experience were equally complex and multi-faceted for our group of oral history interviewees.

Economists and historians are not the only practitioners of migration theory. There have also been significant contributions by anthropologists, demographers, geographers, sociologists, psychologists, and ethnographers, among others. As well as assessing the reasons for migration, they explore how immigrants fit into the host society. For example, two theoretical frameworks that merit consideration are those of assimilation and acculturation (see Chapter 4). Structural theorists focus on economic change, demographic change, and government and institutional policies. In general, theoretical interpretation in the postwar period involves an evaluation of a range of factors, including the demise of the agricultural sector, the emergence and relative demise of manufacturing, the growth of the service sector, globalization, changing age profiles of the resident population, the growth of metropolitan areas, and so on.

Judging from earlier oral history studies of immigrants, the process of integration into a new society also involves the reconstruction of immigrants' sense of national identity. This field has similarly provided a range of theoretical interpretations, and some of these, like the work of Anderson, Gellner, and Smith,[16] can beneficially inform our understanding. New theoretical interpretation is emerging all the time, often in light of new work and changing migratory patterns. One important development is the increasing prominence of transnational migrants in the later years of the twentieth century. These transnationals, sometimes referred to as "transilients," were frequently skilled workers, managers, or entrepreneurs who crossed national boundaries to go where there was a demand for their expertise.[17] The existence of these transnational migrants, in turn, has generated new theories concerning "alternative forms of adaptation of foreign minorities in advanced societies, based on the mobilisation of their cross-country social networks."[18] To what extent were these new forms of immigrant adaptation adopted by English "transilients" in Canada? And was this adaptation directly or indirectly related to the emergence of new technologies? In *Ten pound Poms,* one of the rare studies about English immigrants, Hammerton and Thomson found that the "transformation of transport and communications technologies...changed the way in which migrants moved from one country to another, and altered relationships within extended families."[19] Whether these findings are corroborated by our oral history recordings will be seen in later chapters. In their important contribution to current thinking, Boyle and Halfacree explored the gender power relations that lie behind the decision to emigrate and the effect that long-distance migration has on career prospects and the labour market.[20] They concluded that there are still more questions than answers. The testimonies of our interviewees will go some way toward filling this gap.

It would be an understatement to say that the use of migration theory is somewhat problematic. According to Massey et al., "at present there is no single, coherent theory of international migration, only a fragmented set of theories that have developed largely in isolation from one another, sometimes but not always segmented by disciplinary boundaries."[21] This view is widely held. A further criticism of migration theory is that there is "simply a lack of good representative data...and that the quantity and quality of information are generally inadequate."[22] Even when data are available another general criticism is that relatively few attempts have been made to link theoretical considerations to empirical data.[23] Clearly there will be a role for some aspects of migration theory in the analysis of our data. It would be unwise, indeed impractical, given the confused and contested state of theory, to base our methodology on a single theoretical framework.

That migration has attracted the attention of theorists is hardly surprising, given the massive scale of migration across international borders and internally within countries. Humankind was on the move. As in the early years of the twentieth century, the numbers departing England in the decades immediately after the war were high, especially when compared with lower numbers during the Depression in the 1930s and toward the end of the twentieth century. Precise statistics are difficult to obtain. In the U.K. there was no official method of recording emigration. A scheme involving the use of emigrant departure cards was introduced in 1957 but was accepted in 1960 only by shipping companies. Significantly, the scheme was not adopted by the airlines, leaving us only with Overseas Emigration Board estimates of around a quarter of emigrants departing by air.[24] A joint committee from the Treasury, Home Office, Commonwealth Relationship Office, and the Ministries of Aviation, Labour, and Transport presented their best estimates of emigration to the British Cabinet in 1961. Emigration to Commonwealth countries between 1946 and 1960 amounted to around 1.6 million, but to this figure one would need to add those who travelled by air and, additionally, those who travelled to non-Commonwealth countries. The committee did not have those statistics.[25] The Commonwealth country that attracted the largest number of migrants was Canada at 582,787, followed by Australia, New Zealand, and the Federation of Rhodesia and Nyasaland. The same report identified that the vast majority of emigrants tended to be under forty-five years of age and that they tended to come from skilled and professional backgrounds. One final word of caution about these statistics: the committee was measuring British and not English migrants. Among the flow of immigrants from England was a special group, the "war brides." They numbered some 54,000, the majority of whom were English-born. War brides are not considered in this book because they are already the subject of an extensive literature and because most of them emigrated as Canadian citizens, having married members of the Canadian military.

Regardless of the problematic nature of the collection and interpretation of migration statistics, there was a postwar social climate in England in which the idea of emigration crossed many people's minds and where almost everyone in the population knew someone who had emigrated or was considering emigration. Churchill's fears were realized. What created these conditions? How did this climate influence people considering emigration as a life-changing choice and subsequently affect the behaviour and experience of newly settled immigrants?

World War II and its aftermath

After experiencing the horror, trauma, death, and destruction of World War II, Gordon Jones explained his decision to emigrate to Canada as follows: "We are not going to have our children in a war again." Gordon emigrated to Canada in 1954, followed by his wife and children in 1955. Gordon Jones's wife, Sue, painted a vivid picture of how the experience of war influenced some immigrants' decision making. She recalled an occasion in London when she was kissing her husband-to-be good night after a date:

> I said, "Turn around, look. It's sunset there but it's not the sunset," and then it dawned on us that the East End[26] was burning. It looked, everything was red and then the next day I went to work and you had to get [there]. They closed the Tube, they had closed it all off, you couldn't go through it so you had to get out at Piccadilly, walk across the bridge, Westminster Bridge, get on another train and then I was on the other side and that's how I did it. But that morning it had been so bad that people were coming in, one girl came in screaming and screaming, she was in a terrible state; another one came in just telling us all about it. "They, [German bombers]" she said, "they picked out, the bombs picked out the railway lines and they blew up and flew around." You know I mean people could get killed obviously, by doing those kind of things.

May Preston, who landed in Canada in 1956, had equally vibrant memories of her wartime school days on the east coast of England. She recalled:

> When I was at the primary school, when I was ten, we had a raid. We had a siren that would go, you probably seen movies, you know where the siren it wails, "whooo, whooo," that's the siren. Well, that tells you that the planes are twenty minutes away, gives you time to prepare if you want to go into a shelter or what else. Then there's a crash warning, which is usually on factories or buildings and it's a lower "whooo-ooo" and three minutes and they're going to be above you, so if you do listen to the siren, listen to the crash because before you can move they're there. We used to leave [school], come out at twelve o'clock, and there was a shoe factory just down a little way from our school from the side entrance. We'd come out when the siren goes. The school children had to leave. We never waited for the crash

[siren] because in a school there's too many children to evacuate. So as soon as the siren went, teachers said, "Okay, single file," and then very, very strictly, "Single file march"—out from the class, out from the side door, down the [corridor], past the classrooms, through the gate to the shelter. Well, meanwhile the people are leaving from the factory and this German fighter is above and he [fires] machine guns. I was last but one, the teacher was behind the last one, the teacher was always at the back and the kids were all coming down the steps to the shelter, and Mr. Scarlett, he shoved the boy behind me who pushed me and we went down the steps. If he hadn't pushed us maybe we wouldn't have been hit, but the chances were that we might have been.

In the early years of the war, hundreds of thousands of children were evacuated from cities threatened by bombing to live with foster parents in areas considered to be safer. Children were also evacuated to Canada, some 3,000 through an official government scheme and 10,000 privately. This child "emigration" did not last for long. It ended in 1940 after the SS *Volendam* and SS *City of Benares* were torpedoed and lost seventy-seven children.[27] Sadly, there are no figures available that show how many child evacuees returned to Canada as adult immigrants. Some emigrants certainly followed this pattern, as we found from the testimonies of three of our interviewees. For some, like Jenny Carter, it was all an adventure. Jenny was evacuated along with fifty pupils from her school, Roedean. She recalls playing the piano onboard ship; a communist steward with a runny nose, whose feather duster made them sneeze; and being more worried about seasickness than marauding U-boats.

The significance of World War II in persuading people to emigrate is considered in more detail in the next chapter, along with an evaluation of the influence of other wars, such as the Korean, Vietnam, and Cold Wars. Though the atomic bomb was not dropped in the standoff between the West and the USSR, it created a climate of fear that may have been a stimulus for emigration. The Cold War certainly created a climate of suspicion in both Britain and Canada. In the case of the Joneses, Sue recalled that their neighbours were visited by the Royal Canadian Mounted Police (RCMP) after she had submitted her family's immigration application to Canada House in London. Apparently the RCMP wanted to check whether the new applicants read the left-wing *Socialist Worker*. They did, but this did not prevent them from being admitted to Canada. John King was another immigrant who attracted the attention of the security services. When King was an undergraduate at Cambridge University he became a member of the Communist Party of Great Britain. With his background in the development of radar during the war, he was offered a position by the Patent Commissioner in Ottawa. King recalled being interrogated by a colonel in the Defence Research Board. King admitted being a member of the Communist Party but only when he was a student. The outcome of the interrogation was that King received a letter saying he "was ineligible for the job."

After six hard years of war, many people found it difficult to find employment and housing in England's bomb-scarred cities. The British economy was in tatters and depended on American handouts, courtesy of the Marshall Plan. For ordinary families, this meant living in austerity, weighed down by restrictions of rationed food, furniture, and clothing. If that was not bad enough, fuel shortages and a winter of Canadian proportions in 1947 made life even more miserable. The cold conditions and shortages in England did not escape notice in Canada either. In 1947, one of the coldest and snowiest English winters on record, George Drew, the premier of Ontario, handed out food parcels from the people of Canada to hungry residents in Suffolk.[28]

How did the state of the economies in both England and Canada influence migration? After all, economic factors receive most attention from the theorists. While this book is not an economic history—our emphasis is on letting the migrants tell their own stories—it is necessary to examine, albeit briefly, the context of the economy. Were the English and Canadian economies creating the classic conditions for "push and pull"? In waging war, Britain had acquired debts of £3 billion. Domestic capital had deteriorated by the same amount and the country had used overseas investments to the extent of £1 billion. Additionally, exports had fallen to a third of pre-war levels. Financial assistance came in the form of U.S. loans, but the conditions attached to these led to a series of sterling crises, the first as early as the autumn of 1947.[29] There was a devaluation of sterling in 1949, and the 1950s witnessed a series of balance of payments crises and "stop-go" economic management. There was an upturn in the later 1950s and Prime Minister Harold MacMillan was able to boast, "We had never had it so good."[30] The 1960s, however, saw a return of economic slump, and another devaluation of sterling in 1967. In the 1970s inflation reached record highs. There was further industrial decline and unrest leading to the three-day work week.

As we have seen, most migration occurred in the late 1940s, throughout most of the 1950s and the late 1960s. These were periods when the English economy was mostly in the doldrums. Many had difficulty finding employment and housing—problems that had been exacerbated by destruction of large swathes of housing stock during the war. Individuals and families, after years of deprivation during the war and earlier during the Depression, felt that their desire for a better life was being frustrated. A permanent reminder for every citizen in the land was the continuing constraints of "austerity." Shortages of supply meant that rationing continued in the years following the war, with ration coupons not being finally scrapped until 1954. Rationing and shortages affected almost every commodity used in daily life: coal, petrol, cars, clothes, footwear, furniture, bedding, toys, and above all, food. Rose Uttin, a Wembley housewife, listed her privations in December 1947, in a diary kept for the Mass Observation Project: "Our rations now are 1 oz bacon per week—3 lbs potatoes—2 ozs butter—3 ozs marge—1 oz cooking fat—2 ozs cheese and 1 s [shilling] meat—1 lb jam or marmalade per month—lb [sic] bread per day. My dinner today 2 sausages which tasted like wet bread with sage added—mashed potato—tomato—1 cube cheese and 1 slice bread and butter. The only consolation no air raids to worry us."[31] One aspect of austerity that will be examined when we consider interviewees' testimonies in later chapters is the way rationing bore most heavily upon women—an observation made by Ina Zelwiger-Bargielowska in her important work, *Austerity in Britain*.[32]

Meanwhile, in Canada, while there was wartime rationing, most Canadians had access to a much more nutritious diet than did their allies in England and, ironically, those south of the forty-ninth parallel.[33] Canada's postwar economic problems were much less severe, too. According to J.M. Bumsted, "the period between 1945 and the early 1970s was a period of unparalleled economic growth and prosperity for Canada."[34] There were, naturally, periods of downturn, and some economic sectors, like agriculture, and geographic areas, like the Atlantic Region, did not perform so well. Overall, however, most economic indices moved in an upward direction. There was a substantial rise in the standard of living, with unemployment running at relatively low rates. Indeed, at the end of the war, there were critical labour shortages in spite of the boost from troops returning to a peacetime economy.

The economic disparity between Canada and England provided near-perfect conditions for a push and pull, demand and supply explanation for migration. Some of our interviewees recognized these influences. Peter Whilesmith recalled that after a visit to Canada, he thought it was "the land of milk and honey.... Then we decided it was time we got out [of England]. And that's what we did." Peter came to Canada with his wife in 1952. A word of caution is required here. Even though economic conditions in England and Canada were influential, immigrants' motivations were more complex, as the next chapter will reveal.

Government policies

What did governments do to stimulate and facilitate migration? Did they discourage it or attempt to change the composition or flow of immigrants? Did their policies and actions influence the scale and nature of migration? At the end of the war, both Canada and England required workers for postwar reconstruction. We have already seen what Churchill thought about people leaving England at such a critical time. In contrast, Canadian prime minister Mackenzie King made the following parliamentary statement in Ottawa: "The policy of the government is to foster the growth of Canada by the encouragement of immigration. The government will seek by legislation, regulation and vigorous administration, to ensure the careful selection and permanent settlement of such numbers of immigrants as can be advantageously absorbed in our national economy.... The people of Canada do not wish as a result of mass immigration to make a fundamental alteration in the character of our population."[35] This speech is frequently quoted as a statement of the general principles of Canadian immigration policy until the 1960s. The immigration minister expressed the same views with specific reference to the U.K. in 1955: "We try to select as immigrants those who will have to change their ways least in order to adapt themselves to Canadian life and to contribute to the development of the Canadian nation. This was why entry into Canada is virtually free to citizens of the U.K., the U.S., and France so long as they have good health and characters. That is why deliberate preference is shown for immigrants from countries with political and social institutions similar to our own."[36]

In pursuit of these policies Canadian immigration authorities invested heavily in a U.K.-wide promotional infrastructure, most of which was in England. There were six offices in England, with the headquarters located in London. After the war, until 1950, the Canadian overseas immigration service came under the control of the Department of Mines and Resources. In 1947 an Immigration and Labour committee was established in Ottawa, with representatives from the Departments of Mines and Resources, Labour, External Affairs, and Health and Welfare. This committee was given the task of determining labour needs in Canada. In 1950 responsibility for immigration was transferred to a new Department of Citizenship and Immigration. Further reform came in 1966 with the establishment of the Department of Manpower and Immigration.[37]

Of the six Canadian immigration offices which operated in England in the twenty-five years after the war, London was open during the war; Liverpool opened in 1949 and closed in 1968; Leeds opened in 1957 and closed in 1968; Bristol opened in 1957 and closed in 1968; Birmingham opened in 1966; and Manchester opened in 1969. Two other offices in the U.K. were in Scotland and Northern Ireland.[38] Staff in these offices vetted applications, supervised medical testing of potential immigrants, assisted with passage arrangements, and sold the benefits of Canada to people interested in emigrating. The latter involved ongoing advertising in national newspapers, showing filmstrips and promotional films, and distributing a range of brochures and pamphlets. A display advertisement in *The Times* in 1960 painted a picture of Canada as a land with a variety of opportunities open to adaptable people with training. The advertisement emphasized that "the person with professional talent or vocational skill is always in demand and is indeed welcomed." The text went on to say that there was help available throughout Canada to assist immigrants in setting up their own business. It highlighted the fact that Canadians were the greatest homeowners in the world and that this increased the "probability" of immigrants owning their own home; in addition, they would benefit from a high standard of living and enjoy "the freedom of the great outdoors."[39] Other advertisements concentrated on similar themes under headlines like "Canada is a good place to go!"[40] "Canada is the answer,"[41] and "There is opportunity for you in young dynamic Canada."[42]

Immigration officials, however, were not wholly satisfied with the promotional materials available for their use. Freda Hawkins in the first of her three tours of European immigration offices, including that in London, noted that, "the staff at all Canadian Offices in 1964 expressed bitter feelings about the information materials and films they were obliged to use."[43] She cited as an example that visa offices were having to use a ten-year-old "Trans-Canada Airlines travelogue with a commentary by Christopher Plummer, extolling the natural grandeur of the Canadian scene, but saying nothing about jobs, housing, cities, education or government in Canada, and with a good deal of out-of-date material in it."[44]

Immigration promotion was largely a federal government initiative, but provincial governments were also involved. The government of Ontario had a recruiting and processing office at Rainbow Corner near Picadilly Circus in London. The province ran advertisements with similar inducements to those in the federal government's advertising. Eager to obtain British immigrants immediately after the war when ocean transport was scarce, Ontario's premier George Drew initiated the first scheme for emigrants to travel by air. The first thirty-nine airborne immigrants from England arrived in Toronto on a Skymaster aircraft run by Transocean Air Lines in August 1947.[45] As discussed in later chapters, air transport heralded a significant change both in the way emigrants travelled and the way in which extended families could keep in touch.

Over the years, Canadian immigration policy changed, as did the organization of the immigration service, as a result of changing patterns of demand in the labour market as well as notable cultural shifts in Canadian attitudes. The latter involved a subtle yet fundamental reordering of the way society perceived itself, the interpretation of which is much contested: the official recognition and general social acceptance of multiculturalism. "In a short time," José Igartua observed, "English Canada shed its definition of itself as British and adopted a new stance as a civic nation, without ethnic particularities, and erected this as the Canadian model."[46] This significant change in identity is what Igartua called the *Other Quiet Revolution*. This revolution was much quieter than the Quebec revolution—so quiet that it has not been seriously investigated by historians. Yet its manifestations were widespread, perhaps the most iconic being the replacement of the Canadian Red Ensign flag with the new Maple Leaf flag in 1965. Another manifestation was the dramatic change in immigration policy, though it needs to be recognized that this transformation was also related to structural industrial change, changing demands for labour, and the availability of immigrants.

It is not necessary to chart the extensive changes in Canadian immigration policies; these are widely covered elsewhere.[47] Of most significance for potential English immigrants, however, was the shift from a white European bias to a points-based system that emphasized education and skill rather than ethnic origin. The Canadian points-based system was fully introduced in 1967. Assessment units were allocated to applicants; to be successful they had normally to obtain fifty out of the 100 units available. The 1967 assessment units were later revised in 1974, 1978, and 1985. The 1967 immigration regulations gave most importance to education and skills:

1—Education and Training: Up to twenty assessment units to be awarded on the basis of one unit for each successful year of formal education or occupational training.

2—Personal Assessment: Up to fifteen units on the basis of the immigration officer's assessment of the applicant's adaptability, motivation, initiative, and other similar qualities.

3—Occupational Demand: Up to fifteen units if demand for the applicant's occupation is strong within Canada whether the occupation is skilled or unskilled.

4—Occupational Skill: Up to ten units for the professional, ranging down to one unit for the unskilled.

5—Age: Ten units for applicants under thirty-five with one unit deducted for each year over thirty-five.

6—Arranged Employment: Ten units if the applicant has a definite job arranged in Canada.

7—Knowledge of French and English: Up to ten units dependent upon the degree of fluency in French and English.

8—Relative: Up to five units if the applicant has a relative in Canada able to help him become established but unprepared to sponsor or nominate him.

9—Employment Opportunities in Area of Destination: Up to five units if the applicant intends to go to an area of Canada where there is a generally strong demand for labour.[48]

Changes in immigration practice significantly altered the social and ethnic composition of immigration to Canada. These changes also occurred at a time when numbers of English-born immigrants were on the decline. Policy changes had an impact but it would be unwise to assume they were the sole cause of this decline.

For most of the years immediately following World War II, emigration from England took place on a massive scale. Canada was not the only country trying to attract the attention of potential emigrants. Among a number of nations appealing for emigrants Australia and New Zealand provided the stiffest competition for Canadian immigration officials. Although geography gave Canada a natural advantage, eliminating the thought of a month-long sea voyage to the other side of the world, the Australian and New Zealand governments created a distinct competitive advantage over Canada through the provision of subsidized passages. The Australian and United Kingdom governments forged a free and assisted passage agreement in 1947, popularly known as the "ten pound pom"[49] scheme. Each selected adult could travel for only ten pounds, with five pounds charged for each child between the ages of fourteen and eighteen, and younger children travelling free. This scheme lasted, with minimal change, for some twenty-five years. According to the authors of *Ten pound Poms*, the scheme was hugely popular, with over 400,000 people registering with Australia House in London in 1947.[50] It appealed to working-class migrants unable to afford passage and seems to have drawn a larger proportion of those migrants to Australia.

New Zealand, too, introduced a new scheme in 1947, offering free and assisted passages to immigrants deemed to be necessary to fill vacancies in key occupations. These assisted immigrants "were bonded for two years in a job to which they were directed by the [New Zealand] Labour Department." Like the Australian scheme, these arrangements lasted until the 1970s.[51] In contrast, Canada did not offer immigrants reduced passage fares, although it was forced to respond to competitive pressure, especially the popularity of the ten-pound-pom scheme. In 1950 the Canadian government introduced an assisted-passage loan scheme in which selected immigrants were offered interest-free loans. This scheme was not restricted to U.K. migrants but was open equally to many continental European migrants, who took greater advantage of it. Between 1950 and 1970, more than $50,000,000 was provided for immigrants, largely from Europe, with a repayment loss of only 2.2 percent.[52]

Providing financial assistance for migrants was not a new postwar initiative. A range of programs had supported British emigration since the nineteenth century. In the interwar years the British government had worked with the Dominions of Australia, Canada, New Zealand, and southern Africa on programs to develop an Empire self-sufficiency scheme which linked migration, investment, and tariffs to counter competition from other countries.[53] In the context of Empire, the British government played the role of the mother parliament enhancing British character and contributing to member countries of the Empire and the Commonwealth. Key to this endeavour was a series of Empire Settlement Acts, the first of which reached the statute books in 1922. The arrangement was renewed in subsequent years. Through the Empire Settlement Acts, the British government cooperated on a fifty-fifty basis with the federal and many provincial governments in Canada, and with certain migration societies such as the Salvation Army and the Society for the Oversea Settlement of British Women, to assist selected British migrants to Canada. The funds provided for passage loans, reduced passage fares, and after-care for migrants.

After the war, however, the British government provided financial assistance only to Australia, and for former military personnel who wanted to emigrate. The Canadian government received no financial assistance for migration from Britain. In 1956 the British Overseas Migration Board agreed on a policy whereby "the United Kingdom should continue to encourage migration to other parts of the Commonwealth provided there was no radical change in those migrating according to age, sex and occupation or in the economic position of the country."[54] In 1962 the British government confirmed this approach of "giving facilities for recruitment of emigrants by other Commonwealth Governments, and of giving general encouragement to emigration to other Commonwealth countries."[55] The role played by government(s) was undoubtedly significant. During a period of heightened interest in emigrating from England, governments in Canada and Britain, as well as in Australia and New Zealand, contributed to a climate in which migration was viewed as an attractive proposition, and there were few barriers obstructing the realization of one's dreams. In addition to governmental initiatives a number of corporations, including some in transportation, aerospace, engineering and energy, were also active in immigrant recruitment.

"How we lived then"

In the postwar years, when emigration from England was such a popular lifestyle choice, what was society like and how did social conditions contribute to the propensity to emigrate and to the ability to settle into new homes?[56] These questions are nearly impossible to answer. Social and cultural affairs, however, cannot be ignored in our quest to explain the nature of this phase of English migration to Canada. Arthur Marwick began his seminal work *British Society Since 1945* with an apology, "inevitably in a book of this size much gets left out."[57] His book was over 500 pages long. We will have to be even more selective. Our analysis is guided by the nature and content of the reminiscences of our interviewees, along with some surprising silences. We will need to consider contextual issues related to family and gender, social class, welfare, race and ethnicity, sensory perception, technology, and popular culture.

Much will be made of the mundane, reflecting the importance of the ordinary in everyday life and its potential impact on the experience of both emigration and immigration. The reactions of a young Canadian who arrived in London to study in 1954 illustrate the importance of the mundane. In a letter home, she provides the impression that she had arrived in an alien world. Lynn Seymour wrote:

> I bought some Kleenex and a roll of toilet paper. The kind the Fishers [her landlords] have is like the paper for dress patterns. In fact the toilets themselves are so odd. You have to pull a little chain or string.... I have a little radiator in my room and it goes on after you insert a shilling and light a match. The heat stays on a couple of hours and you must repeat the process.... There are a lot of odd characters in London.... Eccentricity is tolerated here far more than at home.... Don't forget to send vitamins, instant coffee and Breck shampoo.... We usually have sausages and piles of potatoes at the Fishers because meat is so expensive. I dream of having a lean juicy steak.[58]

Lynn, who went on to become one of Canada's greatest ballerinas, was staying with the Fisher family while on a scholarship at Sadler's Wells.

After so much death, destruction, sadness, and separation during the war, family life assumed heightened levels of significance. According to Marwick, family was the essential glue in the social fabric.[59] What, therefore, was family life like in England after the war? And, how would family life influence the migration experience? A competition was held in Brighton in 1951 to find the typical British family. It was won by the Newcomb family from Hemel Hempstead in Hertfordshire. The local paper, the *Brighton Evening Argus*, reported a model of happy family life, reflecting assumptions of appropriate domestic gender relations:

> They must enjoy the simple pleasures. Mrs. Newcomb likes best a quiet evening at home with her husband relaxing and making a mess with his pipe and the family watching television, or walking in the country with their dog Rover.
>
> A husband who doesn't drink, except for a sherry at Christmas, and who doesn't grumble.
>
> A wife who, although told by her employer that she was a career girl who would never enjoy married life, makes a success of it, and who loves making such dainties as lemon meringue pie and fruit flan for a most appreciative husband.
>
> A husband who doesn't mind doing the washing-up on his Sundays off.[60]

Of course, there was no such thing as a typical family, although the popularity of marriage remained consistently high between 1951 and 1971. Taking the whole population over the age of nineteen, in 1951 more Britons were married or had been married than were single: 24.8 million were married; 21.6 million were single, of whom 3.7 million were widowed or divorced. In 1971, 28 million were married and 23 million were single, of whom 3.9 million were widowed and 500,000 were divorced.[61] Compared with later years, marriage rates were high, and divorce rates were low. "Illegitimate births" were only about 5 percent in the mid-1950s.

In the years following the war, the family in England was essentially patriarchal in nature. The wife was the homemaker—or to use the language of the time, a housewife—mother to her children and occasional part-time worker. The husband was the breadwinner who was looked after by his wife at home. This picture of family life is fully corroborated by extensive research and through the oral history interviews carried out by Elizabeth Roberts and Natalie Higgins.[62] "A woman's place is in the home" was a phrase that was commonly used and one which achieved a 79-percent approval rating in a

1957 Mass Observation survey.[63] Men, and often women as well, tended to disapprove of married women going out to work. Even a young Margaret Thatcher acknowledged and accepted this form of discrimination. In 1954 she sought to be nominated as the Tory parliamentary candidate for the eminently winnable Orpington constituency, but failed. Leading local Tories thought that, "her candidacy would be incompatible with having two small children." She later wrote to the Conservative Central Office, saying she would "abandon further thought of a parliamentary career for many years."[64] In a remarkable U-turn, however, Mrs. Thatcher became an MP in the 1959 election when her twins, Carol and Mark, were only six years old.

Immediately after the war there was a baby boom, with the birth rate peaking at 20.5 per thousand of the population in 1947. By the beginning of the fifties the birth rate stabilized at around sixteen per thousand. This compared with twenty-nine per thousand at the outset of the twentieth century and fifteen per thousand in the 1930s. The rate grew relatively quickly in the 1950s and early 1960s, peaking with a secondary baby boom, at 18.8 per thousand in 1964 before falling back to fifties' levels by 1971. Family size was considerably smaller than in Victorian times and varied by region and, importantly, by social class, as working-class families tended to have more children. According to a number of contemporary groundbreaking sociological studies, members of the working class tended to be part of large extended families where the maternal grandmother and nearby relatives played supportive roles in childrearing. The nuclear family, often stereotyped as Mr. and Mrs. Average with 2.4 children and perhaps a dog or cat, was a more middle-class phenomenon.[65]

Social class is one of the most highly contested areas of academic scholarship. It could be argued that scholars like Marx, Weber, and Durkheim, along with their followers, detractors, and revisionists, have created more confusion than illumination. Fortunately, the so-called man or woman in the street often had a much clearer perspective on social class—a perspective that was especially significant in the postwar years. The minute someone opened their mouth they told the world to which class they belonged. Ferdinand Zweig in his 1952 survey of the British worker noted, "a working man speaks a language of his own, while a middle class man generally speaks the King's English."[66] In her study, *"Talking Proper": The Rise of Accent as a Social Symbol,* Lynda Mugglestone argued that "accent was itself to be regarded as a marker of social acceptability, facilitating or impeding social advance; it alone could secure deference or disrespect, acting as an image of 'worth' in a culture increasingly attuned to the significance of phonetic propriety."[67]

Clothing was another giveaway. People from different class backgrounds dressed differently, and in the years after the war it was much easier than it became in later years to detect the social origins of a person by what they wore. Class difference was classically illustrated in a sketch on the satirical television program *The Frost Report* in 1966. In it, the tall John Cleese with a bowler hat, pinstripe suit, and rolled umbrella represents the upper class. The average-height Ronnie Barker, wearing a trilby hat and off-the-peg suit represents the middle class, while the diminutive Ronnie Corbett wearing a flat cap and muffler represents the working class. In a witty yet perceptive dialogue, Barker says to Cleese "I look up to him because he is upper class, but [turning to Corbett] I look down on him because he is lower class." Corbett replies, "I know my place."[68] The social class a person was born into determined his or her life chances, educational opportunities, employment, earning potential, leisure pursuits, and so on. While upward social mobility existed, it was difficult. Very often, migration offered an easier way to move up in the world.

People were particularly sensitive about their class position. A 1952 study by the Coventry City Council Planning and Redevelopment Committee observed that the inhabitants of an essentially working-class district "showed themselves highly aware of social distinctions."[69] Sometimes class differences surfaced in the form of social and political tension. A 1957 *New Statesman* article claimed that the middle class perceived the working class to be "irrational, hostile, nihilistic, getting more for doing less, making each wage increase a preface to a wage demand, refusing to accept the need for higher production, breaking agreements, flouting the law, rejecting elected leaders, enjoying the benefits of full employment and housing subsidies and health services and threatening the economic system from which the benefits derive."[70] This was strong stuff. There was evidently a latent climate of class bitterness, especially during the strikes and industrial disputes that were fairly common throughout the postwar years, as well as later. We shall explore, in the following chapters, whether and how class conflict contributed to a desire, for some, to emigrate.

The *New Statesman* reference to health services acknowledges a significant social change implemented by the Labour government in 1948. The concept of a "welfare state" was much discussed during the war, and in 1942 the Beveridge Report summed up British aspirations. William Beveridge sought to rid the country of the five giants of "want," "sickness," "squalor," "ignorance," and "idleness."[71] The Beveridge Report aimed to provide a comprehensive system of social insurance "from cradle to grave." It proposed that all working people should pay a weekly contribution to the state. In return, benefits would be paid to the unemployed, the sick, the retired, and the widowed. Beveridge wanted to ensure that there was an acceptable minimum standard of living in Britain below which nobody fell.[72] This philosophy influenced government policies for years to come in the fields of social security, housing, employment, education, and health. A new National Health Service (NHS), which provided health care free at the point of need, was a popular innovation, although there were initial problems with shortages of hospitals and medical staff. Funding also proved problematic, and charges for prescription medicines and spectacles were introduced in the fifties. Such was the NHS's popularity and the high demand for its services that one might have expected prospective emigrants to doubt the wisdom of abandoning the shelter of its benefits, especially as Canadian social security provision and health services were less generous, even after the extension of universal medicare to all Canadians in 1972.[73] Strangely, not one of our interviewees mentioned the issue of welfare or perceived its poorer provision in Canada to be a reason for not emigrating. Sue Jones, shortly after her arrival in Peterborough, Ontario, in 1955, had reason to regret not having access to the National Health Service, but did not mention it. She said:

> There was one time when one of my children had toothache and
> we hadn't any money and in the end I thought, well I've got to do
> something about this so I went to the dentist and I said, "he [her son]
> has the toothache and I can't afford anything more than having his
> tooth seen to." So he [the dentist] took him in and when he came out I
> said, "Can you please tell me how much I owe you?" and he said, "You
> don't owe me anything and I've seen to all of them [her son's teeth]."

Sue thus encountered the concern of some Canadian doctors and dentists who occasionally provided free care to needy patients, subsidizing it in part through fees charged to more affluent patients, who usually had private health plans. Sue was lucky in her choice of dentist but typical in hesitating to seek medical care because of the family's lack of money.

While social class was a longstanding division in English society, race became an increasing source of tension in the postwar era. One of the early problems facing the National Health Service was the shortage of doctors and other trained medical staff. This problem was partially solved by recruiting trained professionals from the Commonwealth; this brought an influx of doctors from the Indian subcontinent and nurses from the Caribbean. Ethnically, until the 1950s, England had been an essentially white country. The arrival of 493 immigrants from the West Indies on the MV *Empire Windrush* in 1948 was an important milestone. These immigrants were the forerunners of tens of thousands of other black or "coloured" people from the Caribbean, India, Pakistan, and elsewhere in the Commonwealth. Unlike the NHS recruits, the majority of new immigrants were skilled or unskilled workers. The migration debate initiated by Winston Churchill in 1947 sharply turned its focus from emigration to immigration. Before a cabinet meeting in 1954, Churchill said, "Problems will arise if many coloured people settle here."[74] His remarks proved to be prescient. Racial tensions emerged. Discrimination was widespread, particularly in housing and employment. London's Notting Hill district was the scene of the first serious race riot in 1958.

Intolerance surfaced at all levels of society, from the workplace to the House of Commons—and even to the Church of England. Racism was sometimes insidiously subtle, as in the case of Carmel Jones, a future Pentecostal minister who arrived in England in 1955. After attending his first church service in England the vicar said to him, "Thank you for coming. But I would be delighted if you didn't come back." Asked why, the vicar responded, "My congregation is uncomfortable in the company of black people."[75] Very often, however, racism was more violent, as in the case of the aforementioned Notting Hill riots. In 1968, MP Enoch Powell created a furor with his vitriolic "Rivers of Blood" speech in Birmingham. Powell's main concern was about what he perceived to be the "preventable evil of black immigration into England." He cited the fears expressed by one of his Wolverhampton constituents:

A week or two ago I fell into conversation with a constituent, a middle-aged, quite ordinary working man employed in one of our nationalised industries. After a sentence or two about the weather, he suddenly said: "If I had the money to go, I wouldn't stay in this country." I made some deprecatory reply to the effect that even this government wouldn't last for ever; but he took no notice, and continued: "I have three children, all of them been through grammar school and two of them married now, with family. I shan't be satisfied till I have seen them all settled overseas. In this country in 15 or 20 years' time the black man will have the whip hand over the white man."[76]

In all likelihood this was an empty threat from Mr. Powell's constituent. We do know, however, that xenophobia surrounding postwar black immigration in England is likely to have been one of the many factors that influenced some people to emigrate. Peter Semple, who arrived in Canada in 1966, thought: "In my day, when I was in my teens and early twenties, we complained because there were too many West Indians, too many … Pakistanis, Indians, West Indians. You know cities like Bradford were more black than they were white. And the U.K. was never that kind of country. And this country [Canada] does not have the same racial problem. Not the same racial problem as the U.S. Fortunately, we are reasonably free, we're reasonably open about stuff, whether your face is black or white."

Many other themes and issues also emerged from the oral testimonies, including the importance of sensory perceptions. For example, take the sense of smell. Towns and cities in postwar England smelled quite differently than in later years. Smoke from coal-burning fires used to heat houses filled the air and contributed to urban pollution and smog. Marian Raynham recorded in her Mass Observation diary her experience of London in December 1952: "It was simply dreadful. Visibility about six feet. And it got down the nose & throat & stung like pepper. The Automobile Ass. says it is the worst they have known. All buses etc are suspended. I tripped on a curb & fell on my poor old bosom, left side."[77] "Pea soupers," a term used in England for dense smog, were relatively short-lived, diminishing with the introduction of legislation on smokeless zones and the adoption of gas-fired central heating systems.

Another form of smoke invaded postwar nostrils, however; it came from tobacco. Smoking was widespread, as can be seen from contemporary newsreels of football matches, where a pall of cigarette smoke hung over the flat-capped crowds on the terraces as well as in cinemas and elsewhere.

Although smoking was also common among both men and women in Canada, English cigarettes smelled different, especially in the damp polluted city air. The sensitive nose of seven-year-old Michael Ignatieff (future leader of Canada's Liberal Party, 2008–11) sensed the difference between Canada and England. He recalled his arrival in Southampton with his parents: "Fog closing in.... All the English spaces being different; the railway carriages being narrow, different smells, Woodbines [cigarettes] in the air, the pervasive dampness, fog and chill everywhere, characters in cloth caps, incredibly gnarled old gents carting your luggage to the train." He described London as a "cramped, struggling, grimy, dirty old world" where he lived in an "absolutely freezing apartment" and where there were "these huge red buses looming out of the fog with their lights all smeared by the fog."[78] The importance of the sense of smell for new immigrants has been cleverly demonstrated by the curators at the Ulster American Folk Park in Northern Ireland. Visitors start their tour in restored houses from the potato-famine era before moving to recreated immigrant homes in North America. One is struck by the olfactory experience of moving from aromatic peat fires burning in the Irish homes to the more acrid wood smoke in the North American dwellings.

Another smell no longer found in the streets of English towns and villages is that of horse dung. After the war, horses were still used by haulers to carry goods. The sight and smell of the milkman, coal merchant, and rag-and-bone man were relatively common until the end of the fifties, by which time horse transport had been largely replaced by the internal combustion engine. Private car ownership, however, was still relatively rare after the war, even though the number of registered motor cars rose four and a half times between 1948 and 1965.[79] By 1971 there were some 19 million cars on the road,[80] approximating to one car per household. The subject of cars was raised in many of the oral testimonies. Private cars were an aspirational purchase. Furthermore, there were significant differences between the two sides of the Atlantic. In the postwar years the British motor industry still dominated the home market with cars bearing the badges of Morris, Austin, Hillman, Sunbeam, and Standard. These cars, designed for Britain, tended to be smaller and less exciting than North American cars. Even American-owned British-based manufacturers, like Ford, designed different cars for the British market.

The growth in the use of cars is a manifestation of two factors: a consistent increase in disposable income leading to a general improvement in standards of living, and the emergence of new technologies. The application of scientific knowledge for materialistic advance was not limited to the field of transport. Increasingly, appliances like twin-tub washing machines and refrigerators reduced the housewife's domestic burden. These developments did not happen overnight; in 1956 only 8 percent of houses had refrigerators; ownership rose to 33 percent by 1962 and 69 percent by 1971.[81] Conglomerates like Unilever and Proctor and Gamble invested heavily in research and development, resulting in innovations in disinfectants, detergents, and food technology. On the new commercial television channel, soap manufacturers of Tide, Daz, Surf, and Persil fought to advertise the whitest washes. Meanwhile, the output of research into food oils, textures, and artificial flavours slowly began to change what appeared on the nation's dinner plates. The launch of Bird's Eye frozen fish fingers in 1956 was an early, and ultimately highly successful, venture in prepared convenience foods.

Many interviewees reminisced about the differences between the U.K. and Canada in food and food shopping, and about the shortages and austerity they experienced in England. Food retailing remained largely unchanged in England for a decade or so after the war. Food was bought from relatively small specialist shops, like grocers, butchers, bakers, fishmongers and greengrocers. Most of these were independently owned; chains like Liptons and the Co-op were the exception. Joan Priestley, a Nottingham housewife, described where she shopped in the St. Ann's district in the 1950s: "Farnsworth's pork butchers, Barnes Dales little dairy sold Colwick Cheeses, Barber Len for son's haircut, Coupes Furnishing and round the corner into the Square was Plunkett's Gents Outfitters, Atkins Wine Shop ... Briley's Ladies and Children Wear ... the Co-op Butchery and Greengrocer, Morley's Cake Shop, Deans for Ladies fashion, past the Cavendish Cinema, then there was Mr. Ash an excellent Fishmonger."[82] This pattern was typical in most towns and cities in England during this period. Self-service stores were being introduced slowly, and they were not always popular. In 1956 Tesco opened the first full-blown supermarket in a disused cinema in Maldon, Essex. Out-of-town shopping centres with their checkouts and *bogof*s (Buy One Get One Free) were a long way off in the future.

Beyond food, other technologies had a bearing on English migration to Canada. Examples include telecommunications, atomic energy, and aerospace along with aircraft engineering. In the years after the war, few people in England had telephones. Before subscriber trunk dialling was introduced in the sixties, making a call was difficult and involved going through an operator. Calling was also expensive. In 1951 only 1.5 million households had a telephone, increasing to 4.2 million by 1966. In spite of this growth, less than half of all households had a telephone in 1970.[83] As we shall see, the telephone became increasingly important in maintaining family contact.

In a different way, the development of atomic energy also linked England and Canada, and fed the impetus for migration. In 1956, Queen Elizabeth opened the Calder Hall Magnox reactor in Cumberland. This was the first nuclear power station in the world to provide electricity for domestic and industrial purposes through a national grid. Britain secured a significant commercial advantage, and the know-how of its scientists and technicians was much sought after in other countries, including Canada.[84] Many English-born immigrants were recruited to help develop the nuclear facility at Chalk River in Ontario. Indeed, the nearby town of Deep River incorporated a number of English design features, including a cricket pitch, to make the new arrivals feel at home.[85]

Aerospace was another sphere where Britain could boast technological leadership. The development of commercial jet aircraft revolutionized both tourist travel and immigration. The first British passenger jet, the Comet, came into service in 1952. Unfortunately for its manufacturers, the Comet was prone to metal fatigue and suffered a number of crashes. These problems allowed American-owned corporations, Boeing and Douglas, to dominate. As the transnational field of aircraft and aerospace development expanded, however, the expertise of skilled British workers became a prized commodity. Companies in Montreal, Winnipeg, and elsewhere in North America deemed England to be a fertile recruiting ground for immigrants. Such was the feeling of loss that contemporary newspapers in England routinely ran stories about the "brain drain."[86]

In this brief survey into "how we lived then" we have touched on the senses of sight, smell, and taste. Turning to sound, in 1956 Bill Haley and the Comets hit the charts with *Rock Around the Clock*. This presaged a musical revolution. Haley was quickly followed by Elvis Presley, Lonnie Donnegan, and Cliff Richard, among others in the late fifties, to be followed by the Beatles, the Rolling Stones, and many others in the "swinging sixties."

Their music was widely embraced by teenagers, a word that came into mass use at the end of the war.[87] Assertive youth culture emerged in the mid-fifties, first as Teddy Boys with their duck's arse hairstyles, long colourful jackets, drainpipe trousers, and thick crepe-soled shoes. They were followed by mods and rockers, then the free love, long hair, and the flower-power counterculture of the sixties.

British society went through significant attitudinal change, often creating generational conflict. David Kynaston described the fifties as a time when deference, respectability, conformity, and trust were probably more important than piety.[88] He also asserted that Britain was an authoritarian, illiberal, and puritanical society. In the years after the war there was indeed a culture of respect. Men tended to touch or doff their hats when meeting women; school children called male teachers "Sir"; and some would argue that corporal punishment in schools maintained discipline in much the same way as national service in the forces did until it was scrapped in 1960. One area where there is little room for disagreement is that there was near-universal respect and pride in the Royal Family, the British Empire, and the Commonwealth. How significant was the Commonwealth connection in generating emigration to Canada? Answers will emerge when the immigrants tell their personal stories in the next chapter.

Conclusions

Marjory Harper and Stephen Constantine, in their recent book *Migration and Empire*, concluded that at one level migration to Canada "was the story of personal decision-making, in which the principal actors were the migrants." The authors found that "migration reflected personality, ambition and/or anxiety, and was affected by the specifics of family finances, relationships, networks, practical opportunities, and sometimes random information flows."[89] Migration was also influenced by cultural, social, economic, and political factors beyond the control of the individual. It is the latter that we have sought to explore in this chapter. In so doing we have endeavoured to paint a picture of what society and its institutions were like, mainly in England but also in Canada, during the postwar years. Inevitably with such a large canvas our efforts are more in line with an impressionist than a figurative painter. It would take a whole gallery of paintings to reveal the mass and complexity of the issues and factors that created the climate that encouraged half a million English people to leave England to live and work in Canada.

World War II had a devastating effect on British society; its economic impact was huge and long-lasting. After the euphoria of victory there was a near-stampede to emigrate to Commonwealth countries and elsewhere. Although this exodus incurred the ire of Winston Churchill, the propensity to emigrate continued and was particularly strong through to the 1970s. This interest was encouraged by the immigration policies and promotional activities of Commonwealth governments, particularly Canada and Australia. Postwar austerity measures and the stop-and-go nature of Britain's economic performance proved frustrating for many, and escape was sought through emigration. In addition, uncertainties created by social, structural, and cultural change sometimes stimulated ambition, or alternatively created a sense of alienation among individuals and families struggling to make a life for themselves in postwar England. In the "how we lived then" section, we attempted to highlight some of these issues. Most of them are raised, in one form or another, in the immigrants' oral testimonies. While this section is no more than a sketch, our intention is to provide a route map to aid understanding and interpretation of the testimonies revealed in later chapters.

Chapter 2

WHY EMIGRATE?
WHY CANADA?

By coming to Canada, we'd improve our lives.[1]

*Well, it was an adventure. You know, when
you're in your twenties, it is an adventure.*[2]

Let's give it a try.[3]

In February 1956, journalist Noel Taylor left Oxford, England, for new opportunities in Ontario, Canada. In a 2007 interview with Murray Watson,
Taylor characterized himself as an economic migrant. At the same time,
his recollections reveal that his decision to emigrate was more complicated
and, in some respects, more personal than what the term *economic migrant*
generally conveys. Taylor was well educated and had interesting employment in England. The son of a bank manager and a mother who stayed
at home in accord with middle-class standards of the interwar period,
Taylor went to a private school in Somerset. He left school in 1945 with the
academic qualifications for university but was not able to gain admission
because returning servicemen were taking the available places. Instead of
university, Taylor fulfilled his national service obligations by joining the
navy for more than two years. Because English had been his best school
subject, Taylor next obtained a position with the local newspaper in his
home community of Andover. He progressed to another newspaper in
Bournemouth and finally to the *Oxford Mail*, which he described as being a good paper in the mid-1950s. Although his career was advancing,
Taylor felt dissatisfied in Oxford. He now had a wife and a baby boy, and

the lack of suitable housing forced the Taylors to live with another family. The accommodation problems undoubtedly contributed to his frustration that life in postwar England seemed "stultified," that "we didn't feel that we were getting anywhere." In his memory, ten years after the war "we were still worse off than we were maybe even during the war, certainly as far as eating was concerned."

Although Taylor did not comment on the significance of place, his move to Oxford increased his chance of meeting Canadians living in England. The academic reputation of Oxford was a magnet for aspiring Canadian students, scholars, and writers. Taylor became quite friendly with Morley Safer, later to become well known as a reporter on American television. In 1955, however, Safer was a Canadian reporter for a London, Ontario, newspaper and had obtained a grant to go to Oxford. In conversation one evening, Safer pointed out to Noel and Noel's wife Lin that they were not travelling anywhere and that the only way they would be able to travel would be to migrate somewhere. He offered to assist Noel by providing him with references and introductions for Canada. Consequently, as Noel remembered, "almost on a whim we said, 'Let's go, let's do it.'" They thought about cheap passages being provided by Australia, but Morley's Canadian help seemed more valuable. To obtain information and confirm their decision, Noel and Lin went to Canada House at Trafalgar Square in London. They found so many people lined up on the stairs for an interview that they were not able to get into the building. Returning another day, they were more successful. Not only did they obtain an interview but they also received a very positive response to their enquiries and were made to feel really wanted. Taylor's impression of the Canadian officials was that "in those days, emigration from England was a big deal for them. They were glad to have us because we were fairly well educated, fairly well trained in our jobs, and so on."

Noel Taylor crossed the Atlantic in advance of his wife and child to find a job and a place to settle in Canada. Because he was an educated Englishman with sufficient resources and good prospects for employment, he had not needed either a specific job offer or sponsorship to be accepted as an immigrant. Taylor's journey to Canada gave him more travel adventure than he had anticipated. The old Cunard ship on which he sailed broke down in the mid-Atlantic and had to be towed back to Britain. The passengers were transferred to the *Queen Mary* which, after a rapid Atlantic crossing, sailed at night into New York Harbour past the illuminated Statue of Liberty and the lights of the city. Coming through the most celebrated gateway to the New World, Taylor felt he had truly participated in the immigrant experience. As he stated, "It was quite a bonus for me because I knew how immigrants should arrive and I came over on a boatload of immigrants." Taylor proceeded to Toronto, where he could use the newspaper contacts Safer had supplied. Declining the possibility of a position in Sudbury, he obtained a referral to Peterborough, Ontario, where he was interviewed by the newspaper editor, Robertson Davies.[4] Davies was another Canadian who had gone to Oxford, so the Oxford connection created an instant bond. Taylor recalled how "his eyes lit up and I knew immediately I had a job, because he was so interested in having someone from Oxford working there." Taylor started work two weeks after arriving in Canada, and ten weeks later Lin and the baby joined him in Peterborough.

Noel Taylor's story illustrates the complexity of intertwining motivations and concerns that our oral interviews reveal. In Taylor's case, discontent with continuing economic deprivation in England became linked with a desire to travel that could be fulfilled only through emigration. "It was a sense of adventure, a little bit, coming into it and a sense of wanting to see a bit more of the world, which we couldn't do because we were sort of stuck in England and we were not that well off." Friends and family also had an important influence on Noel and Lin's joint decision. Morley Safer not only suggested migration but gave the couple reassuring aid and a personal connection with Canada. In contrast, ties to family in England made migration more difficult. From Noel's perspective, Lin was close to her mother, who lived in the New Forest area of southern England. While Lin shared Noel's interest in expanding their horizons, she was unwilling to make a permanent break with family. Noel explained, "She said if we're going, we're only going for two or three, for two years just to get some travelling in and do all this…and it's what a lot of people do." Migrating even temporarily to another country was a major decision for the Taylors, who were a couple in their late twenties with the responsibility of a baby, but they also sensed that they needed to take advantage of the opportunity before more time passed. True to their agreement, the Taylors returned to England after two-and-a-half years in Canada. Noel, however, was not satisfied with his newspaper work back in Bournemouth. A good job offer in Ottawa drew them once more to Canada, this time to settle permanently, even though the parting with Lin's mother was still difficult.

The economy and society of both England and Canada changed significantly in the three decades between the end of the war and the mid-1970s. Postwar austerity in Britain continued into the 1950s but eventually gave way to better times in the late 1950s, only to be replaced by a return of economic problems in the 1960s. Conversely, Canada emerged from an economy devoted to the war effort into an unexpected era of postwar prosperity and affluence geared to a growing consumer and technological society. This image of progress dominated the international reputation of Canada in the decades after the war, in spite of a recession that was especially worrying in the early 1960s and, as in Britain, increasing inflation and unemployment in the early 1970s. Gender expectations and roles were also in transition in the postwar decades even though the major impact of the women's movement on family and the workplace did not happen until the 1970s.

Motivations for migration in part reflected the changing times. For example, with 1940s and 1950s migrants, austerity featured strongly as a push factor in interviews, whereas some later migrants would declare, "There was nothing driving us to leave" or "We were not emigrating to get away from England." Nonetheless, several important factors shaping individual migration decisions form recurring themes through the interviews. These include: the desire for better employment and standard of living, or simply transatlantic opportunities in a technological society; frustration with either the class structure or socialism in England; an interest in travel and experiencing more of the world; encouragement from family or friends with a Canadian connection; and an assumption that Canada as a dominion in the British Commonwealth would provide a relatively familiar place to live, not too remote for contact with England or possible return. In sharp contrast to Australia, the main alternative destination for postwar English migrants, the weather in Canada did not feature as an attraction. How potential migrants responded to varying combinations of these motivating influences depended on personality and ambition, hopes and fears, as well as the particular circumstances of each individual. Most of our interviewees, like the majority of English migrants to Canada in this period, were in their twenties or early thirties. Unattached single migrants, however, had more flexibility of movement and more freedom to give priority to adventure than married couples with children. Our interviewees included working-class migrants, hoping for a better future for their children as well as for themselves, along with the educated middle-class migrants that postwar Canadian immigration policy increasingly sought to recruit. Social class affected not only migrant attitudes but also the resources that enabled individuals to contemplate migration to Canada. Gender, too, made a difference. In spite of women undertaking non-traditional roles in wartime in both England and Canada, the dominant middle-class belief that men should be the principal breadwinner had not changed. Ingrained beliefs regarding appropriate sex segregation in the workforce meant far more career opportunities were available to attract male migrants than female migrants. Women had primary responsibility for home maintenance and the raising of children, so when couples debated migration, wives were more often the reluctant partner, loath to lose family or community ties.

Memories of austerity: "A fairly grim and miserable place"

Many migrants, like James Roland, remembered postwar England as "a fairly grim and miserable place." During the six long years of war, sacrifice for the survival of the nation had been expected and accepted. Victory brought an end to destruction, bombing, and wartime loss of life, but it did not lead to economic recovery. Continued austerity in the peacetime decade after the war was demoralizing and far more difficult to endure than wartime restrictions. In migrant memories, two issues related to basic human needs—housing problems and food rationing—epitomized the austerity that oppressed lives and seemed indicative of England's decline.

When he was discharged from the navy in May 1946, Charles Hall could find no accommodation in London for himself, his wife, and baby other than one room in his parents' house. Charles's father had little formal education apart from the technical training he received in World War I, but he had a good steady job. By betting on the horses he had won the money to purchase a house in East Finchley, where Charles grew up. Aged seventeen when the war started, Charles became a pilot in the Royal Navy. He met his Scottish wife, Ellen, who was serving with the Land Army when he was stationed at the airfield in Ayr, Scotland. Theirs was the whirlwind wartime romance of couples who feared there might be no tomorrow. They were engaged on their second date and the wedding was arranged when Charles returned to Ayr nine months later. Having survived the war, unlike nearly 80 percent of his squadron comrades, Charles Hall sought the security and stability of a home of his own. As he explained, "It was so important to get a grounding…to have a house, somewhere to live…that was more important than anything. No matter what, that's what you've got to have, you know." When he was not able to find a flat in London, Charles turned to emigration as a means of obtaining a home. He had personal experience of North America while serving with the Royal Navy, having passed through Canada and trained for several months at an American air base. Although he made a point of stating that his knowledge was limited in some respects since he had not been inside houses in Canada, he assumed there were opportunities. In addition, Ellen's sister had gone to Canada as a war bride, having married a Canadian serviceman. Not only could she provide the sponsorship that Charles and Ellen needed, but her presence in Canada made the prospect of migration acceptable for Ellen, as the two sisters were quite close. While personal knowledge and family connection were obviously important contributing factors in the Halls' decision to migrate, the primary motivation for Charles was the need for a home. "We started looking, searching for a flat, and realized there was *nothing* available," he recalled, "and that's when I said to my wife: 'Well, I liked what I saw in the States and Canada, and your sister's there.'" The Hall family sailed on the *Aquitania*—a troop ship, they were surprised to learn—and arrived at Pier 21 in Halifax on 21 December 1947. They were among the earliest postwar English migrants to obtain passage to Canada.[5]

Dissatisfaction with inadequate housing in England was most acute during the immediate postwar years, when finding any accommodation could be difficult, but the relatively high cost and scarcity of housing remained an incentive for migration throughout the following decades. Like the Halls, Agnes and Frank Butcher married during the war while Frank was serving in the navy on a mine sweeper. Having gone to work at age sixteen to help support his widowed mother, Frank knew the value of money and wanted to ensure that Agnes, as his wife, would have his pension if he should be killed during his dangerous war service. After the war, Frank did manage to rent a house for his family fairly cheaply, but only because it was owned by his new stepfather's mother, who was relatively wealthy. Agnes and Frank soon "got fed up" with the old drafty Victorian house that was similar to countless other dwellings in the London suburb of Croydon, but they had no hope of being able to afford a home of their own. Agnes had worked as a secretary until she was seven months pregnant but she strongly believed that a mother's place was in the home. With only one breadwinner and soon two young sons, the Butchers could not accumulate savings even though Agnes shopped carefully. When asked to explain their migration, Agnes immediately said, "We came to Canada to improve our lives. Where we were in that old house in England it was, you know, pretty cold, hard living in that house and we thought by coming to Canada we'd improve our lives." Frank added, "It's a lot different now, but at that time…no way we could buy a house; you'd have to double the wages for people."

By selling an old Austin car that he had bought with a small inheritance and fixed up himself, Frank managed to scrape together the fare for a passage to Canada on the *Empress of Scotland* in 1952. Agnes similarly sold the house furnishings for airfares so she and the boys could follow. She arrived in Canada with twelve dollars, which she spent on an iron so she could iron the boys' clothes. Looking back on the reasons for their emigration from the perspective of more than fifty years in Canada, Agnes and Frank agreed on the importance of getting better housing but diverged slightly on the aspects that they emphasized. Agnes, who stayed at home with the children, remembered the comfort of warm Canadian floors on which the children could crawl, in contrast to the cold stone floors in the English house. Frank, the breadwinner, contrasted the inability to buy a house in England to the ease with which they bought twelve Canadian houses over the years. For him, the impossibility of home ownership in England was symbolic of the difficulty of making progress during postwar austerity. As he noted, when they needed a washing machine because of the baby, he had to spend the last nine pounds in the bank, and "that kind of thing got on my back after a while."

The shortage of housing handicapped couples who wanted to marry after the war as much as those who married during the war. Richard Nash used to enjoy raising eyebrows by declaring that he and his fiancée had to get married quickly. Then he would quell gossip by continuing with the reason. They had been engaged for nearly three years when a friend told them a room was coming available. He believed that long engagements were not unusual, because such an inside tip was almost the only way to get scarce accommodation: "There'd been no building, the houses had been destroyed, and if you tried to look around and find a place, anything the council was able to offer went of course to people with three or four kids…and if you'd put your name on a list you were *way* down at the bottom somewhere." He and his fiancée went to look at the accommodation—simply one small room with a place to sleep in the hall. Not particularly impressed, they were going to leave when they were told that if they did not grab the room it would be gone in the afternoon. In the early 1950s co-habitation was not yet socially acceptable, so taking the room thrust them abruptly into marriage, with the third reading of the bans being on the day of the wedding.

The cramped living quarters became more gloomy and unhealthy as a result of smog, which persisted outside their one little window during the winter of 1952–53: "It was a terrible time," Richard recalled, "because that was the year they had that killer fog in London, and 4,000 people, apparently, died and it was the most *awful* thing.... It was typical of that time with the coal fires, and it was sulphur and dust, coal-dust; everything you touched was filthy." During these appalling conditions, the Nashes were listening to the radio one night and heard commentary on the Canadian budget, including projections for the coming year. Although Richard did not elaborate, obviously the Canadian prospects were much brighter than

1. A young English couple contemplating emigration at Rainbow Corner in London. Photo credit: Archives of Ontario, RG 9-7-4-1-3, Ontario House Records.

conditions around London. Within a week Richard and Heather were at Canada House to obtain information, and a short time later they jointly decided, "Let's give it a try." While the poor accommodation in itself might not have impelled Richard to migrate, the combination of terrible pollution and unsatisfactory housing laid the foundation for leaving England.[6]

Rationing, which continued into the early 1950s, also featured prominently in migrant memories of austerity in England. A war-weary people found the prolonged rationing difficult to tolerate. Indeed, the rationing of some basic items became more severe in the late 1940s than during the war. Butter and meat rations were cut (by half, for bacon), and potato rationing was introduced for the first time in 1947. Bread, soap, and petrol rationing ended by 1950, but a wide range of traditionally favoured foods remained on the ration, including meat, cheese, fats, sugar, sweets, and tea.[7] A currency convertibility crisis that resulted in a major devaluation of sterling also affected the availability and cost of imported items such as bananas. Children as well as adults suffered in these conditions. Austerity and food scarcity became embedded in childhood memories, helping to shape the response to life in England both at the time and in later years. In 1951, at age eleven, Tom Knight migrated to Canada with his family, who had Canadian relatives. The son of a stonemason in Birmingham, Tom remembered their limited diet in the postwar years. Offal helped to stretch out the rationed meat supply, so the family ate steak and kidney pie, and liver. Tom thought the liver resembled leather and had a "dried up, yucky taste." Later in Canada, when served liver at the Royal Military College, Tom was surprised to find that "you could actually cut it and chew it and it actually had some flavour." The difference in food, and especially in the liver, represented for Tom a difference between England and Canada.

When her family immigrated to Canada in 1948, Emma Bulmer was too young to have many personal memories of life in England, but family stories of English austerity shaped her childhood knowledge of her background: "Part of the stories growing up was how there was not enough coal to heat the house, so we slept in the kitchen and that was really cold, and putting the baby in a drawer to sleep because there wasn't enough money to buy a certain thing like a crib, and of the ration books, having to have rations for different things." Emma's family also had a difficult time during their first years in Canada because exchange controls prevented her father, an office clerk, from bringing to Canada the money he had obtained from the sale of their Staffordshire house.

Childhood memories of an austerity that melded the war and postwar years rarely faded completely. Such memories continued to influence some who migrated in the 1960s and 1970s because of disillusionment with England, either economically or politically. In 1968, Pat Connor, a single mother with one son, joined her aunt and uncle in Ottawa because the London-based agency for which she was working as the equivalent of a computer operator was moving to Cheltenham and she did not want to leave London. Lacking formal qualifications in her field, Pat had difficulty finding another London job. Her life had already been scarred by the death, during the war, of her father, a regular soldier, and by the subsequent difficulties faced by her mother in trying to provide for five children. Pat only later understood why she and her two sisters temporarily had the trying experience of being placed in an orphanage with strict discipline. Memories of austerity augmented her recollections of a difficult life in England that might be overcome by a fresh start in Canada:

> The one thing I most remember about the war years and years after
> is rationing. It was awful....There was hardly any food, and there was
> no sugar and no fruits…and we had dried eggs, ugh, and we had
> to bake with them, and I don't remember having candy—well no,
> that's not fair, I mean we did get rations and they, parents, would try
> to make candy for you, you know. So we would get treats, I mean
> they were really treats then, because they just weren't available....
> So we grew up without, but because of not having a proper diet
> in growing, it affected a lot of things, like especially with English
> people, especially in my generation, their teeth was one in particular,
> you know, there was no toothpaste.... Because we couldn't get the
> vegetables…we ended up having problems like rickets which you
> know is bowed legs in children that are not eating properly.

As Pat's testimony of her difficult adulthood made clear, the physical consequences as well as the emotional impact of earlier austerity could continue through life.

Alastair Stone, who migrated to Canada during the economic downturn of the 1970s, similarly linked the immediate problems he was encountering with the background of austerity after the war. Unlike Pat, Alastair had an intellectual more than an emotional perspective; he attributed the intensity of the economic difficulties to unsatisfactory political management. Born in 1947, Alastair grew up in what he described as a middle-class family, living in a typical English suburban semi-detached house first in Norbury in southeast London and then in Bromley in Kent. His father was in sales, working for a major London glass importer, and his mother was a house-wife. Supported by the stable home environment that Pat Connor lacked, Alastair proceeded from grammar school to a three-year university degree followed by two years of post-graduate education, and then, "Oh boy! [I] joined British industry in 1970." Alastair's exclamation drew attention to the precarious state of some industry in England in the early 1970s. Nonetheless, Alastair had suitable employment in research and product development until 1976, when he learned that the site where he was work-ing would be closing. He applied for various positions, including one with Bell Northern Research in Canada, which he saw advertised in the *Sunday Times*. He was offered two or three jobs in Britain as well as the Bell North-ern Research one, but the latter paid exactly twice what the best British job paid. While the Canadian salary was a pull factor, what Alastair regarded as the collapsing state of the British economy was an important push fac-tor for accepting the Canadian offer: "It was just about the point where we thought Britain was about to be rolled up and towed out to sea because it was so disastrous in the economy. There were daily strikes, and the whole country going for a three-day week because there wasn't enough coal to power the coal power stations, so you couldn't have electricity in industry for more than three days a week. What a weird way to live, eh?" Alastair pointed to incessant labour strife and the huge inflation that eliminated any expectation of improvement in the standard of living. Although he had experienced good times in the intervening years, the "long and dusty run" in the 1970s brought back memories of the austerity of the early 1950s: "I remember my mother taking us to the shops for the food shopping and so on and she still had ration books. Up until well into the 1950s the wartime rationing process was still in place in Britain. It was one of the last countries to ever get rid of that, and it was no excuse. For eight years after the end of World War II we were still being treated as if we were at war." Alastair thus filtered his childhood memories of austerity through his adult knowledge of political economy. The resulting disillusionment with Britain's inability to manage its economy disposed Alastair to look favourably toward Canada.

He was also encouraged by rave reviews of Toronto and Oakville from his mother and sister after they visited family friends who emigrated to Canada in the early '70s. Consequently, 1976 became a hectic year for Alastair Stone and his wife because "we bought a house, got laid off, got married, sold a house, and emigrated all in six months."

Class tensions and social attitudes: "I didn't know your sort knew about Turner!"

As Alastair Stone indicated with his comments on strife and strikes in the 1970s, class divisions in English society did not vanish as a result of World War II, even though it was known as the "people's war," nor indeed as a result of the cultural innovations of the "swinging sixties." Class has been described as "a difficult and messy subject"[8] and the exact composition or meaning of the English class structure is open to debate. Our interviewees either voluntarily identified their class position in England as part of their life story or could readily do so in response to questioning, and in some cases showed an awareness of the ambiguities of class identity that are debated by historians.

Migration to the new world offered opportunities to those who felt that class attitudes restricted their lives in the old world. Although the myth of "America" as a classless society had long been discredited, an emphasis on individual opportunity for those who would work pervaded Canadian immigration advertising. In our interviews, class issues sometimes simmered beneath the surface of economic frustrations, thus contributing to a general dissatisfaction with prospects in England, such as that felt by Frank Butcher, a self-made man who could not get ahead as he wished. At other times, class tension became the principal trigger for the decision to migrate. Such was the story of Tom Martin, who left London for Toronto in 1970. Tom referred to his parents as ordinary working-class or perhaps middle-class people as his father was a fireman and his mother was a nurse until she resigned to look after the family. Education, as Tom later realized, was an important prerequisite to advancement as well as to personal fulfillment. Unlike most working-class children, Tom successfully passed the "eleven-plus" exam, the results of which determined whether a pupil went to a grammar school (the academic stream) and hence potentially to higher education, or was sent to a secondary modern school that led to the termination of education at age fifteen. Tom attended a reputable grammar school but one that gave little attention to non-élite pupils. In his words,

Tom "bombed out." He left school as early as he could to work as a lab technician, first at a research lab at St. Bartholomew's Hospital Medical College and then at the School of Pharmacy in Brunswick Square, central London. While working with a PhD student at the School of Pharmacy, he observed a gorgeous sunset outside the window. Wanting to share the pleasure, he said to the student, "Isn't that gorgeous? That's like something that Turner would have painted." Instead of agreeing, the PhD student exclaimed, "Good Lord, I didn't know your sort knew about Turner!" Tom could laugh when recounting this episode forty years later, but he also commented, "If there is a point at which you say, 'Okay, I'm out of here,' that was probably it." Although a minor episode in a lab conversation, the PhD student's attitude highlighted the class divide that Tom knew he could not overcome in England. Admitting that the incident was one of his favourite stories that he might have embellished over the years, although he did not think so, Tom said, "You would hear those sorts of things quite a lot and so that system was really quite well in place and I would often sort of feel that there was a ceiling above me that I couldn't push through." Tom attributed the constraints on his life not only to the class system but also to his inability to proceed to higher education because of his laziness when at grammar school. Believing that he could not find a remedy in England, he sought a solution in emigration. Connections with Canada made the decision easy for him. His grandmother's family had migrated to Toronto and every year through the war to the early '60s they would send a large Christmas parcel full of goodies his family otherwise never saw, such as canned pineapple, whole chickens in tins, and peanut butter. Then Tom's brother moved to Toronto in 1967 and wrote constantly about Expo 67, Trudeaumania, and the Toronto Maple Leafs winning the Stanley Cup. Canada sounded much more attractive than England, especially since Tom did not have a close relationship with his parents. Sponsored by his relatives, he bought a one-way ticket and flew to live with his brother in Toronto, thinking of one of the top songs of the period, "Leaving on a Jet Plane."

Two weeks before he left England, Tom Martin met his future wife, Joan, at a Valentine's party. As Joan commented in the interview: "It's horrible, you know. 'Where did you meet your husband? Oh at a Valentine's party.'" Joan was equally eager to escape the class culture in London, but for different reasons from Tom's. Although Joan was born in London shortly after the war, she spent her formative teenage years in Trinidad when her father, an agricultural research scientist, was invited to work on projects there. After completing her schooling in Trinidad, Joan returned to London to train as a nurse at the Middlesex Hospital. Unlike Tom, Joan did not feel scorned or constrained because of her class position. Unusually for the time, both her parents were university graduates and had professional careers, and Joan herself had a good academic foundation. Instead of class prejudice, she experienced culture shock when she returned to London from the more relaxed and informal society that she knew in Trinidad. She had no doubts about her feelings: "I did not like England, a very, very cold place, very emotionally cold, very physically cold." In Trinidad she could have a casual conversation with a total stranger in a grocery line or be given helpful advice by someone at a gas station, whereas London society frowned on such behaviour. Although she did not reflect on the reasons why Londoners seemed unfriendly, she was encountering the guarding of privacy in the public spaces of a large city, as well as the careful social distancing that not only arose from class boundaries but also preserved them.

Joan made no secret of her displeasure: "My whole aim and object was to get out of England." Indeed, Tom joked that she picked him for her future husband at the Valentine's party because of his emigration plans: "she found some guy who was leaving England: 'Oh yes, great, I'll go with him.'" Joan and Tom corresponded, and Joan visited Tom in Canada. Back in London, she applied for Canadian immigration papers but was turned down. Unwilling to remain in England, Joan rejoined her parents in Trinidad for a period, again came to Canada on vacation, and this time quickly married Tom. Their marriage at City Hall two days before Tom's pay day left them with no money after they had paid ten dollars to the "nice man" to marry them and bought their two witnesses a beer. Then Tom lost their marriage certificate, which he had stuffed into his back pocket; he later found it lying in the street with a large boot mark on it. In spite of this slightly inauspicious beginning, not only did their marriage survive, but their immigration strategy also worked: Joan was allowed to stay in Canada.

Working-class and lower-middle-class migrants, like Tom Martin, who aspired to a better life, could particularly dislike being fitted into a box in the English class system. They also were vulnerable to rejection if they ventured outside the box. Teenagers sometimes had an even more difficult time because they were subject to family decisions rather than their own choices. Pamela Austin, who migrated with her family to Montreal in 1957, knew the pain of rejection at school. She identified her family as lower middle class. Her mother was a skilled seamstress, a strong woman, and the driving force in a matriarchal family. Her father was an unskilled manual labourer who drove a steamroller for the Borough of Hornsea in north London. When Pamela passed her "eleven-plus" exams, her mother chose to send her to an "upper crust" grammar school in the area rather than the school generally attended by girls from backgrounds similar to Pamela's. Pamela was miserable at grammar school, "totally a fish out of water." She felt she did not fit in at all with the other students, whose fathers were bank managers or in insurance. An educational system that was intended to promote advancement on scholastic merit thus failed Pamela, as it may have failed Tom Martin, because of social attitudes. Other studies have found that some teenagers rebelled against family migration decisions that forced them to part with close school friends.[9] In contrast, Pamela was delighted to escape from her school when her mother decided that the family should emigrate to Montreal.

Pamela's mother was "a true East Ender"—a descendant of strong women who knew that they were lifetime wage earners and, growing up as the only girl in a family of seven boys, "tough from the day she was born." She made parachutes during the war and continued to work after the war even when her three children were young. Far from being a reluctant or passive female participant in the family migration process, she initiated the move. She replied to an advertisement by the International Ladies' Garment Workers Guild, which was hiring workers in London to relocate to Montreal. She thus seized the opportunity for improvement and some travel adventure at the same time. Pamela believed that her father was quite willing to acquiesce in the decision; he had little choice other than to stay behind. Pamela characterized her mother's migration decision as "the best gift that she could have given us."[10]

Class tensions in England had a major impact upon politics in the postwar decades. Profoundly divergent visions of the role of the state in managing the economy, redistributing wealth, and providing social services led to a polarization of power between the Conservative Party on the right of the political spectrum and the Labour Party on the left. The victory of Labour in the general election of July 1945, defeating the popular wartime prime minister, Winston Churchill, heralded an era in which Labour governments (1945–51, 1964–70, 1974–79) alternated with Conservative governments (1951–64, 1970–74). Ironically, Canada seemed more attractive than England to migrants at both ends of the political or philosophical spectrum. One of our interviewees came from a pacifist, socialist family. Her father, a dental surgeon, had been affected by his experiences in World War I, and both her parents were "utterly convinced of the wrongness of a class system." One of her main reasons for preferring Canada as a place to live was that class distinctions were much less oppressive than in England. In her family "there was a strong feeling that the privileged structure of so much of English life was an ugliness that should be stamped upon. Now it's not that Canada has no class and social distinctions but one thing that's …clear to me was that they were much less—*controlling* is the word that I would use." On the other hand, a number of our interviewees readily identified themselves as refugees from socialism. Canada had a social democratic party, the Cooperative Commonwealth Federation (CCF), which had been born in the depths of the Great Depression of the 1930s and in 1961 reconstituted itself as the New Democratic Party (NDP) but, although more successful in some provinces, it had never formed a national government. In postwar Canada, the alternation in federal government was between the two centrally aligned political parties, the Liberals and the Progressive Conservatives. The testimonies of those who perceived themselves as refugees from socialism, however, showed more concern with the political scene in England than in Canada. While they may have been reassured by the absence of a Labour government in Canada, they were primarily attracted by a more general equation of economic growth with a North American capitalist economy.

Peter Whilesmith began investigating possibilities for emigration in the late 1940s because he was frustrated with England's lack of postwar recovery, which he associated with the socialist government in power. Peter had been born in Sheffield, Yorkshire, to parents who were both teachers. He went to grammar school in Wakefield, Yorkshire, and with the beginning of war joined the air force at age seventeen as an apprentice technician, eventually becoming a flight engineer. At the end of the war, he transferred his engineering skills to a job in Bristol. He also married Rosemary, who had contributed to the war effort through secretarial work on a large farm near Peter's air base. By 1949 they had two children. Peter noted that rationing continued in England, and he believed a general lack of spirit to be the major problem. He blamed the stagnation to a large extent on the policies of the socialist government. He knew that Japan and Germany were recovering faster, even though they had theoretically been defeated in the war, and he assumed they had suffered even more devastation. So he asked why England was not picking up as it should in the postwar years. His answer: "It was a socialistic government at that time and they went a little bit overboard; they nationalized the railways, they nationalized the airlines, they nationalized the road transport. And the unions were terribly strong, and they weren't only fighting with employers but they were fighting among themselves."

Like Tom Martin, Peter Whilesmith made one small personal incident the turning point in his life. He had gone to Canada and the United States on airline business. When he returned to England he immediately noticed a major difference in people's willingness to provide service:

> The thing that finally drove me to immigration was that I went into
> a shop in Bristol on a Saturday morning once. Men's clothing shop. I
> went to buy a shirt. And there were two young men standing in the
> shop talking about cricket. So I stood at the counter and listened. And
> I stood there I suppose three or four minutes whilst they talked about
> cricket. So I eventually said, "are you two young men… interested
> in selling anything?" "Oh yes, yes sir, what would you like to do?"
> "Well I've been standing here for three minutes waiting to buy a shirt
> from you and you've just lost a sale." And that was not an uncommon
> attitude. There didn't seem to be any drive for entrepreneurship, or
> if the owners had entrepreneurship drive, the people they employed
> sure didn't...and I went back home to Rosemary and I said, "We're off."

Rosemary was decidedly less keen than Peter to emigrate; her reasons for coming to Canada were simply "I came because Peter came." Both sets of parents were also sad at the parting, although they were good about it when Peter explained, "I realize it's tough and I don't like doing it but I think for my sake and the family's sake…we've got to go somewhere where there's more spirit, where there's more spirit to succeed than there is here." Peter had no trouble finding a job in Canada because the Canadian aviation industry was expanding after the war. He accepted a position in engineering with Air Canada in Montreal and the family moved to Canada in May 1952. For Peter Whilesmith, the small incident in the clothing shop encapsulated the ills of English society that the socialist government in power may not have created but was certainly exacerbating rather than solving.

Some opponents of Harold Wilson's Labour government in the 1960s were vehement in voicing their objection to socialism as a guiding economic principle. Peter Semple was a qualified chartered accountant in Leeds with a wife and young child. He was glad that his studies had exempted him from national service, but by the early '60s, life and work had stopped being fun for him. The prospect of living under the first socialist government in a long time sealed his desire to seek alternatives. As he explained, "I come from a long line of capitalists. I don't believe in socialism and I think it's the wrong, the wrong bent. My bent is different. It's capitalism. And I decided I didn't really want to live under the then government of the U.K. I looked around at alternatives and one of the alternatives on the front of my local paper one day which I was reading in the local pub, was to go to Canada." Semple had a comfortable life in England but was not satisfied: "We got a nice house out in the country at that point, nice walk from the local pub. I played cricket with a local team. You know, all the good stuff. Used to take my cat to the pub at night. She used to sit on my shoulder and walk down to the pub and go around and see everybody, but it sort of wasn't enough." He was restless, staying home when some of his friends were seeing more of the world. While the desire to expand his horizons obviously had an important influence on his decision to find work in Canada, the motivation that he first presented in his story was his objection to socialism.

John Steven, who emigrated to Canada in 1969, explicitly described himself as a "refugee from socialism." John had a higher-level scientific education and was quite mobile. He grew up in northwestern England, attended the local grammar school in Southport in Lancashire, studied physics on a scholarship at Oxford, and then completed a PhD at Liverpool. In the late '60s he was disillusioned with life in England: "The Labour government was in power; the Unions were in full swing; the place was described as England being the 'sick man of Europe' at the time." Given his distaste for socialism, John initially considered emigrating to the United States but discovered that he would have to register with the draft board at a time when the Vietnam War was being fought. Instead, he came to Canada with his wife and baby, making a career switch from working with electricity supply in England to joining the space industry in Canada. He found that Canada was much more politically aligned with his way of thinking than England had been, although, looking back, he commented that later everything changed.

Some migrants were motivated by the impact of the government's economic decisions rather than by ideological preferences. Those with professional or scientific qualifications often worked in fields of expertise or for companies with transatlantic connections. Business trips to Canada, such as the one made by Peter Whilesmith, could provide an introduction to material conditions in Canada and to some of the culture. More importantly, Canadian industry and Canadian governments actively recruited trained personnel in England by advertising in daily newspapers, as noted by Semple, or in specialized magazines, or through transatlantic networks of communication that passed along information about job requirements and potential applicants. These educated workers generally received encouragement during enquiries with Canadian immigration agents in England; they were exactly the type of trained migrant favoured by Canadian postwar immigration policy, especially after the changes introduced in the 1960s, which gave points for education and skill and eliminated explicit selection by ethnicity or national origin (see Chapter 1). Thus Canadian options were readily available to some displaced from employment or seeking job moves in England.

In the early sixties, Kenneth Cecil, an aircraft engineer, contemplated emigration because he felt he was not getting ahead financially as he should. After paying his house installments, food, and other bills, there was little money left in the bank for himself, his wife, and their two girls. He found that the decision to go to Canada was made much easier when the Conservative government was replaced by a Labour government and it became clear that production of the TSR2, reputedly one of the most sophisticated aircraft ever built, was going to be axed.[11] He remembered that recruiters started interviewing engineers to tempt them to take jobs in places like Boeing in Seattle and Canadair in Montreal. Kenneth, along with a number of his friends, chose Montreal.

Robert Baldwin similarly became worried about his job when Harold Wilson began cancelling aircraft projects. Robert moved to a mechanical engineering research laboratory at Leicester, planning to get a PhD in connection with his research. His plans did not come to fruition because, as he explained, "Along the way, I had interviewed for a job in an aviation magazine, didn't get the job but the editor had passed my name to someone from Canada who was in London on business and looking for an assistant.

So he interviewed me and a bunch of other people and he offered me a job in Montreal and it sounded like an interesting job." The offer led not only to travel but also to marriage more quickly than he had intended. If he were married, the company would pay his wife's passage, too, so he quickly proposed to his girlfriend and she accepted while they were on their way to visit Robert's parents. His mother had a ring that she was keeping for such an occasion so the pact was sealed and the wedding and a short honeymoon were fitted into the brief time before departure for Canada.

Travel and adventure: A working holiday?

An interest in travel threads through many of the migration narratives. Individuals who were fearful of going places or dealing with the unfamiliar were much less likely to move voluntarily to another country on the other side of an ocean. Frequently, our interviewees characterized themselves as "adventuresome" or wanting to experience more of the world. As we have seen, those who left England for economic or social reasons often linked these motivations with a desire for travel. Noel Taylor, whose story introduced this chapter, is an excellent example of a migrant who combined a wish to escape economic stagnation in England with the fulfillment of a sense of adventure. An expectation that the move to Canada need not be permanent made immigration as a form of travel much more acceptable. While couples with children, like the Taylors, took advantage of the opportunity to expand their horizons through employment in Canada, it was young single women and men or sometimes young childless couples who developed the concept of the "working holiday."

It was not new in the postwar era for young English women to fulfill their dreams of travel and adventure through going to Canada to work. The thousands of young working-class women in England recruited for domestic service in Canada in the 1920s included those who mainly wanted to see more of the world, such as the Southampton woman who yearned for a voyage on the ocean liners that she viewed in port. Similarly—although in much smaller numbers—female secretaries, teachers, and nurses welcomed the opportunity to have new experiences by working in Canada.[12] For these 1920s migrants, though, work prospects were not incidental to their decision and they would not have described their intentions as a working holiday. Working as part of travelling was a product of changing attitudes toward leisure, an evolving youth culture, and greater mobility in the postwar decades.

Isobel Sinclair, who migrated to Toronto in 1956, explicitly described her idea of having a working holiday in Canada. Coming from "a working-class family," she had no possibility of achieving her desire to attend university, even though she could have obtained scholarships. Her parents thought they had done wonders to allow her to remain at school until age sixteen. When working at Barclays Bank in London, Isobel and a colleague decided to visit Vienna, an exciting place where her colleague had many contacts. Isobel started working during her one Saturday off each month and eventually accumulated enough extra days for a terrific holiday in Vienna. On her return to London she realized she was not going to have a single hour's holiday for over a year. At age twenty-one, she became obsessed with this bleak prospect. In retrospect, she judged the fixation to be the key factor propelling her immigration to Canada. As she explained, "the idea was coming for a holiday...a working holiday." Even if she had more money she could not have taken it from England because of the exchange controls. The only way she could afford to stay in Canada for a period of time was to work, and to be allowed to work she had to be an immigrant, not a visitor.

Isobel's London bank manager, who had been in Canada on business, took an interest in her welfare and arranged a job for her at the Imperial Bank in Toronto. Obviously concerned about a young woman travelling independently, he warned her, "It's a wild country and those men there are rough." Trying to understand her youthful impulses and emotions, Sinclair speculated that living through the London blitz as a child and then the fear of nuclear annihilation had had an impact. She recalled clearly the huge areas of bombed places still not fixed up while she was in London, and the maps in the newspapers that showed the radius of London that would be wiped out by an atomic bomb. She wanted to experience life while she could. Later she felt that she had participated in an important movement: the spike in the immigration charts formed by the huge exodus from England to Canada after the 1956 Suez crisis. In Toronto, Isobel was not satisfied with her dull job at the Imperial Bank and soon found different employment with a small pension firm. She also did not travel to various places in Canada as originally contemplated. Although she did not have sufficient schooling to become a teacher in England, Isobel discovered that she could qualify for training in Ontario because of the shortage of teachers. Exactly one year after she landed in Canada she entered Toronto

Teachers' College. The friend who emigrated with her returned to England, but Isobel's working holiday was diverted into permanent settlement.

Mary Irvine also came to Canada as part of the growing wave of English immigrants in 1956. Mary's father was in the Royal Navy, and Mary's leisure activities as well as her upbringing reflected her middle-class background. Like Isobel Sinclair, Mary was motivated by her desire to travel and her migration too was affected by childhood experience of war, although in a quite different way. Growing up at Torquay in South Devon, Mary observed the various troops passing through the port, including Canadians, Americans, Poles, and French, and this acquaintance sparked her interest in travelling. At school her favourite subject was geography, and particularly that of North America. She could remember "drawing in the map of Ontario and putting in the Welland Canal; and I said to a friend who was sitting next to me, 'I'm going to see that someday.'" She kept telling friends that she intended to go to Canada, and initially everyone seemed eager to join her. By the time she was eighteen or nineteen, however, many of her friends were falling in love and were not prepared to leave England.

One night, while working in London, Mary Irvine passed through Trafalgar Square and, looking up at the statue of Nelson on top of his column, almost told him, "Okay, I'm off on my own." The hero of British naval ventures seemed to give Mary the courage to believe that she, too, had the independent spirit to conquer the world—or at least to travel to Canada on her own. That evening she told her parents that she was returning home to Torquay to work, in order to save money to go to Canada. Mary did not leave England entirely on her own. A casual friend with whom she played squash in Torquay said she would love to go as well, and they sailed together in June on the *Empress of France* from Liverpool. Mary now is amused by her photographs of their departure on the train from Torquay. Aged twenty-two, they were dressed as proper young ladies, wearing hats and gloves and looking different from the way youth now would travel. Like Isobel Sinclair, Mary Irvine obtained a job in Toronto, courtesy of a businessman sponsor with transatlantic connections. As she explained: "I had an introduction to Canadian Pacific because when I was in Torquay I had worked at the Imperial Hotel as my last job there and the man who was in charge of CP in London, Mr. Arkle, used to be a visitor there and he sent a letter of introduction to Toronto and as a result of that I became secretary to the Vice President and Treasurer, two separate positions, two separate men at CP Express in Toronto."

On the boat, Mary and her Torquay friend met another English young woman uncertain about her future plans and the three of them decided to share an apartment in Toronto. Mary intended to remain in Canada only two years and during that period to take advantage of the opportunity to travel within Canada. As she said, "My plan was certainly not to stay a long time in Toronto." In the first summer, she travelled to northern Ontario to visit several English students she had met on the boat, who were going to work on the Trans-Canada highway or in mining. At New Year's she went to Mont Tremblant in Quebec for skiing, and the following summer she travelled around much of the eastern United States on a Greyhound bus. The friend with whom she travelled to Canada married an architect and moved to Kitimat, BC, where her husband became a town planner. After two years in Canada, Mary took the train west to see the Calgary Stampede. In Calgary, Mary met her own future husband, a British Olympic skier. In 1960, after a six-month working visit to England, Mary married the skier at a marvellous June wedding in Calgary.

In *Ten pound Poms*, analysis of interviews with English migrants to Australia in the 1950s revealed a distinction between the motivations of single women who saw Australia as an opportunity for travel and adventure, and those of young single men, who placed more emphasis on work and career because of a male work ethic bolstered by a collective memory of poverty and insecurity. In the 1960s the difference faded as young single men also gave more priority to adventure.[13] Therefore, it is probably not by accident that our most outstanding accounts of the working holiday come from young single female migrants. Yet single women could not necessarily rely on marriage being their future career. May Preston, another 1956 immigrant to Canada, was a single woman in her mid-twenties who sought adventure but also valued the work experience she would acquire. Coming from a working-class family in Norwich, she knew poverty during the Depression and the trauma of bombing during the war. Her father, a factory worker, was on short time during the Depression so the family had to manage on little. The war experience, though, was foremost in May's memories of childhood and youth. Because her home was in a region of the east coast subject to heavy bombing during the war, May and her younger brother were supposed to be among the child evacuees sent to Canada where they would live with their father's cousin in Winnipeg. They were all packed and waiting for word to depart for the port; they waited and waited and the telegram never came. May later learned that children had been drowned when the ship before theirs was torpedoed by the Germans and Churchill had decided that "if our children will die they can die at home with their families." As a result, May and her brother remained in Norwich during the war.

During the interview May described in considerable detail the impact of the war on her family and community. Her family erected an Anderson shelter of corrugated iron in their garden, and she and her brother spent their nights in the shelter. Sensory impressions are often long-lasting, so many years later May recalled quite clearly the sounds of that experience:

> We had bunk beds; we used to say good night to our parents, go out, close the back down, and walk down to the garden and go into the shelter and I was up top and my brother was at the bottom and we would sleep through the air raids. Sometimes we would wake up if the bombs were near and if they were further away we just slept all night. Sometimes there was a lot of noise and it wasn't always the bombs. There were big anti-aircraft guns around and they made a lot of noise when they were shooting at the planes. Sometimes we'd wake up and my mother would be sitting in a chair and you knew then that it was serious 'cause otherwise she wouldn't have come down.

May's mother was responsible for the safety of the children at night because May's father, a member of the Home Guard, popularly called "Dad's Army," would often be out on fire patrol. May's schooling also was severely affected by the bombing. When she went to school in the morning she might find empty seats where classmates were missing. For a number of months, May had her lessons on the tennis courts if it was sunny and in the shelters if it rained because her school had been partly destroyed by a direct hit by a fire bomb.

Having survived the war, May obtained a thorough training as a nurse, including midwifery, and a post-graduate chest course at the Brompton Chest Hospital in London. After nursing for seven-and-a-half years, she was restless: "I didn't want to get stuck in a sister's post...and get into a rut." May did not elaborate, but she was undoubtedly feeling confined by some of the strict discipline, rules, and social hierarchy that still characterized hospital nursing in the 1950s. May noted that she was "kind of adventuresome," so she looked into several options. She chose Canada because the secretary of the nursing council whom she consulted arranged that she receive a job offer from a Toronto hospital: "When I came it was for two years' experience, and I promised my mother I would go back after two years." The promise was not kept. May's plans changed abruptly when after about two months in Toronto she met her future husband and decided to stay. When asked how she felt coming to Canada after her experiences in England, she replied, "Oh, well it was an adventure, you know; when you're in your twenties it was an adventure...and I had a job to come to, somewhere to live in residence." May did not indicate that she was hoping to enhance a career in nursing through two years of experience in Canada but the security of the work was nonetheless important to her. After her wedding, May continued to work in doctors' offices for four years until her son was born.

In contrast to the single women, young single men in England had their lives interrupted by two years of compulsory national service in the 1950s. Britain's military involvement in the Korean War in the early 1950s prolonged the imposition of national service, which did not end until 1960. The response of our interviewees who experienced national service ranged from viewing it as a waste of time to believing that it expanded their horizons and enabled them to meet different people. Robin Lanson erroneously thought that national service would be abolished by the time he finished university, so he was too late for the Air Force. Instead he reluctantly served the Queen for two years in the Royal Signals in Yorkshire at Catterick Camp, which he considered "pretty much of a dump," although the surrounding countryside was beautiful. Nearing the end of his service, he started anticipating escape and looking for jobs. He found both in the form of a journal advertisement for a hospital physicist in Halifax, Nova Scotia. An only son, he assured his mother, "Don't worry. I'm only going for two years. I'll be back." He firmly believed that he would return to England in two years but instead he met a woman in Halifax whom he married two years after his arrival and he settled in Canada.

Unlike Robin Lanson, James Leonard had no expectation of evading national service; he simply filled in time after leaving school at age sixteen until he was conscripted at age eighteen. He thought he was lucky because, out of 140 conscripts at Brighton, he was one of sixteen accepted for the Air Force. James spent most of his two years' service on bases in Germany, experiencing new surroundings and different people. Following his military service, James worked on his family's Sussex farm that James's father had taken over after being employed as head gardener on a large Sussex estate. Getting "a bit fed up" after the more exciting life in Europe, he wanted to go somewhere else; he chose Canada to please his mother, who thought Australia was too far. He needed a job to satisfy Canadian immigration authorities so accepted work on an Ontario farm. Looking back, he recognized the importance of youth in explaining his motivations: "Well, when you're young, you want to see something different. I mean, when I'm out for a walk I always like to see what's around the next corner, and it's that sort of thinking, you always want to see what's around the next corner, that sends you off somewhere. You know, I didn't necessarily intend to stay but I have, and I don't regret it." James Leonard and Robin Lanson did not talk about immigration as "adventure" in quite the same language as the young single women, but they were equally interested in seeing more of the world. National service had disrupted the pattern of their lives and thus helped to prepare them for other moves.

By the 1960s and early 1970s, technological advances in transportation combined with greater consumer affluence increased mobility. More people owned cars that they could use to travel greater distances, not only in Britain but on the continent. At the same time, the distance across the Atlantic seemed drastically reduced as plane travel became faster and more common. A jet plane could connect London and Montreal in a few hours, whereas an ocean liner took a week to make a similar journey from Southampton or Liverpool. Changes in culture were equally important. The 1960s became known for an assertive youth culture whose demands for greater freedom and independence from authority increased generational differences. The music of the Beatles, whose career took off from Liverpool after 1962, dominated English popular culture. Clothing styles also changed in accord with the youth movement, emphasizing greater informality, denims, and, by the mid 1960s, the miniskirt that looked most attractive on a slim youthful figure.[14] Although much was happening in England, the youth movement also reinforced the excitement of discovery through travel.

The general meaning of changing times is not always fully grasped by those living through them, especially if they are young and more self-centred. In telling her story, Margaret Bell tried to recapture how being young in the 1960s affected her immigration to Canada. Married to a student, Margaret came to Calgary in 1968 because the only expert for her husband's rather obscure master's degree topic happened to be in Calgary. She was happy to accompany her husband to Canada; to live near the Rocky Mountains was definitely an adventure. She could not remember anything about how she told her parents that she was leaving England: "It didn't really seem like a big deal to me. I was twenty-two...I don't think most twenty-two-year-olds really think about the significance of what they are doing or what might be happening to them or what's going on in the world at the time. In my case it was the sixties and we knew that we were having a good time, but I don't think we knew that the sixties were going to be quite as significant as they turned out to be, once you start looking back." Margaret grew up in Brighton but lived in London while obtaining a BA in geography at King's College. Her leisure time included frequent attendance at the theatre, concerts, and clubs in London, as well as rock climbing in North Wales and the Peak District with a mountaineering club. For her, flying to Calgary was an extension of these good times.

Demonstrating the greater ease of travel, Margaret and her husband were able to afford a return visit to England on a charter plane ten months after their arrival in Canada, even though they had limited income. At least in retrospect, Margaret realized that while she regarded going to Calgary simply as an adventure, her mother had been quite upset. A few years earlier, her mother felt she had lost her favourite sister when she migrated to Australia; now, Margaret's mother was convinced that she would never see her daughter again. Margaret was happy that she was able to prove that "more than 3,000 miles across the Atlantic really wasn't the end of the world."

A few 1960s migrants managed to convert a passion for travel into an occupation. After completing grammar school near London, Hannah Marriot took a course in hotel catering and from age seventeen worked at various resort hotels in England. "I liked to move around," she explained. "I was single, fancy-free. I owned a Lambretta (scooter) so I was mobile." Then Hannah decided to work in French hotels in order to perfect her spoken French. The British Hotel Association finally found a placement for her at a small hotel in the Jura district of eastern France where nobody spoke English but they needed an English person on staff to deal with English tourists. Because of currency restrictions in the early 1960s, English people organized motoring trips in their own cars to the French and Italian Riviera by purchasing, in England, prepaid vouchers for meals and hotel accommodation. Hannah's hotel was on one of the organized routes.

At the French hotel, Hannah met her future husband, whom she persuaded to join her when she returned to England even though he did not speak any English. Hannah and Daniel married in Norwich, where they refurbished and managed a small hotel that had been owned by a distant relative. They too enjoyed good times in the mid 1960s. They were happily settled in Norwich, "really enjoying hotel life, making quite a good living, able to save quite well; we had a small car, a Mini." At this point in late 1964 or early 1965, they saw a great many newspaper advertisements for emigration to both Australia and Canada—"full-page ads, making both countries sound like paradise, offering all kinds of advantages, including financial help even to get there." Hannah described herself as part of a peripatetic family; her parents, who were in business, travelled frequently; her sister worked as a legal secretary in Geneva; and her brother was completing a degree in Boston. Although no longer single, and perhaps not quite so fancy-free, Hannah and her husband were both excited to take advantage of an opportunity to move to Canada. Enjoying an ocean holiday en route, they sailed to Montreal with three large steamer trunks full of stuff and found employment in a resort hotel in the Laurentians. Their work in the hotel industry enabled them to continue travelling during their first years in Canada. Not only did they return to England for a visit, but they also had a working holiday in the Bahamas for a winter and travelled across Canada by train and bus. Marriage had not impeded their mobility, but with the approaching birth of their first baby, they decided that they should "stop this continual moving around and travelling" and settle down in Montreal.

Although from a quite different social background than Hannah Marriot, Roger MacKay also enjoyed the youthful freedom to travel in the 1960s. A passion for flying brought him to Canada in 1968 at age twenty-two. Born in Sittingbourne, Kent, Roger was a men's hairdresser for a time after he left school. Getting "fed up with that," he worked in various factories and other places. With a friend, he travelled around Europe for a year with a car and a tent, and by the time he returned to England, he said, "I'd got travel fever." Roger had become interested in flying while he was at secondary school. At age fourteen, he had the chance to go to glider camp with the Air Training Cadets and had to make three solo flights. Although it had been a frightening experience, Roger became hooked on the excitement of flying. He took flying lessons at Rochester Airport, but flying in England was expensive. Roger was investigating several countries where flying would be cheaper when a friend returned from Canada on a visit and conveyed good impressions of that country. A couple of months later, when he obtained his private pilot's licence, Roger decided that the time was right for emigration to Canada. Unlike Hannah Marriot and her husband, who took three steamer trunks, Roger bought a one-way plane ticket to Toronto and travelled light with two suitcases—and "the stuff that wouldn't go in the suitcases I put on and wore over." The day after he arrived, he found a job in a shop in downtown Toronto and contacted the flying club. Roger had no money for a return ticket to England, so he gave himself five years to get into the commercial aviation business in Canada. Neither Roger MacKay with his dream of a permanent career in commercial aviation nor Hannah Marriot with her cumbersome steamer trunks fit the image of a forerunner of the modern backpacking generation seeking self-discovery and adventure through temporary migration. In both cases, however, their emigration to Canada was the culmination of youthful mobility and travel in Europe. In separate ways their lives were linked to the growing popular enthusiasm for the more affordable travel of the 1960s.

Why choose Canada? "In England now the snowdrops are out"

When deciding to leave England, some emigrants knew without question that they wanted to go to Canada. Chain migration and family sponsorship were much less important in shaping the postwar migration of the English to Canada than with some other ethnic groups, such as the growing number of Italian immigrants in the postwar decades. Nonetheless, the presence of family and friends in Canada could serve as a magnet in determining the destination of certain English migrants, while for many others it was an important influence supporting other motivations. As testimony in this chapter has already indicated, however, English migrants often considered a range of possible options before selecting where to go. For our interviewees, the main choice was between Canada and other Commonwealth countries, especially Australia and to a lesser extent New Zealand, Kenya, and South Africa, or sometimes between Canada and the United States.

Snow tended to characterize the dominant vision of Canada held abroad. Lamenting in his late February interview that the snowdrops were already blooming in England, James Leonard drew attention to the infamous Canadian winter that was both longer and colder than in England. Since the mid-nineteenth century, Canadian immigration promoters had struggled to overcome an image of Canada as a land of ice and snow, with a few Mounties and beavers added. Canadian immigration literature over the years commonly featured lush summer pastoral settings or bountiful fall western harvests. Advertising tried to attract British immigrants by contrasting Canadian sunshine and blue sky implicitly or explicitly with dull, damp Britain. One example is the 1920s Ontario pamphlet, *Sunny Ontario for British Girls,* directed at young British women.[15] But no amount of government advertising could make the Canadian winter disappear. English migrants to Australia interviewed for *Ten pound Poms* included those who had rejected Canada as "too cold." Australia, with its pictures of long sandy beaches and ocean surfing, was definitely the preferred destination for those who gave priority to sunshine and warmth.

2. The long Canadian winter: September snow in Calgary is fun for one English immigrant. Photo credit: By permission Rosemary Sloan.

The trump card that Canada held in the competition with Australia for English migrants was distance. Canada might be "too cold" but Australia was "too far." Travelling to Australia, whether by sea or by air, was a much longer journey than to Canada. To deal with the disadvantage of being too far, Australia negotiated the ten-pound assisted passage scheme in 1947. For the duration of the scheme from 1947 to 1982, selected British migrants could travel to Australia for only ten pounds per adult while children had lower fares and were free in the 1960s. The "ten pound Poms" had to remain in Australia for two years or they would be required to reimburse the balance owing on the passage fare.[16] Most of our interviewees were aware of the cheap passage scheme for Australia, although sometimes their memories were incorrect regarding details; one thought that all accepted on the scheme travelled free to Australia, and another believed that the Australian government paid immigrants ten pounds to go to Australia. What is important about the memories is not whether the exact details are accurate but rather the general knowledge that passage to Australia was much cheaper than to Canada. Canada had an assisted passage program, but it simply provided a loan that had to be repaid from earnings in Canada; it did not reduce the actual fare. In spite of the cheaper Australian passage fare, for many of our interviewees Australia was still "too far." Many migrants were uncertain how long they would remain in Canada or came intending to return to England in two or three years. The return passage fare was not covered by any government program and definitely would be lower from Canada than from Australia. Being in Canada also was regarded as permitting more regular visits with family back in England. In various cases, parents—and mothers in particular—were more willing to accept their children's migration to Canada than to Australia.

Although the Canadian climate was not a particular attraction, Canada could compete with Australia in offering open spaces to those interested in outdoor recreational activities. In 1966, Jeremy Plunkett came to Canada to pursue advanced studies at the University of Western Ontario in London, Ontario. He also had a good offer from the University of Chicago but he declined the American offer because he feared that he would become involved in protests against the Vietnam War and neglect his academic work. Instead, he opted for what he believed everyone described as "nice, peaceful, boring" Canada. In the back of his mind, though, he also had a more positive reason for selecting Canada. While attending technical school, he and a friend spent their weekends hiking on the moors; early on, therefore, he came to enjoy running and climbing around hills: "When I was on top of the moors I used to try and pretend it went on forever, and that it wasn't an island of wild heather and rocks surrounded...by mill towns in the valleys." Looking at a map, he realized that Canada was the reverse of England—little islands of civilization surrounded by vast empty lands and wonderful landscape.

Similarly, in 1976, Rob and Jean Watson were drawn by the greater expanse of outdoor space in Canada. Rob told how a camping holiday in Canada had made them more aware of differences between Canada and England: "My wife and I were very keen on camping and hiking and that sort of thing, and it was getting more and more and more restricted in Europe to what it is here in Canada. We were used to camping sites where virtually your ropes crossed over the next person's. We came to Canada on holiday and saw the provincial parks where really there's a big gap of trees between you and the next site and it seemed awfully wonderful. So that was one of the things that I guess motivated us." Open space was not sufficient in itself to bring Rob and Jean Watson to Canada. Rob, a systems analyst, was also frustrated with the economic restrictions in England and feared how upcoming changes in the educational system would affect their children. Nonetheless, the appeal of being able to feel a little more alone with nature was important.

The frequent comparison of Canada with Australia occurred because migrants leaving England often chose to stay within the Commonwealth. Ties of empire had a long history. Generations of imperial migration linked Britain to its former colonies and now autonomous countries within the Commonwealth. In the interwar period, the Empire Settlement Act had promoted the concept that "overseas settlement" was simply moving within greater Britain. In spite of political realignments and growing independence in the postwar era, a sense of Commonwealth identity as well as institutional connections continued to reinforce the bonds created by migration. When May Preston, the London nurse who was not ready to settle down, began looking at options such as joining the forces, another nurse suggested, "why don't you go to one of the Commonwealth countries?" May actually received a job offer from Nairobi, Kenya, but her mother pleaded with her not to go because of the Mau Mau uprising. Others similarly considered but rejected South Africa because of racial tensions. More made their choice from among Canada, Australia, and New Zealand.

In the case of one of our interviewees, the selection of Canada was quite accidental. In 1966, at age twenty-one, James Roland decided "it was time to see the world." He went to London, and as he recalled, "I sort of had this idea of Commonwealth in my mind." He planned to go to the Australian, New Zealand and Canadian High Commissions to learn about emigrating. He came to Canada House first and never got any further. There he found a huge room of people all wanting to go to Canada and waiting for several days to be processed. In contrast, when an immigration officer discovered that Roland had a degree, he was fast-tracked and emerged three hours later, having had a medical examination and obtained an assisted passage and landed immigrant status. He did not bother to investigate Australia or New Zealand.

While it is important to recognize the impact of the accidental, even in making important decisions, interviewees who chose Canada over Australia and New Zealand generally had specific reasons. They were concerned about distance, as already seen, or had connections with relatives or friends in Canada, or believed their employment prospects to be better in Canada. The united war effort of Britain and Canada gave some migrants more personal knowledge of Canada. Spending part of the war in Canada either because of war work or evacuation, they later wanted to return. One coal miner from Newcastle in the Northeast of England had a more unusual wartime connection with Canada. Captured at Dunkirk, he spent the rest of the war in a German POW camp, where he became good friends with a Canadian from Nanaimo, British Columbia, also known for its coal mines. After the war, when it seemed the Tyneside coal mines might be closed, he brought his family to Nanaimo to join his friend, who had constantly been urging him to migrate to Canada.[17]

Conclusions

As many examples in this chapter illustrate, personal contact remained significant in influencing the choice of Canada, by would-be emigrants in postwar England. Such contact ranged from chance meetings with casual acquaintances who were visiting from Canada, to friendship with Canadians temporarily living in England, to regular letters and parcels from close relatives in Canada. Those considering migration often thought such personal sources particularly useful in providing information as well as encouragement. Of course, personal sources could be unreliable.

One migrant chose Canada, even though her two brothers had gone to Australia; the second brother to emigrate discovered that the first one had completely misrepresented his success. Immigration history contains many such examples where immigrants did not want to admit failure or worry their family at home. Our interviewees did not complain about friends or relatives trying to deceive them, but some realized on arrival in Canada that they really knew very little about the country.

Careful economic calculations regarding employment could also lead to the selection of Canada. Kenneth Cecil, the aircraft engineer who felt in the 1960s that he was not getting ahead as he should, knew that there was considerable emigration to places like South Africa, Australia, New Zealand, and Canada, so he got as much information as possible from High Commissions in London and Liverpool. He explained why he and his wife decided on Canada:

> Australia and New Zealand, we considered them but decided they were too far to travel; we wouldn't be able to get back to see our families on a regular basis, and they wouldn't be able to see their grandchildren. Another important fact was that the engineering opportunities weren't nearly as great in those countries as they were in South Africa or Canada, and when I looked at the funding ratio, the cost of the house divided by the annual salary of an engineer, in Australia it was going to take me twenty-four years to buy a house, twenty-four years of salary; in Canada I could do it in six. That's why we decided if we go anywhere it would be Canada.

English emigrants viewed Commonwealth countries as having the advantage of being English-speaking. Before 1970, few of the English emigrants that we interviewed took account of Canada's francophone culture in making their decision, even if they were planning to live in Montreal. Hannah Marriot, who had lived in France, and her French husband were significant exceptions, but it was their French connection that made them interested in the bilingual culture of Quebec. Most others, like many English Canadians, took for granted the English-speaking culture that prevailed in most of Canada, and indeed even in the business world of Montreal.

The United States was also English-speaking and, like Canada, was not "too far." The United States had emerged from the Second World War as the economic and political leader of the western world and offered attractive economic and professional opportunities. Although most of our interviewees selected Canada from among Commonwealth countries, some had a North American perspective in considering emigration. A number of young men were interested in economic or educational possibilities in the United States in the 1960s but chose Canada because they feared involvement in the Vietnam War. As we have seen, Jeremy Plunkett thought he might spend too much time participating in student protests against the war, whereas others were afraid that they would be drafted to fight. At a time when many young American men were fleeing to Canada because of their opposition to the war, these young English men decided not to risk emigration to the United States. Other interviewees considered migration to Canada as a possible backdoor entry to the United States. Isobel Sinclair, in search of her working holiday, came to Canada with a friend who wanted to go to the United States but had not been able to obtain sponsorship. Originally they told Canadian immigration authorities that they wanted to go to Hamilton because it was close to the United States, but they were persuaded to choose Toronto instead because it provided better accommodation and employment. Abbi Andrews came to New Brunswick in late 1946 when her father obtained a position at the University of New Brunswick. A scientific expert in permafrost, her father was anxious to move south to the States because the main experts in permafrost were at MIT in Boston. Within two years he had achieved his ambition but Abbi remained in New Brunswick, where she had acquired friends. Similarly, some of the professional migrants to Canada in the 1960s and 1970s thought connections in the aviation or aerospace industry or other business links might lead them to the United States.

The migrant narratives call attention to the significance of advertising in shaping the decision to move to Canada, especially when seen at a critical moment for making life choices. Some, like Hannah Marriot and Peter Semple, who were dissatisfied with life in England or simply interested in travel and new experiences, were attracted by large newspaper ads promoting the rewards of emigration. In other cases, migrants responded to more specific advertisements for well-defined employment opportunities. As already noted, Pamela Austin's mother replied to an advertisement by the International Ladies' Garment Workers Union, Robin Lanson in the Yorkshire military camp found a journal advertisement for a hospital physicist in Nova Scotia, and Tom Walsh saw an advertisement in the Sunday papers for a Montreal engineering job that was almost identical to the one he had in England. In a somewhat different twist on advertising, Charlotte Hinton's husband, a shipbuilder, had his interest in emigration reinforced by the magazine *Popular Mechanics*. As Charlotte explained, "*Popular Mechanics* always had fabulous things you could build if you were in America or Canada. And he wanted so much to have this house that was in Canada. So eventually we moved to Canada."

The departure of young people from England documented in this chapter became noticeable shortly after the war. Nella Last, living in the town of Barrow-in-Furness in northwestern England, was one of the most faithful and prolific of the diary keepers for the Mass Observation project, which had been collecting the perceptions and thoughts of ordinary Britons since 1937. An acute observer of daily life, Nella Last wrote in her diary in August 1947, after listening to Churchill's voice on the radio: "I share his concern about so many who want to go abroad, but what can we do? Youth is so fleeting. This generation has lost so much, and dear God they ask so little—just that chance to work and see something for their labours, a share in those simple good things in life in the way of food that the colonies have to offer. I've never yet heard anyone speak of making a fortune or of big wages, only the chance to get on."[18] The migrant narratives confirm how a desire to get on, for a combination of reasons, continued to motivate both women and men in their twenties and thirties to leave England in the following decades. Having made the decision to leave, migrants next faced the journey and transition to a new country.

Chapter 3

CROSSING THE ATLANTIC

"A magnificent future awaits in Canada."[1]

Seventeen-year old Anne Graves, along with her parents and younger brother and sister, emigrated from Newcastle-upon-Tyne on England's northeast coast to Port Alberni, on the west coast of Vancouver Island, British Columbia, in 1956. Their move involved a complex journey of 6,500 miles and took the best part of a month. For Anne and her family, this was an exciting and traumatic time, though Anne acknowledged their journey was not as difficult as that faced by the first English settlers who "came here on a sailing ship that took six months round the Horn."[2]

As we saw in the previous chapter, Anne's father, a miner, had been persuaded to come to Canada when his friend Bill Ross, a miner but from Vancouver Island, invited him. The men met when they were both prisoners of war. Bill wanted Anne's father, Jack, to emigrate in 1947, but Jack chose to wait until Anne had finished her schooling. According to Anne, the decision to emigrate was her father's alone. Her mother was reluctant to leave her family and was fearful she would never see her mother again. Anne could not recall her parents arguing about emigration but was sure that her mother would have tried to persuade her husband to stay in England. But, Anne observed, this was in an era when "you go where your man goes."[3] Moreover, the pits were closing and coal mining in the Northeast was in decline. Jack decided that a move to Canada would be a move for the better, and he had a sponsor in Bill Ross.

Once the decision to emigrate had been made, preparations got under-
way. Applications had to be made to Canadian authorities for permission to
emigrate. This took the whole family to their nearest Department of Citizenship and Immigration overseas office in Glasgow, Scotland. Anne was too
young to remember all the formalities, but she has distinct memories of the
circumstances. Mother, father, and the three children travelled to Glasgow,
more than 150 miles northwest of Newcastle. They all had to get passport
photographs taken, and Anne's aunt bought her a new dress especially for
the occasion. On the way to the immigration office Anne's eight-year-old
brother lost his balance on a trolley car and fell off. Another trauma befell
the family when, with the exception of Jack, mother and children all fainted
when they had their shots at their medical examinations. Anne, who had
just started her first job as a comptometer operator for Vickers Armstrong,
had a rosy vision of Canada and was excited about moving there. While at
school she had seen pictures of Canada depicting the prairies, trees, and
Mounties. She also remembered being sent apples from Canada after the
war. Canada, she said, "was like Camelot to me."[4]

For most immigrant families the decision to emigrate would have
been the main topic of conversation among friends and members of the
extended family, but not so in the case of Anne's family. To avoid upsetting
Anne's grandmother, Anne's mother insisted on secrecy, only to be undone
when somebody revealed that the family were selling their furniture prior
to departure. Family separations are poignantly emotional and traumatic
for both emigrants and those left behind. Forty-odd years later, through
tears, Anne recalled how her grandmother reacted to finding out why the
furniture was being sold: "When she saw my Mum, she said to her: 'I might
as well say goodbye because I'll never see you again,' and that came true...
and I am going to cry!"[5]

Anne's was a close-knit family. Because her father was incarcerated as a
POW, she did not see him until just before her seventh birthday. Her first
recollection of her father was of sitting on his knee and feeling his rough
army uniform and rough beard. She had been living in her grandmother's
two-bedroom house with her mother and aunts, sharing a bed with her
grandmother and Aunt Molly. After the war she would see her grandmother,
aunts, and cousins every weekend. Saying goodbye to everyone was difficult. Making the arrangements to travel also involved selling their house
and furniture, and giving "a lot of stuff," some of it with sentimental value,

to family members. The house was a valuable asset and provided capital for Jack to buy a house in Canada. After the war Jack's increased income from his promotion at the pit had enabled him to buy a large house with two attics, three bedrooms, a box room, bathroom, sitting room, dining room, kitchen, and scullery. According to Anne, her mother "hated" this "huge" house mainly because she had to spend all of her time cleaning it and cooking for the family. Nonetheless, Anne's mother did not want to leave her close family. In an attempt to mollify her, Jack took the unusual move of buying expensive first-class tickets for the family's passage.

After the farewells at their grandmother's house in Newcastle, Anne's family travelled to Southampton, stopping in London to say goodbye to Jack's sister. The family departed Southampton in July 1956 on the luxury liner SS *Homeric*. When they boarded the ship, the crew, hearing their working-class Geordie accents, directed them to steerage until Jack furnished the first-class tickets. Mum and Dad, together with the two younger children, shared a cabin, and Anne shared with a French-Canadian woman in her twenties. In her notes about the voyage, written on the back of menu cards, Anne recalled a good crossing and recorded a lot about the food: "I talk about a steak that my Dad had that filled his plate! I mean, I'd never seen anything like that before!" Sadly, her mother did not enjoy the unaccustomed luxury, being laid low with seasickness and spending most of the voyage in her cabin. Anne did not remember much about her arrival in Montreal other than the enormous and busy arrivals shed. She did, however, remember the four-day railway journey on the old CPR—the food, the different colours of the houses, and the fact that they were made of wood, which she perceived as a fire risk. Bill Ross met the family in Vancouver and then it was onward by ferry to Nanaimo, where they boarded a bus to Port Alberni. Anne recalled, "It was probably a couple of hours, [but] it seemed like such a long way, and we went around Cameron Lake; I'd never been that close to a lake...the scenery and everything really enthralled me."[6] Bill's son met them at the bus depot and took them to his home which, according to Anne, was "in the middle of nowhere, right in the bush where there were only trees."[7] The new immigrants had arrived.

3. A sad and emotional farewell at London's Northolt airport. Photo credit: Archives of Ontario, RG 9-7-4-1-14, Ontario House Records.

Anne's story highlights the emotion and life-changing nature of her last days in England, her journey, and her arrival in what she perceived to be the middle of nowhere on Vancouver Island. For most immigrants, getting to Canada was a mélange of anticipation, fear, excitement, and regret, as well as a range of other emotions. The complex process of leaving their country of birth and getting to Canada involved considerable upheaval for all those involved. There were the immigration formalities before departure; arranging and financing transportation; packing, selling goods, and disposing of housing; consolidating assets; resigning from employment; and much more. These activities were followed by saying goodbye to family and friends. Then came the actual journey to the port of entry, followed by immigration formalities before their onward journey. What were their first impressions? And, how did the whole experience colour their approach to settling in and adopting Canadian cultural mores and values? This chapter considers the significance of what was an epic journey from the old world to the new. It also introduces themes central to the immigrant experience that will be considered in greater depth in subsequent chapters.

Getting ready to go

For the majority of immigrants, their first point of contact with Canada and Canadians was at one of the six Canadian immigration offices in England. While some of our interviewees initially contacted an office simply to obtain information while deciding whether to migrate, all eventually had to pass assessment at an immigration office before being accepted for entry into Canada. The nature of their experience could affect their attitude to Canada or to migration. According to Freda Hawkins, compared with the Canadian civil service, the overseas immigration service were the "poor relations or second cousins."[8] While some of the architecture of Canadian immigration offices was most impressive—as in MacDonald House, the former American Embassy in London's Mayfair, and later Canada House in Trafalgar Square—internal furnishings and office equipment left prospective immigrants and employees with a poor impression. A 1964 article in the Toronto *Financial Post* reported, "Our immigration offices abroad have been described as 'tatty,' 'filthy,' and 'second rate,' by depressed officials. Compared with the smart, attractive offices of the Australian Service, Canada cuts an unattractive figure."[9] The attitude of the staff and the service that they provided also had an impact. Hawkins's investigations found that the Canadian overseas service employed a low grade of staff, management was not of the highest calibre, communication with Ottawa was poor, and staff morale was not as high as it should have been. Morale was at an all-time low in London in 1962–63 when the numbers of immigrants from England dropped to their lowest level since the war. This decline created despondency, which led High Commissioner George Drew, the former Ontario premier who had initiated the air transport scheme in the 1940s, to demand action from Richard Bell, who was the new Minister of Citizenship and Immigration in the Diefenbaker government formed in 1962.[10] What became known as "Bell's Resurrection" was the outcome. Bell decided to put his department in the U.K. back in business and sent new staff and special instructions to London to get moving again.[11] Within five years, numbers of English-born immigrants increased fivefold. Overall, however, improvements to the Canadian immigration service between 1945 and 1970 tended to be slow and sporadic.[12]

Despite the internal departmental struggles, our interviewees found immigration officers in England to be generally diligent and helpful. Personnel in the English offices performed a range of tasks. Their first job was to sell the benefits of Canada even though, as we saw in Chapter 1, they were not always happy with the promotional material at their disposal. This stage was followed by counselling prospective immigrants, providing advice on a wide range of topics from housing to employment, education, the passage loan scheme, and more. In Hawkins's opinion, the officers tended to exhibit a positive bias toward English and other U.K. immigrants. This practice was a consequence of familiarity, tradition, history, and to some degree government policy. Kerry Badgley documents one revealing example of this bias, as well as the bureaucratic ineptitude that at times infiltrated the service, in an article titled "As Long as He is an Immigrant from the United Kingdom: Deception, Ethnic Bias and Milestone Commemoration in the Department of Citizenship and Immigration, 1953–1965." By studying government papers Badgley discovered that ministers and officials sought to commemorate, in a blaze of publicity, the arrival of the millionth postwar immigrant in 1954. Given a skeptical and somewhat xenophobic Canadian public, the government wanted to show the benefits immigrants brought to the country. In a rash of interdepartmental communication, photogenic and other attractive candidates were put forward to represent the ideal immigrant. The majority of the proposals given serious consideration were English men and women, supplied by the High Commission in London. Because of the contrived nature of this publicity stunt the plan was eventually dropped, with government officials fearing media ridicule.[13] The role of England-based immigration officers became somewhat less subjective after October 1967. The introduction of the points-based scheme for the assessment of potential immigrants introduced a new regime of objectivity, emphasizing education and skills rather than ethnicity.[14] As Hawkins observed, it became much more difficult to accuse immigration officers of discrimination and poor judgment. Nonetheless she did concede that the immigration officer still retained a fair amount of responsibility in the selection process.[15] Once the prospective immigrants had completed their formal applications and had passed their medicals, it was the responsibility of the immigration officers to screen the applicants. They were assisted by locally based RCMP officers who conducted security screening, as we saw in the case of the Joneses in Chapter 1.

A common memory shared by our interviewees was of waiting among crowds of aspiring immigrants at the overseas immigration offices. Journalist Noel Taylor recollected both the crowds and the favourable reception given English immigrants:

We went up to Canada House one day [in 1956], and [laughs] we had
to line up. I can remember the place now. Canada House is in Trafalgar
Square, big building, several storeys. There were a lot of people lining
up, all the way up on the stairs just sitting on the stairs waiting to
get in for an interview. We needed an interview of some kind just to
find out how interested we were and how interesting we would be to
them, so to speak. So we couldn't get in the first day and we went again
another day and finally got in and everything went okay. So that was
no problem; it was not a question of "we want to keep you out, we
really want you to come in" sort of thing. In those days emigration from
England was a big deal, for them. They were glad to have us because
we were fairly well educated, fairly well trained in our jobs, and so on.

Ten years later, in 1966 as the point system was being introduced, James
Roland found that immigration officers were operating a form of triage in
the selection and fast-tracking of desirable educated immigrants:

I recall going up the stairs [at the Canadian High Commission in
London] and it was on the second level and there was a huge room full
of people all wanting to go to Canada. I think this was historically just
at the end of rather a large period of immigration from Britain, and
certainly not knowing that at the time, but just had this impression
of this large room crammed with people, and I got to the front of
the first queue, which was just to get a form to fill in. So I filled in the
form, and I recall while I was there sort of talking to people, and they
were saying, "Well I've been here two days" and "I've been here three
days" and this horrible feeling. Well, I got the form filled out and got
into the next queue, got to the front of it, and the chap looked at it and
said, "Oh you've got a degree," and I said, "Yes". He said, "Okay, I'll take
your form, please go back and wait." And then five minutes later an
announcement came: "Will Mr Roland please so and so." So instead of
two or three days, in three hours I was out of there having had a medical
and having an assisted passage [sic][16] and landed immigrant status.

On the whole, interviewees' memories were of a positive experience in their dealings with the Canadian immigration service, but that is to be expected; the self-selecting nature of the interviewees meant that we were interviewing successful applicants only. Nonetheless, some did experience difficulties. It is evident from James Roland's testimony that many aspiring immigrants were subject to prolonged scrutiny. Pat Connor recalled that, "it took a year for my paperwork to come through." Not all applicants were successful. As shown in Chapter 2, Joan Martin, in spite of being English-born, initially experienced rejection from the immigration authorities. After having her immigration application turned down, Joan returned to her parents' home in Trinidad. Sometime later she visited her boyfriend Tom, who had been given landed immigrant status, in Toronto: "I came up here [Canada] on vacation and just stayed. So we got married and then we went and told the Immigration and at that point they said okay and they let me stay."

After securing permission to come to Canada, the newly approved landed immigrants faced an extremely busy period in their lives. The logistics of emigration were complex. The first step was usually to book and pay for the passage. In the years immediately after the war this proved to be difficult, given the loss of shipping during the hostilities and the fact that available ships were still being used as troop carriers for returning Canadian soldiers, as well as transport for war brides and displaced persons. Demand outstripped supply and Charles Hall admitted having to pay a bribe of five pounds, then the equivalent of a week's wages, to secure a booking on the *Aquitania*, which was still configured as a troop ship. This meant that he was separated from his wife and daughter, who shared a cabin with forty other women on the starboard side while he shared with forty men on the port side.[17]

Canada did not subsidize emigrants with free or low-cost fares. Some employers, however, paid for the moving and travel expenses of their new employees and families, as in the case of Jeremy Charles, who came to work for Canadian Avionic Electronics (CAE) in Montreal. Such employers often placed conditions on expense payments, requiring the subsidized employee to work for a minimum period, a stipulation faced by Robert Baldwin, who also came to work in the aircraft industry in Montreal. Most immigrants had to fund themselves. Some, like Robin Lanson and Peter Semple, took advantage of the Canadian government passage loan scheme. Others, like Frank and Agnes Butcher, had to save. Frank recalled:

My fare was going to be £100 on the *Empress of Scotland* and we put a couple of ads [for my car] in the paper. It was easy; some guy at 6 o'clock in the morning was knocking on the blooming door to buy it. We sold it for £87. That was about what I spent on it, you know, 87 quid, and then I had to wait three months; I had to wait while I could save enough money to get the damn £100. That's how bad it was, and we didn't waste any money. Agnes was a fantastic shopper, even at that age. We didn't waste any money at all, but it took me another three months to get my £100, and that's what I paid to come here on the *Empress of Scotland*.

In some families even children became involved. The father of six-year-old Alan Thoms auctioned his son's toys to start a bank account for him on his arrival in Calgary. Alan remembers that his sixty-three dollars "was a lot of money for a kid in 1957." Homeowners tended to have the best source of realizable capital, but many emigrants were tenants or were still living with their parents. Even for those owning property or having access to other sources of capital, there were periodic problems in the shape of exchange control regulations. Because of the perilous state of the British economy, from time to time restrictions were imposed on taking sterling out of the country. Isobel Sinclair discovered that the existence of exchange control regulations in 1956 meant that "you couldn't take money out [of England]," and unless you were "independently wealthy with foreign connections," you would have to have work. Emigrants also sold or had to give away furniture or other goods they did not take with them. Some travelled light; Roger MacKay, for example, had only a one-way ticket and two suitcases, and the layers of clothes he was wearing. Others, like Florence Foster and John King, took considerable amounts of luggage with them. Florence Foster, her fisherman husband, and two adopted sons landed at Pier 21 in Halifax with twenty-two suitcases.[18] John King, who came from a well-travelled, upper-middle-class family, recalled experiencing difficulties with his heavy luggage even before embarkation at Southampton in 1947:

I had to find something to pack my stuff in to ship. I remember we had a lovely wooden box which I had for years, which was made in the USA with handles on the ends, and it had a nice lid with a rubber seal around the top...and I put all my junk in it and it had to go down to Waterloo [Station] to be delivered to the agent of the shipping company to be transferred to Southampton by rail. So now the box was full it weighed, I can't remember, about 200 pounds or something and so it took two able-bodied young men to lift it. So I persuaded some colleagues of mine to come down to the railway station in Malvern and load this on to the train for me, because when we got down there…the porters said, "We are only allowed to lift 100 pounds with two of us." So [my colleagues and I] lifted it on the train and I went down to London with this thing. And, I had buddies who were in London working at the universities there, and so one of them turned up to meet me off the train. So the two of us lifted this thing onto a trolley…because the porters wouldn't do it for us, took it out to the front, and found a taxi to go to Waterloo. I remember we said to the taxi driver, "We don't know whether you will want to take this great big heavy thing." "Oh that's all right," he said, "just put it up here beside me…I'll tie it up here." And off we went with this box which nobody on the Great Western Railway would lift for us, down to Waterloo. And we get there and the guy comes up…with his little two wheeled trolley and we said, "It's a great big heavy box." "That's all right," he said and he flipped it on to his two-wheeled trolley and off he went to the place I had to go…to send this thing off.

There were two other important elements in the departure process. The first, which we will consider in Chapter 5, involved terminating employment in England and finding work in Canada. The other, saying goodbye to family and friends, was the most difficult part of "getting ready to go." We have already seen how Anne Graves's grandmother was convinced that she would never see her daughter and granddaughter again. In the days before the introduction of jet aircraft, fear of not seeing relatives again was common, though given the relatively high rates of return and chain migration, the fear was not always justified. Separation anxiety was a near-universal phenomenon and most of the interviewees' testimonies reflected the sadness of departure, including the emotional turmoil of those left behind. Tears and anguish, mixed with a sense of excitement and anticipation, were commonplace.

Maisie (née Goat) Lugar and her brother Stanley Goat experienced a double dose of family separation.[19] During the war, their parents arranged for the two children to be evacuated to Canada. Stanley remembered thinking that their sojourn in Canada would not last long:

We boarded the train from Middlesbrough to the place from where we
had to board the ship. There were hugs, kisses, and tears, and I remember our parents running like mad from the platform…to a railway
crossing, where the train would go through, and waving at us. We had
our youngest sister Sheila, who stayed back with our parents in England.
As far as we can recall my parents were reluctant to send any of us so far
away, and they had to keep at least one of us with them, and they kept
Sheila. Unfortunately she died from natural causes during the war.[20]

Stanley did not return to his hometown until 1951, by which time he was in
the Canadian army serving in Germany. Maisie continued her formal education in New Brunswick, where the social welfare officer had found foster
parents for her and Stanley. Maisie wrote to her birth parents every week and
once spoke to them on a live radio broadcast from Moncton on a program
called *Hello Children*. She admitted, however, "We were so comfortable and
well treated by our foster family that it didn't take us long to almost forget
our parents."[21] At the end of the war, to save money and because Stanley
was halfway through his degree course, his birth parents agreed to let him
stay on in Canada. Maisie, just graduated from high school, was persuaded
to return to Middlesborough, even though, as Stanley recalled, their foster
parents much regretted that decision. Her return lasted only four years and
in 1951 she returned to Canada and soon married a Canadian.

Sometimes parents and occasionally spouses were hostile to the idea of
emigration. Mary Charles, whose husband had been offered a job by CAE,
recalled: "My mother said, 'What on earth are you doing taking two children
to a place you don't know?' and as he had to go quickly…we came to a deal."
Her husband should go for three months. From an employment perspective,
that was an impractical proposition and created a real dilemma for the family.
Until the job offer, Mary "had no thought of leaving England whatsoever." At
the same time, "there was no money in the bank at the end of the month and
we had an eight-year-old car and two young children." Yet Mary remained
reluctant. "Leaving friends and the kids having to give up their friends…it
seemed not just like a quarter of the way round the world but the other side
of the world." In the end Jeremy went on his own. Mary recalled:

> I remember it well—big tears to dry up after he had gone. Three
> months later, he came back to get us, and looking back on it I don't

know how on earth we did it. We did manage to sell the house, and the day we sold the house and walked out and turned the key on it, we got in a car and were driven to the airport and got on a plane and came to Canada. Two kids that had never been on a plane before, aged seven and five. We had eighteen pieces of hand luggage, the rest had all been packed up and was being shipped over here.

Getting there

Until after World War II, the only way emigrants could cross the Atlantic Ocean was by ship. In the years immediately after the war, however, there was a shortage of berths given the demand from returning troops and displaced persons. Capacity problems also resulted from the loss of ships during the hostilities and from the need to reconfigure passenger ships that had been converted for wartime purposes. Passengers from England usually embarked from Southampton, Liverpool, Bristol, or London. Canadian ports of arrival included Saint John, Pier 21 in Halifax, Quebec City, and Montreal. Some emigrants entered Canada via the United States after

4. Inspecting new arrivals in the Immigration Examination Hall, Pier 21, Halifax, March 1952. Photo credit: Chris Lund / National Film Board of Canada Photothèque Collection, Library and Archives Canada, PA-111579.

having sailed to New York, Boston, or occasionally Philadelphia.

John King was an early postwar immigrant who found a passage on a former troop ship destined for New York. After his travails with his heavy box, King boarded the *Marine Falcon*. He recalled:

It had come from Cherbourg I think and so it was already full of European postwar camp refugees who had managed to get admission to the United States. So I guess a whole lot of people joined it from Britain, of various sorts of people, at Southampton, and then it sailed off to Cork in Southern Ireland, and there a whole lot of people came out on a tender and boarded the ship, all Irish, and then we sailed off across the Atlantic. Well it was kind of interesting because we were on a former [troop ship], the GI brides, I think there were about 150 or so of them perhaps… with all their kids up in the cabin accommodation, the rest of us were down below in two tier bunks, open, not in cabins, all in between the bulkheads in about three decks underneath these women and their children. And, the eating facilities, the cafeteria was upstairs where the women were. So off we went [laughs] and I remember it because when we went up to our first meal, breakfast next morning…there was unlimited amounts of bacon and eggs and coffee and toast and so forth. I had come from wartime Britain where you got one egg a week. The second thing I remember about that was that there was a big Scandinavian American who sat at the end of the line you got to with your trays, and he sat on the top of the counter, I can still see him with his legs crossed, and he poured the coffee into your mug as you went by….

We get around the southwest corner of Ireland, and we ran into a huge gale so we are like this for the next, virtually ten days. In fact I think when we were two-thirds of the way across, south of Newfoundland or somewhere, the ship actually hove [to] for two days and just didn't go anywhere. The only thing they could do was keep the head into the sea, it was so high nobody was allowed to go on deck, so you can imagine what it was like down below. I had been across the ocean many times and so I wasn't sick, but I would say that 90 percent of the people were sick…and they never went up on deck from the day after they rounded the southwest of Ireland to the day they got to Long Island and New York Harbour.

The other thing I remember about it was they had a store, and you went there and you could buy chocolate and soft drinks and stuff like this. And…particularly I remember the Irish. The Irish had come along with Irish money, they didn't have any American money, and the guy that ran the store refused to give them the exchange rate for their money….I think the exchange rate at the time was supposedly four U.S. dollars to the pound and I think he gave them two or something like that, and they were outraged, I remember that. And… there was no recreational facilities of any sort, there was just a big open space on one of the decks down below where they had a few chairs and some seats….There were a lot of Jewish people on board from the camps and of course they had their Jewish holiday in March while we were on board ship and I can still remember them. One wall of this room was the Wailing Wall and they all had to do their stuff there at the wailing wall…. There was a table there and I used to go and sit and watch, I never played, where they played poker, a lot of people playing poker. And I still remember there was a guy sat there who played poker, and he used to win quite a lot of the time. And so they were playing poker with Bill, probably mostly British and American currency, and I remember every time he had won a game he would pick up the money and stick it in his shirt pocket. And, this went on for the ten days that we were in this part of the trip and people figured he had made enough money at the poker game to pay for his passage. I think I paid…twenty-eight or thirty pounds for a one way trip on this ship to New York….

Any rate, we get to New York. And, the next thing that happened was we had to go through the Immigration on board ship…and I and the guy that slept on the bunk above me or below me, I forget which, was going to Toronto. He had decided he was going to take the Greyhound bus across the US and back before he went to Toronto to whatever job he had to go to there….I had my ticket, from Canadian National, I was taking the CN train up to Montreal and the guy had wisely said to me "it's an overnight train so if I were you I would have a roomette, a bunk on the train," so I had that. I remember we were lined up, the two of us together on this lineup. He reaches the immigration officer. The immigration officer says to him, "how long are you staying in the United States?" and he says to him, unwisely I guess, "I wanted to stay long enough to take the bus across to the west coast and back before

I get to Toronto." So I can still see him; he stamped his passport and visa and said forty-eight hours. In other words, "Get the hell out of here." I came up behind him and he asked me how long I was going to stay, and I said I am taking the CN night train up tonight.... So I came up on the CN train overnight...got to the border, was admitted to Canada, arrived in Montreal, took the train up to Ottawa.

John King's memories of the voyage were vivid ones, as were those of many of the interviewees who travelled by sea. Following years of rationing and austerity the immigrants commented often about the quantity, variety, and choice of food. The weather, rough seas, fog, and the occasional iceberg also featured in the oral testimonies, along with memories of seasickness. By the 1950s a sea voyage became more comfortable as former troop ships were replaced by passenger liners, although there were significant differences in comfort levels depending on whether the immigrants were travelling first class or steerage.

The young, single, and adventurous Mary Irvine sailed on the *Empress of France* from Liverpool to Quebec City in 1956, with her friend Trish:

The two of us set off from Torquay, waved farewell to our parents at the station.... We went up to Liverpool, and our cabin was down in the depths of the *Empress of France,* which had originally been called the *Duchess of Bedford* and was known as the drunken Duchess, it was so tossed around on the sea. Anyway, Trish went to sign up for a table in the dining room, which you had to do in those days. She came back and she said, "Oh, I've met a nice girl and her brother and we're going to share a table with them," and sure enough, Sue and her brother Mike were going off to visit a cousin in Toronto. Michael was a student at Cambridge, and he was going to be a doctor, and he was just going for the summer. Sue didn't know how long she would go for. I was only planning to come over to Canada for two years at that point but you still had to emigrate from England if you wanted to do that. And we got on well. I actually spent the first three days being terribly sea sick and then Sue and I sat out on deck and chatted and before long we became good friends as you do on a ship, I think, and she decided to share an apartment with Trish and myself when we got to Toronto. On the boat there were a great many students. It was the time that the Trans-Canada

Highway was being built and a lot of the fellows on the boat were going
out to work during the summer on the Trans-Canada. There were other
students from the…Imperial College in London, and they were going
out to Elliot Lake, which was a big mining area at the time. We had a
ten-day crossing and we all became very good friends…and we landed
at Quebec City, and it was just lovely walking round there, the Chateau
Frontenac…. Anyway we went the next day, the boat continued on,
and we actually went up the river to Montreal…on the *Empress of
France* and then transferred on to a train and went to Toronto.

What is significant about this part of Mary's testimony is the amount of socializing she enjoyed on board ship. Mary made new friends and met a young
woman with whom she shared an apartment. Other immigrants, including
those with young children, also forged relationships with fellow passengers,
which helped prepare them for their new lives in Canada. Significantly, this
opportunity was not open to postwar immigrants who travelled by air.

First impressions of arrival in Canada featured extensively in the interviewees' reminiscences. These memories were an important part of their
life stories and were largely positive, often revealing a sense of anticipation
and excitement. They helped to symbolize the new life to which migrants
had come and would influence the process of settling in and adapting to
Canada. We have already seen how Anne Graves was struck by different-
coloured wooden houses, trees, and wide open spaces. Sailing up the unexpectedly long and wide St. Lawrence River, or arriving at Pier 21 in Halifax
created lasting impressions. Janet Cecil sailed to Canada after her husband,
Kenneth, had flown over in advance. He had been surprised by the heat: "I
remember the airplane was very hot on the approach: it was uncomfortably
hot and I thought the air conditioning had broken down. When we got
off, it was 85°F in the terminal in April and we were just absolutely hit by
this tremendous heat and humidity." Travelling later, after a fairly rough
crossing on the *Empress of Britain*, Janet recalled:

We got off at Quebec City, went through the customs, and I
walked all round the little town and they all looked pointy houses,
brightly coloured. And we got back on, and I came to Montreal.
Kenneth [had] told me how hot it was there [but] when I got off
the boat it, was freezing, and when [Kenneth] took me back to this

apartment there were no doors on anything, only the bathroom, and I found it cold. There was heating so he had to persuade the landlord to put the heat back on because I was so cold.

Differences in food also made an impression on many of the new immigrants. Shortly after her arrival Isobel Sinclair recalled:

There were certainly new foods. I remember going with some friends when I was working at that bank and we went for lunch somewhere, and people were ordering buttermilk. I said, "Oh what's that?" They said, "Oh, it's delicious!" [laughter] So I ordered it, but wanted to throw up. I'd never had that…. And the other thing that was different was eating out casually, which we didn't often do in England…because of the money, but if you did, there wasn't much choice of places to go to, and the kind of food that you got…well, the cheapest thing was usually baked beans on toast—that was a popular item and then you'd have tea…. When I left [England] we still didn't have a big variety of things in stores, like fruits and vegetables, and that was a big change here—a lot more things.

Another common memory was the experience of passing through customs and immigration. In 1951 the Department of Citizenship and Immigration employed 1,282 officers in the Canadian Field Service, at border controls and ports of entry. Ten years later, this number had increased to 1,485.[22] These officers gave final approval for the immigrants to enter Canada and stamped their papers as landed immigrants. This was a positive experience for most new arrivals. Many remember how welcoming they found these officials. Florence Foster and her husband Chris landed in Halifax on a Sunday afternoon in early January 1951. The immigration officer asked them where they were going and who would meet them. Florence said they didn't know anyone, and they didn't have anywhere to go. The immigration officer, hearing that Chris was a fisherman, told them to go to Water Street, to National Fish.[23] He also told them about Gerrard Lodge on Barrington Street.[24] The snow was deep and they didn't know where they were, but they eventually found the lodge. They rented one room for the night at seven dollars. In the morning they went to Woolworth's for breakfast. They also bought their sons warmer clothes and walked around Halifax to get a feeling of the city. The next day, Chris went to National Fish and got a job on a boat right away.[25]

Hannah Marriot, the young hotel worker we met in Chapter 2, and her French-born husband remember their particularly helpful immigration officer, a Mr. Chauvin:

> He asked us about ourselves and our experience and the type of
> work we would want to do and where we would want to be, and
> suggested that the following day he was going up into the lower
> Laurentians by car to see…a German youth that he had placed in a
> Volkswagen garage in St Jerome; if we liked we could go with him,
> and he would take us to a few hoteliers that he knew in the Laurentian
> area as the resort season was just beginning—it was mid-June—and
> introduce us to a few of these hotel proprietors in the region.

Jenny Carter immigrated with her parents when her father obtained a post at the University of New Brunswick:

> We arrived on January first 1947 to a tremendous welcome. One of
> the immigration officers, who was well known for helping people—his
> daughter was at UNB and she alerted her father that we were coming,
> and so he really welcomed us, took us to his home, his wife gave
> us dinner, and then they put us on the train for St John. And, then
> we spent the day in St John and being with the parents we spent it
> at the New Brunswick museum and then we went by train up to
> Fredericton to be met by [the university president] Milton Gregg
> and his wife…. So it was really a tremendous welcome to Canada.

In 1966, an unnamed senior official who had been employed by the Department of Citizenship and Immigration in the 1950s observed that the department consisted largely of "self-made men," and that university graduates or those with professional qualifications were not hired. He admitted that these employees "had limitations" but that "there were many who had a great deal of dedication." He went on to say that these officers "were doing a good job for Canada, which was unappreciated."[26] They may well have been unappreciated by politicians and sections of Canadian society, but for many of our interviewees the opposite was the case. And according to anecdotal evidence such as that cited by John King (above), the Canadian immigration service compared favourably with that of the U.S. Nobel Laureate John Steinbeck concurred. In his best-selling travelogue, *Travels with Charley*, he wittily described his experience with U.S. and Canadian border officials in 1960.[27] According to the Californian-born writer, "the Canadians were kind," while the U.S. officials were like the "Gestapo."

In contrast with immigrants who came by sea, those who came by air had much less to say about their journey. Air travel took less time so airline passengers were not able to meet and mingle with fellow travellers, or enjoy a series of sumptuous meals, or look at the view, or engage in other activities. These differences may explain why, for those who came by air, the actual journey had less significance in their life stories. The first commercial passenger flight over the North Atlantic was inaugurated by Pan American World Airways in March 1939. During World War II the crossing of the Atlantic by air became commonplace, with RAF Ferry Command delivering a steady stream of U.S.- and Canadian-built combat aircraft to the United Kingdom, crossing from Gander in Newfoundland to Prestwick in Scotland. Aircraft technology improved during the war years, and airfield runways were lengthened to accommodate long-range aircraft.

As noted in Chapter 1, the Ontario government initiated the first scheme for emigrants to travel by air in 1947. This program used a propeller-driven Trans Ocean Airlines Skymaster aircraft. Prop-aircraft were slow, noisy, and an uncomfortable means of travel. Ron Inch recounted how he came in 1948 on a British Overseas Airways Corporation (BOAC) North Star four-engine "prop job." "Sixteen hours!" he said, laughing. "Oh God I remember that."[28] The flight stopped for refuelling at Reykjavik, Goose Bay, and Montreal before landing in Toronto. In 1961 Murray Watson flew, with his teenage sister, from Heathrow to Gander via Shannon, Ireland, on a BOAC four-engined Britannia. As with most propeller-driven aircraft it had an unpressurized cabin. This meant that the aircraft could not fly at heights above 10,000 feet, therefore exposing the passengers to unpleasant levels of turbulence. It also meant that the fuselage suffered condensation problems and Murray remembers that his sister was concerned that the plane was leaking.

The revolution in air travel came in the 1960s with the introduction of jet-propelled aircraft such as VC10s, DC8s, and the ubiquitous Boeing 707. As shown in Table 1, in 1964 the numbers of immigrants arriving by air overtook those who came by sea. This rapid change in the mode of travel had a significant impact upon the whole migration experience, especially the dynamics of extended family relationships. Long-distance migration by sea created perceptions that immigrants would never see members of their extended families or friends in the country of origin again. This fear was removed with the arrival of the jet plane.

Table 1 | **MODE OF ARRIVAL FROM ENGLAND**

	SHIP	AIRCRAFT
1957	*50,502*	*26,552*
1958	*11,295*	*5,360*
1959	*8,639*	*3,897*
1960	*8,130*	*3,897*
1961	*6,386*	*5,224*
1962	*8,381*	*6,938*
1963	*12,263*	*11,953*
1964	*13,107*	*15,612*
1965	*16,777*	*22,399*
1966	*21,595*	*40,563*
1967	*18,776*	*42,437*
1968	*8,658*	*27,973*
1969	*5,849*	*24,713*
1970	*3,702*	*14,708*

Source: *Department of Citizenship and Immigration, Annual Reports, Statistics Section.*

Conclusions

Leaving one's home, complying with the bureaucratic demands of immigration officials, packing up to go, and saying goodbye to family and friends before journeying thousands of miles into the unknown was an extraordinarily brave step for emigrants. A sense of uncertainty, excitement, and anticipation coexisted with regret and sadness, all part of an unforgettable period of emotional turmoil in immigrants' lives. This intensity was reflected in the depth and detail of memories of our interviewees. The minutiae of John King's memories, recorded sixty years after his voyage, emphasize how significant the actual process of emigration was. It is noteworthy that the more detailed reminiscences came from immigrants who travelled by sea. Their journeys were longer and so perhaps more memorable than those by air. Furthermore, sea voyages created a greater sense of distance, giving passengers more time to absorb the significance of the life-changing nature of the journey they were undertaking. In two studies about English migration to Australia and New Zealand, memories of the voyage, albeit much longer in duration, also featured prominently in the life story testimonies.[29] Interestingly, both the Australian and New Zealand governments provided on-board education classes for the immigrants. This service was not provided by the Canadian authorities.

The postwar years also witnessed a revolutionary change in the nature of international migration. The introduction of jet propulsion transformed international travel. As early as 1964, air travel surpassed sea voyages as the preferred means of transatlantic migration. This development contributed to an increase in the number of English-born immigrants coming to Canada (even though the rise was short-lived, as numbers declined from the 1970s onward). More significantly, flying changed the nature of the migration experience. No longer did immigrants assume they would never again see the loved ones they left behind. The consequences of air travel and other technological developments will be explored further in Chapter 6. We now turn to the next stage in the immigrants' lives: settling into their new homes and jobs.

Chapter 4

ADAPTATION

You had to feel settled and that is the biggest thing—
to feel that you belong in that place.[1]

For the postwar English immigrants whom we interviewed, the physical journey to their intended Canadian destination was a brief interlude, whether measured in days if by sea or, increasingly, in hours if by air. Their emotional journey, however, continued for the rest of their lives. The excitement and sadness of parting with family and friends lay in the past, but physical separation created enduring anxieties or a sense of loss for many, although sometimes also welcomed freedom from family pressures. The migrants usually had to deal with the break in family connections at the same time as they tried to settle into their new communities. English immigrants, like all immigrants, had to adapt in order to feel at home and be accepted in Canada. The existence of Commonwealth ties and assumptions of a shared British culture made the decision to migrate easier but did not necessarily prepare English immigrants for both subtle and more pronounced differences in the way of life in Canada.

In recounting their life stories, our interviewees welcomed the opportunity to reflect upon the process of acculturation in Canada. They brought a mature understanding to their personal experiences as a result of contemplating them after several decades of life in Canada. Many also compared themselves with other English immigrants or immigrants from different parts of the globe. In a 2006 interview, Rob Watson, a 1970s immigrant working in the computer industry, voiced the cultural tension inherent in belonging to the country of birth as well as the new chosen country:

I think it's the same for anybody, really, who goes to a new country. It's exciting, it's new, way of life is new. There are things available to you that weren't available to you in the place you'd come from. There are things that are quite different in each place. I think most people absorb part of the culture they come into, but never entirely absorb it. They are always attached to part of where they were, and we certainly are. We've probably got a more English way of life than a lot of people who came to Canada.... Partly I think that is because we came a bit later in life; we were in our thirties.... But obviously you have to adapt. That's what you do.

The interviews reveal the individual nature of responses to the opportunities and challenges of living in Canada. They also raise many questions that deal with work, family and community, and national identity. What did adaptation or acculturation mean for English immigrants in terms of daily life or personal identity? Did age or gender or place of settlement make a difference? How did single immigrants or childless married couples fit into Canadian society compared with married couples with children? And, fundamentally, why did the English interviewees decide to remain in Canada even though many came intending to stay for only a limited period of time?

The majority of postwar English immigrants to Canada settled in urban areas. As already noted in Chapter 1, Ontario was, by far, the most popular destination. British Columbia—a province that socially privileged English immigrants had favoured in the early twentieth century—ranked a distant second, followed closely by the province of Quebec. From the 1960s, oil-rich Alberta attracted a growing number of English immigrants, significantly outstripping both Manitoba and Saskatchewan, with their agriculturally based economies. Few postwar English immigrants stated an intention to go to the Atlantic provinces despite their proximity to Britain and the role of Pier 21 in Halifax as an immigrant receiving centre. While English immigrants conformed to general postwar immigration patterns in their regional distribution, they usually differed from most continental European and Asian immigrants by dispersing among the existing Canadian population.[2] Those we interviewed did not come as part of a community or group movement, and they did not seek to settle with other English immigrants. Nonetheless, happenstance and the recruitment of skilled English employees by certain Canadian enterprises produced occasional clusters of English or British settlement. Deep River, the atomic energy community in the Ottawa Valley, was one centre of concentrated English settlement in the 1950s; so were parts of Kanata, the high-tech suburb on the outskirts of Ottawa, in the 1960s and 1970s. Similarly, English immigrants recruited by the Canadian aviation and aerospace industry based in Montreal sometimes discovered that their neighbours included other English immigrants.

While economic or social differences in the various regions of Canada could affect the reception of postwar English immigrants, Quebec posed the most distinct challenges. A number of our interviewees who settled in the Montreal area felt unexpectedly isolated in francophone Quebec. They found themselves in the midst of a powerful resurgence of nationalism in Quebec—the "Quiet Revolution" of the 1960s.[3] Inspired by independence movements in former colonial territories around the globe, and feeling threatened by the invasive presence of anglophone culture in North America, francophones in Quebec demanded increased recognition and preservation of their language and culture. The majority supported the peaceful reforms that dramatically transformed Quebec from a society dominated by the Roman Catholic Church into a modern secular state, with the French language forming the core of its identity. A radical fringe group promoted violence which escalated from mail-box bombings to the October Crisis of 1970. The terrorist kidnapping of James Richard Cross, a British trade representative in Montreal, at the same time as the murder of Pierre Laporte, a Quebec cabinet minister, highlighted in a frightening way the hostile extremist insistence on "liberation" from the control of English Canada, or more generally "the English." Because Québécois had long viewed English immigration as reinforcing colonial ties with Britain as well as strengthening the English Canadian population, it was not an easy time to be an English immigrant in Montreal.

As noted in Chapter 1, two important theoretical frameworks for understanding the integration of immigrants into a new society are assimilation and acculturation. The meaning of "assimilation," however, is ambiguous in the Canadian context. Writing in the 1970s when multiculturalism was becoming government policy in Canada, Howard Palmer set out the "three theories of assimilation" linked with Canadian response to immigrants in the twentieth century.[4] The first, which was dominant at least until World War II, was conformity to the existing society, an approach which required immigrants to reject their own traditions in favour of the values of the receiving society. The second was the American concept of the "melting pot," which envisaged the creation of a homogeneous new society, and indeed a biologically new race, through the melding of the host society with the newcomers. This view accorded more value to the immigrant contribution and gradually gained acceptance from some Canadians who wanted a more tolerant approach to immigrants in their midst. The third theory was "cultural pluralism" or "multiculturalism," which became more popular in the latter half of the twentieth century. Because the term "assimilation" in Canadian discourse had long been associated with the demand that immigrants shed their culture so they would not be a threat to Canadian society, it often continued to carry those connotations even in the period after World War II. The migrants whom we interviewed rarely, if ever, spoke of assimilation; instead they reflected on adaptation, a flexible concept that implies change but not necessarily complete conformity. In our analysis here, we will follow their lead. Similarly, acculturation theory addresses a potentially two-way process whereby immigrants may shape the receiving society as well as be shaped by it. In telling their life stories, however, the English migrants we interviewed were mainly concerned with the evolution of their own lives rather than with the question of whether their coming had changed Canadian society.

Adaptation is a personal and complex process that depends on individual personality and emotion, expectations and fears, as well as such factors as background, family relations, age, gender, socioeconomic status, time of arrival, and place of residence in Canada. Two members of the same family may react quite differently to life in Canada. How migrants believed Canadians were responding to them was important. Whether Canadians seemed to perceive the migrants as different or "other," and, equally significant, whether they made such identification grounds for helping the migrants or treating them with discrimination, affected the adaptation process. So too did the scope of the migrants' own desires to fit in and feel that they belonged in their adopted country.

In this chapter we will examine some of the personal aspects of adaptation through the lens of our interviewees' recollections. Our interviewees' general silence regarding their appearance helps to confirm the invisibility of the postwar English migrant in Canadian society. By contrast, although they spoke English, the dominant language of Canada, many interviewees found that they were set apart by accent and language issues. Because communication is such a central part of life, accent difference was an emotionally stressful component of adaptation for some, although much less so for others. In addition, interviewees who settled in Montreal often felt increasingly uncomfortable because of their lack of competence in French, whether or not they sympathized with the efforts to reinforce francophone culture in Quebec. Instances of discrimination as a result of being identified as English could make a lasting, deep impression but were few in number, occurring mainly in conjunction with immediate postwar economic fears or the 1960s and 1970s turmoil in Quebec. The interviewees, nonetheless, discovered that fitting into Canadian ways and the Canadian environment required considerable adaptation in daily life. They had to acquire a Canadian reference system before they could feel they belonged in Canada. Their place in a Canadian urban consumer society was one major theme; they discussed the new money and financial system they had to use; shopping and cooking; and food and drink, including the absence of the English pub which, for some, had been a cherished social institution. A parallel theme was their adaptation to the Canadian natural and built environment: the almost overwhelming sense of space; the extremes of the climate; the differences in the landscape; and the birds, flowers, trees, and the unanticipated prevalence of bugs. Throughout, sensory perceptions, especially of sight, sound, taste, and smell, informed their personal responses and their memories of adaptation. For some, adaptation occurred quickly and relatively easily in the first months or couple of years; for others it was a lifetime process. Several reported that the "$1,000-cure"—a return visit to England—was indeed the elixir that overcame homesickness and enabled them to feel settled in Canada.

The audible immigrants: Accent in English Canada

White English-born immigrants in the postwar era seldom stood out as visibly different from Canadians. Mainly in their twenties or early thirties when they arrived in Canada, immigrants of this generation tried to conform to changing style trends that spanned the Atlantic. Austerity in Britain in the 1950s did limit the purchase of clothing and other commodities. As a young single woman on her working holiday in Toronto in the mid-1950s, Mary Irvine noted: "What was so lovely was all the lovely clothes. I can remember there was just such a variety of clothes because of course in the UK at that time we were still rationed for certain things." She did not, however, indicate that she felt awkward or apart in her English clothing. Her own choice of clothes obviously differed from that of the "elderly ladies in their tweeds" whom she later encountered when shopping at The Bay department store in Victoria and immediately identified as "so over-the-top English."

Some interviewees did discuss problems with their clothing, not because its appearance made them seem identifiably different but because their English purchases were not suited to the Canadian climate. Barbara and Roy Trueman humorously recalled how, in preparing for Canada, they bought matching gray duffel coats made of a type of blanket cloth and complete with toggles and hoods. They wore them on the voyage but discovered that they were totally inadequate for an eastern Ontario winter. Other memories were less cheerful. Richard Nash's recollections of settling in Montreal included the dreadful commute to work through howling Montreal blizzards: "We didn't have proper clothing. We had bought some clothing when we left, but not clothing that suits the weather here."[5] Pat Connor believed that inadequate clothing for the cold weather contributed to her depression.

Conversely, English immigrants also had to adjust clothing styles to the centrally heated Canadian urban homes, which were much warmer than in England in spite of the blizzards outside. Robin Lanson, who had himself adapted, remembered how he feared that his visiting father might be ill: "I noticed he was…very red in the face and everything, and I happened to be in the bedroom when he was getting dressed one day and…he puts his woolen vest on, a heavy shirt, a pullover, and a tweed jacket. I managed to convince him that all he needed was to walk about in short sleeves but somehow or other he felt this wasn't quite on."

In spite of their invisibility, our interviewees could not remain anonymous; they revealed their English identity as soon as they spoke. As Tom Martin astutely commented, "there was an 'audible minority culture' in that you fit in perfectly until you open your mouth and begin to speak and then you become 'other.'" Accent in England was a marker of social class and often of regional identity as well. In postwar Canada, by contrast, accent was mainly a marker of ethnicity. That marker vanished quickly with children, who were still at a malleable age when language skills were more easily acquired. Sailing to Canada at age twelve with her Cockney seamstress mother, Pamela Austin abandoned her accent in the middle of the ocean.[6] Eager to fit in as soon as possible, Tom Knight, on arrival in Canada at age eleven, stood at the end of a farm lane and practised saying "car" the Canadian way. He noted that his sister who was three years younger made the transition without any effort. Emma Bulmer from Birmingham was told that she came to Canada at age three with a strong regional accent that was rapidly teased out of her. Adults, too, found that they seemed to lose pronounced regional dialects. These lay dormant in Canada but could re-emerge if the immigrants returned to the district of England where they were again immersed in the dialect. May Preston, who had grown up in wartime Norwich, described her experience: "When people here say, 'Oh, you have an English accent, you haven't been here long,' I say, 'Well, I do have an English accent, but I don't have a Norwich accent anymore.' I completely lost the dialect [but] when I go back, within four days I got it, I'm speaking with the dialect. And, when I come back, it only takes me two or three weeks to lose it, and you do lose it." Like May, most adult migrants did not lose an identifiable English accent. It might be modified after years in Canada, but it did not disappear.

Our interviewees discovered that they were separated from English-speaking Canadians by a supposedly common language. Both pronunciation and vocabulary set them apart, leading to communication problems. In his first days in Canada, John King had difficulty with public transport because the bus driver could not understand what he was saying. Margaret Bell, who studied in London before emigrating in 1968, soon felt quite Canadian except for unexpected problems with her accent: "I can remember going to The Bay in Calgary not long after I got there, and asking one of the assistants for something, and she couldn't understand me and yet I just had a Brighton accent. It wasn't like I had this thick Glaswegian accent like the friends that we subsequently met." Initial difficulties with comprehension occurred in the other direction as well. Tom Martin had trouble understanding English-speaking Canadians when he arrived in Toronto in 1970: "For the first week I found people incomprehensible. We were talking the same language, and I couldn't understand what they were saying. It took about a week to get into the rhythm of the language so that I could pick up what they were saying. It wasn't vocabulary, it wasn't idiom and so on. I think it was simply the rhythm. Somebody would say something and I had to say, 'Sorry' or 'I beg your pardon.' So that was a bit of a shock." For certain individuals, the language problems were very stressful. In a vulnerable state because of personal issues, Pat Connor found having to repeat herself constantly strained her ability to cope. In addition, she never knew whether people were laughing at her or with her when they reiterated the well-known language joke regarding the double meaning of "knocking up," which in England referred to getting people up for work, but in Canada meant getting someone pregnant. A number of interviewees also commented on often unanticipated differences in word usage between England and Canada. The English *pavement* was *sidewalk* in Canada, *lorry* was *truck*, the *boot* of a car was a *trunk*, *Sellotape* was *Scotch* tape, *chemist* was *drugstore*, and the list could continue indefinitely. Although such differences in vocabulary formed obstacles to understanding, the new Canadian terms could be learned with relative ease; with practice and time, the Canadian usage would became automatic. May Preston helped to explain more subtle divergences that she found continued to be difficult. Canadian expressions such as "I guess so" or "Is that right?" were not used in England, and words like *controversy* or *advertisement* were pronounced quite differently in Canada. Individual ability to acquire language skills varied widely. In general, though, the interviewees indicated that acute problems of communication diminished relatively quickly as their ears became more attuned to the speech around them, but differences in language usage and pronunciation continued to set them apart.

Although almost all our interviewees were conscious of being identified by their English accent, they responded in various ways to such identification. Many seem to have passively accepted being audible immigrants as an inevitable fact of life. It was a little frustrating to be recognized as English as soon as you opened your mouth, but not a major concern. The journalist Noel Taylor even found his accent, and particularly his wife's accent, to be a positive asset that helped establish common bonds with other English immigrants. Over the years they stopped asking about regional origins, as they used to do, but still retained their sense of commonality with others from England.

On the other side of the spectrum were some immigrants who took action to try to lose their English accent, but with only partial or no success. James Leonard from southern England, who left his Canadian farm placement to join the military, had the assistance of Canadian friends in his efforts: "People had trouble understanding me! In fact, in some ways I was lucky. When I was in North Bay when I was still single we were four in a room; we roomed four guys together. One of the guys was from Hamilton and he took me under his wing and tried to teach me the Canadian way of saying things. Must have rubbed off a bit, but I still have an English accent!" James's use of the word *roomed* instead of the English *shared with* demonstrates his adoption of Canadian vocabulary, even with a self-confessed English accent.

Jenny Carter came from a higher level of the English social scale than most postwar English immigrants. Her family employed a chauffeur and a butler, and she had attended a socially elite girls' school near London. She believed that she encountered an anticolonial backlash in Canada that made an accent like hers unacceptable, even though understandable. As a result, in the mid-1970s she joined other newcomers in taking language courses so she could lose her accent: "I took three courses…and failed all of them, as you can tell…. I forced myself to take these dreadful courses, feeling rather like the girl in Pygmalion, and being so bad at it…. There are just some sounds that my throat refuses to make. And so, there were a lot of people there in the course. I mean all nationalities; it was very very interesting…. I went and I did my best but it just wasn't good enough so I've never lost it [English accent]." Ironically, Jenny Carter told us she did occasional voice-over work for Canadian radio because of her distinctive English accent.

The audible immigrants: Language in Quebec

English immigrants settling in the Montreal area confronted a different and more acute set of language challenges. The ability to function in French became much more important for them than the accent with which they spoke English. A few interviewees arrived either fluent in French or hoping to improve their French language skills as a result of living in Quebec. Hannah Marriot with her French husband deliberately chose to work in the restaurant business in Quebec because of their ability to speak French as well as English. Robert Baldwin was attracted to the job offer in Montreal in part because he hoped that it would provide an opportunity to improve his school French. He regretted that he never did become fluent in French; his work in the aviation industry was entirely in English. Others were surprised by the French presence in Quebec. When Elizabeth Summers was surrounded by French speakers on her journey to Montreal, she suddenly realized she had not done her homework. Arriving in 1960 when the Quiet Revolution was just beginning, Summers had no difficulty working and living in English in Montreal during the next year; she found Montreal a "very vibrant city" with extremely friendly people.

Questions of language and belonging soon became much more troubling and quite personal for our interviewees living in Montreal in the 1960s and 1970s. Quebec was the only Canadian province in which the linguistic minority could function entirely in its own language, with its own institutions. As a result of the dominance of English in major businesses in the province, francophones were limited in their employment opportunities unless they were fluent in English. Québécois nationalists increasingly demanded the right to work in their own language and simultaneously insisted that the French language be protected in order to preserve a distinct Québécois culture. Beginning in the late 1960s, the Quebec government addressed these demands through legislation that progressively enforced the use of the French language in Quebec and eroded the previous freedom-of-language choice in education, advertising, and business. Bill 22 in 1974 made French the official language of Quebec, and in 1977 Bill 101, the Charter of the French Language, streamed all immigrant children into French-language schools. As a consequence, for the first time, English immigrants in Montreal were forced to educate their children in French and to deal with the subordination of English in many aspects of their daily lives.[7]

The following stories of three interview families illustrate a spectrum of emotional response to the increasingly restrictive language legislation and the social tensions surrounding it. Rosemary and Peter Whilesmith, Margaret and Robert Baldwin, and Charlotte Hinton all tried to adapt by becoming more fluent in French while living in Montreal, but none succeeded. They could manage to communicate but did not feel at ease with the language. While the men, including Charlotte's husband, were partially cocooned from language stress because English remained the dominant language in their employment, the women were continually exposed to language issues in daily living. Although all three families eventually left Montreal, their reasons ranged from embarrassment because of their own language ineptitude, to unhappiness with treatment they considered unjust, to acute trauma.

Rosemary and Peter Whilesmith always felt welcome in Montreal but feared that their lack of fluency in French might make them seem unwilling to adapt and fit in. Migrating to Montreal in 1952, the Whilesmiths lived through the dramatic changes of the next thirty years in Quebec society. They liked Montreal and believed that, as outsiders without deep roots in the province, they were more sympathetic to the problems of French Canadians than were many anglophone Canadians. They remembered the strict social control of the Roman Catholic Church in the 1950s, when the parking lots of the large churches were absolutely full on Saturday evening and Sunday morning.[8] Rosemary, like other women in Quebec, could not wear shorts in public. Similarly, their children could not go to movie theatres, although they could get married at a young age. Their kindly French-Canadian doctor, if he believed that patients with children were struggling, did not charge and simply said, "Put something in the hat" that was sitting in the hall. Using French was not a requirement. The Whilesmiths tried to improve their spoken French but had little practice because their "extremely nice" French Canadian neighbours all tried much harder to speak English with them. Rosemary's children did not appreciate her efforts to take French courses at night and told her they wished she could "speak American" like their friends.

In the next two decades, however, the Whilesmiths witnessed an end to the dominance of the Roman Catholic Church and the replacement of religion by language as the central focus of the culture. Employed in the aviation industry where the international language of work was English, Peter was partially isolated from these changes. Nevertheless, he observed that the younger francophones being hired were more upset by the fact that they had to speak English. Like Rosemary, Peter tried to improve his French. He took private French lessons for a long time but "I never got beyond translating and you can't speak a language translating. It has to be in there [pointing to his head]." Although they never felt personally unwelcome, the Whilesmiths became increasingly embarrassed by their lack of fluency in French. After Peter retired, the Whilesmiths moved to Ontario. They reasoned that they would be closer in their old age to their children, all of whom were bilingual, but undoubtedly they also believed that they would feel more comfortable.

Margaret Baldwin interpreted the subordination of English in the public affairs of Quebec not simply as a frustrating inconvenience that complicated her household duties, but also as an attack on her rights as an English-speaking citizen. She felt she was the subject of discrimination, inferior, a second-class citizen. Within the traditional family structure of the postwar era, women who were housewives and mothers were more exposed to language issues in family and community daily life than were their husbands who were occupied at work and sometimes absent travelling. Such was the case of the Baldwins, who had married quickly in 1966 because Robert had received an attractive job offer in Montreal that included transatlantic fares. Like the Whilesmiths, the Baldwins remained in Montreal for over thirty years until Robert retired. Robert enjoyed his engineering work, which was all in English, and relished the proximity of Montreal to excellent ski hills. Margaret, who had primary responsibility for looking after the home and raising the children, felt much more oppressed by restrictions on the use of English that affected her daily life:

> I became more and more unhappy with living in Quebec because first
> of all, there was the language problem. Even though we had school
> French from England, we never really learned to be fluent in French
> in Quebec because it's the patois, it's like another language. It's hard
> to recognize it as French. We didn't live in French areas, and so it
> was almost impossible to learn the language. I mean, you could pick
> up enough on a day to day basis so that when I went in the stores or
> supermarkets it wasn't a problem, but conversational French was quite
> difficult. Then the restrictions became more difficult to cope with, all
> the time making us feel like second class citizens, not being allowed
> to use your own language, not being allowed to put signs up in your
> own language, and if you did it had to be half the size of the French
> writing. I think the final straw was when the flyers that came from the
> newspapers, which I would try to go through because I try to shop
> economically, when the [English] printing in that was such that it was
> half the size of the French, and the French you could hardly read.

Because Margaret did not live in a French area, she did not experience language problems in associating with her neighbours. Instead, she felt oppressed by unanticipated political changes that affected her private life. Margaret noted that their boys, like the offspring of many of their friends, went to university in Ontario and never returned to Quebec. Therefore, when Robert retired, Margaret urged moving to Ontario so they could be close to family and cease being second-class citizens. Robert did not share the feelings of second-class citizenry, but after four years he agreed to move.

In contrast with the Baldwins and the Whilesmiths, who stayed in Montreal until retirement, Charlotte Hinton and her family joined the exodus of English Canadians from Quebec in the 1970s as a result of the FLQ crisis and the escalation of separatist demands. Charlotte's family lived in a French district of Montreal, a choice of housing that Charlotte recognized almost immediately as a mistake. She had many helpful neighbours, but there were a few who would not accept an English family within their community. Therefore, Charlotte's family lived partially in disguise. Her four young children quickly became fluent in French; their language skills, however, were not a source of pride in successful adaptation but a mask that concealed their ethnic identity. Being neither audibly nor visibly different, they did not appear as English immigrants to those who did not know their background. With four children to raise and her shipbuilder husband regularly working overtime, Charlotte had a busy life but was also acutely aware of political developments impacting her family: "You'd wake up in the morning, and the radio would come on, and you'd find out that you'd lost another right. Slowly, slowly, they ate away at all our rights. I mean one day we woke up and found out that English was no longer an official language. This was Canada. And we were in the French area."

Like Margaret Baldwin, Charlotte adopted the public discourse that presented restrictions on English as an abrogation of rights. For Charlotte, though, the consequences affected her neighbourhood life much more directly. Her words implicitly convey her impression that her family unexpectedly found itself in enemy territory in a battle that was being lost. They knew they had to leave, but saving enough money to cover the difference in house prices between Montreal and urban areas of Ontario took a long time even though they lived frugally and never had holidays. Eventually, the day of departure arrived. In spite of tensions, their children, ages eleven to fifteen, were heartbroken at leaving their friends. Charlotte remembered how at their departure party they just sobbed:

All their friends were there, and one little kid said to me, "Why'd you have to go? You're not bad." This is because my kids spoke French. I [always] said to them, you speak English in the house but when you're outside, speak French. And they did. They were completely bilingual as kids. But one of them went to her friend's house and her father was sitting there and the friend said, "Angie's leaving; she's going to Ontario" and he said, "Why does she want to go to a rotten place like that?" and the little girl said, "Well, Angie is English" and he threw her out of the house! She'd been going to the house for two years and he didn't know. It's not that all French are bad, it's

just a few. Most of them are nice. I mean I had the best neighbours
in Quebec, marvelous neighbours. But it's just some of them.

Speaking French fluently, Angie was not recognizable as English by
those unaware of her background. Her young friends, who knew she was
English, accepted her because she conformed to the aspirations of their
society—she was not bad. On the other hand, for the friend's father, Angie
was no longer an individual but a representative of "the English" who had
oppressed Quebec. His reaction helps to explain why Charlotte felt so vulnerable in their particular Montreal neighbourhood. The move to Ontario
was a culture shock for the Hinton children. Charlotte recalled: "It was
difficult because we were sort of damaged, sort of hurt. My kids couldn't
believe that they could speak English outside. They couldn't believe that
they weren't inferior 'cause that's what they'd been taught to believe. Well,
they got over it. I mean, they were delighted. They came home and said,
'Mum, everybody's speaking English!'" Charlotte's references to "damaged"
and "hurt" as well as "inferior" convey her belief that her family had escaped
from a traumatic situation.

These Montreal interviewees experienced, in their daily lives, a modified
form of the language challenges faced by immigrants coming to Canada
who spoke neither English nor French. They felt the frustration and the
restrictions of not being able to deal adequately with a language that was
foreign to them. The interviewees' experience, however, was significantly
different in two respects. In spite of the new language legislation, they could
continue their daily lives in English in Montreal; they could listen to English-language radio and TV stations, read a mainstream English-language
newspaper published in Montreal, obtain health services in English, conduct business in many locations in English, and, if they wished, send their
children to respected English-language Montreal universities. Nonetheless,
the interviewees had not anticipated having to deal with language conflict
as a major part of their adaptation; most thought they had chosen to migrate to an English-speaking country, so often found their circumstances
stressful. For them, the political had become personal.

Perceptions of discrimination

Whether settling in English Canada or in Quebec, adult English immigrants
were identified by their speech. Completely losing an accent was as difficult

as becoming fluent in French. Apart from the issues of acceptance raised by the Québécois nationalism considered in the previous section, experiences of discrimination were seldom mentioned by our cohort of interviewees. By comparison, oral history studies in other countries have discovered that English migrant schoolchildren often were subject to bullying because their accents marked them as different. Such was the case for the English in Scotland interviewed by Murray Watson.[9] Similarly, in their study of British postwar migrants in Australia, Hammerton and Thomson concluded that English schoolchildren probably suffered the worst of the pain and abuse directed against English migrants as the result of a long history of Australian distain for English attitudes of superiority and propensity to complain, whether real or imagined. The "whingeing Pom"—an Australian term of derision for English immigrants—was an iconic image in Australian culture, and children, who could be cruel, turned their parents' prejudices into bullying actions at school.[10] Although we do not have sufficient evidence to make any substantive comparisons, those of our interviewees who came to Canada as school-age children did not report similar school bullying. In fact, Pamela Austin felt much more at home in her Canadian school than in the socially elite English school to which her working class mother had sent her. As we have seen, the child migrants were eager to fit in and quickly changed their accent so they would not appear different.

Canadians were similar to Australians in having a long history of suspicion of the English, whom they singled out among British migrants for special concern. Writing about British migration to Canada before World War I, Susan Jackel noted, "The appellation *English* was not always a term of compliment in Canadian usage, although *British* usually was. Resentment against the English in turn-of-the-century Canada was so marked that 'No English Need Apply' became a common sign in notices advertising jobs."[11] The legendary signs "No English Need Apply" reflected Canadian beliefs that English immigrants thought they knew best and were not adaptable. Some Canadians particularly resented English immigrants of the upper social classes who assumed English superiority, fostered by an ingrained culture of English imperialism and the English class system.

The publication in 1965 of the novel *No Englishman Need Apply* by Denis Godfrey suggests that knowledge of the prejudice was still common in the postwar period. Godfrey set his fictional account of ethnic tension within the corridors of a postwar western Canadian university. Philip Brent, a young aspiring English academic, reluctantly accepts a post at the university because he has no other offer. On arrival, he soon becomes aware of latent hostility toward the English, at least in some quarters, and warns his wife, "Until we're accepted we've got to conform.... We're English, and they don't much care for English people in western Canada."[12] At the university, Philip finds himself in the middle of a conflict between the head of the department, an Englishman who recruited Philip to reinforce the English style of the department, and his archrival, a U.S.-educated Canadian who has an American outlook and "doesn't much care for things or people English."[13] In the ensuing struggle for power, Philip's voice becomes symbolic of his identity as a newly arrived Englishman. The head of the department, who had been in Canada for twenty-five years, muses: "It was the voice, of course, that oh-so-precise, so-well-modulated English voice, that unselfconscious ring of cool authority! After so many Canadian years, the professor could react to it as they [other members of department] did, could sense in them that curious spellbound mingling of envy and dislike."[14]

Looking back on his immigrant experience, interviewee Gordon Bulmer recognized that he came to Canada in 1963, in his early twenties, with an attitude of English class superiority, a belief that he had a better education and that the English way of doing things was best. "I was probably the absolutely worst kind of first immigrant," he said. "We knew best, the way it was done at home. They couldn't do anything right here and I took myself rather seriously." Working for the New Brunswick forestry department, he initially criticized the Canadian method of leaving behind cut wood; in England, it would be cleared out. Later he realized that the Canadian foresters were dealing with a much larger area than English foresters and so had to use different methods. Gordon did not mention suffering any hostility or resentment specifically because of his assumptions of English superiority, but he did recall his defensive reaction when a colleague criticized him for his English class accent: "I got absolutely furious with him. I made some nasty comments to him. I was surprised at how vehement I was about 'don't muck about with my accent.'" Defending his accent so strongly could be interpreted as a way of defending his initial assumptions of English superiority and resisting change. Gordon soon discarded his beliefs in English superiority, not because of the response of Canadians but because of the impact of a visit to his homeland: "After I'd been here for about two years I went back to England for my grandfather's funeral and I was shocked at how wrong I'd been, how much things were better here, there was more space, it was cleaner, the people were about as friendly."

Ironically, given that Canada and Britain had just fought a war together, Canadian prejudices against the English were strongest in the immediate postwar years. With the end of war production, Canadians feared a return to the years of economic depression that had plagued the country during the 1930s. Therefore, some Canadians viewed the English migrants who arrived shortly after the war as unwanted and unneeded competitors for scarce jobs. These economic fears melded with the longstanding resentment of English migrants who claimed superiority. It is significant that the few interviewees who reported encountering discrimination in employment all arrived in the late 1940s. For example, Emma Bulmer, who came to Alberta in 1948 as a young child with her family, later learned that the "English were not being very well received here," and that at the first few places where her father applied for a job he was told, "We don't want any English people working here."

Ron Inch, who came to Toronto in 1948 after wartime service with the British Navy, tried to recapture his feelings at the time of emigration in a manner that was half joking but also serious: "I'd have probably said that I felt like a missionary or something. I'd left the motherland and I was bringing all the good things that I knew to a backward country like Canada. Very egotistical!" From an "average" or working-class background, Ron believed that he was immediately "snapped up" by Massey Harris, a farm equipment company, because he had some engineering skills that he thought most Canadians lacked. He remembered clearly the staff's treatment that followed his hiring: "I ran into quite a bit of resentment by the Canadians. They objected to me.... I'd got preferential treatment! You know, 'You damn Limeys, you come here, why don't you go back home?' And, I got that for a couple of years, and finally I left Massey Harris." Ron was convinced that his treatment was not exceptional; he knew other English workers at other companies who were similarly resented for stealing Canadian jobs.[15]

Barry Broadfoot, drawing from his collection of tape-recorded interviews with postwar immigrants of many nationalities, provides an example that reinforces Ron's view. In 1947, the wife of a newly arrived English immigrant to Hamilton was chatting pleasantly with the local storekeeper when another shopper accosted her: "This woman was just standing there, and she heard my mother's heavy Cockney voice and she just let fly at her.... This woman started to scream that my mother—she called her 'you goddamned English'—that we were taking all the good jobs away from Canadian boys, and it was the Canadians who had gone to England and saved England from the Germans. They'd died at Dieppe and other places. And honestly, I thought that woman was going to hit my mother. She was screaming. Yelling. Cursing." The storekeeper who evicted the screaming customer explained that the customer was upset because her husband had been out of work for months.[16] Opening the employment doors to English immigrants during the period of reconstruction after the war, when many Canadians were anxiously searching for peacetime work, ignited hostilities that later English immigrants did not report encountering because, contrary to fears, the Canadian economy boomed in the postwar years. Ron Inch's second wife, Norma, who migrated to Canada in the mid-1960s, thought that she met similar resentment against Brits, but her experience was significantly different. Norma initially had difficulty obtaining employment because "whatever experience you had was no good, you know, if you didn't have Canadian experience."[17] Norma thus encountered the protectionism that reserved jobs for Canadians and maintained Canadian standards by demanding Canadian training and experience. English immigrants were not a specific target for exclusion, although some felt unjustly treated if their credentials were not accepted. These employment and workplace issues will be explored more fully in the following chapter focusing on work.

Most of our interviewees emphasized that they wanted to fit into Canadian society. Adult immigrants would always be identified as "other" by their speech, but they hoped not to be rejected as a consequence. Educated professional immigrants, who formed a growing majority of English immigrants to Canada in the postwar period, were often quite aware of negative attributes attached to Englishness in the postcolonial world. Apart from Quebec's *nationaliste* politics and the immediate postwar tensions, our interviewees did not remember overt or ethnically explicit discrimination, although some did resent those Canadian regulations that limited acceptance of their English professional qualifications. Nonetheless, many interviewees had a struggle to feel at home in Canada.

Fitting into the surroundings:
"The light switches are backward"

Arriving in an alien world—that is how Canadian ballerina Lynn Seymour remembered her first visit to London, as we saw in Chapter 1. That is also how English immigrants to Canada, having travelled in the opposite direction, remembered their first encounter with the new country. A multitude of small, and not so small, differences in the fabric of daily life affected their integration into Canadian society. Elizabeth Summers was not bothered by the light switches that seemed backward to her, or by the realization that the police in Canada carried guns rather than truncheons. "Everything was different and that was what was fun, really," she said. Doreen and Arthur Wood were more seriously affected when they learned the hard way that having a north-facing house with a driveway sloping to a basement garage was not a good idea in an icy Canadian winter. They had deliberately bought the house because it gave them the sunny southward-facing backyard so valued in England. They did not foresee the hellish struggle they would have to get the car up the frozen northern driveway. Social knowledge and social instincts from England also were fallible because Canadian customs were different. Barbara and Roy Trueman, almost in unison, described their embarrassment at assuming that Canadians shared the English custom of visiting on Christmas morning:

> Barbara: In England at Christmas you go and
> visit your neighbours. And have a little tipple, or a cup of
> tea, or whatever. And so, we went to visit people.
>
> Roy: We turned up at my boss's place at about half past ten in
> the morning. And he was half dressed and hadn't shaved.
>
> Barbara: Obviously that wasn't the thing to do.
> Right? So we didn't do that again did we?
>
> Roy: No, didn't do that again. We were not so well received.

Until the Canadian environment and way of life became natural for them, our interviewees could not feel that they fully belonged. Sarah Walsh, a nurse and housewife who migrated in 1972 with her husband and first daughter, succinctly expressed these emotions: "You had to feel settled and that is the biggest thing—to feel that you belong in that place. It's easy to feel a little lost because everything was different." For the first months or years, the standard of reference for most immigrants was England, and Canada fitted into that reference system by being similar or different. Hannah Marriot, who had lived in France as well as England, was aware of making such comparisons. "A lot of things took getting used to," she said. "We found, for example, that we compared everything with life in England at the beginning, which I suppose is only natural."

English immigrants, like all immigrants, had difficulty assessing the value of items in Canada, in part because of currency differences. James Leonard, who came from an agricultural background, knew that he "had been taken for a ride" when he was charged one dollar for an apple on arrival at the wharf in Quebec City in 1958. "It takes a couple of years to get acclimatized," he continued. "When you're first here, you're always converting…dollars to pounds to get the value of something. Now I don't. I'm thinking Canadian now."

The Canadian banking system also differed from the English. Buying a used car shortly after arrival in Ottawa, Arthur Wood was astounded to find that the car salesman, who had let him drive the car wherever he wanted for an entire weekend, would only accept a certified cheque to pay for it. Wood, who had never heard of a certified cheque, initially thought the salesman meant that the car had to be certified. He wrote a cheque, telling the salesman, "My cheque is my bond," but the salesman refused it and suggested that Wood take the car to get a certified cheque at his bank. Arthur was on good terms with his Canadian bank manager, who had helped him set up his account and transfer money from England, so he had no difficulty in obtaining a certified cheque. The manager, who explained the process of certification, just smiled at Arthur's bewilderment and said, "That's the way of life. They have to be certified." What Arthur did not realize, and was not told, was that in Canada bank accounts were more readily available to everyone; in England, having a bank account was usually a sign of financial respectability, while working-class people with meagre savings most often had post office accounts or no accounts at all.

Our interviewees immediately experienced a new sense of space in Canada. As May Preston from Norwich observed, "It was space, space everywhere." Wide Canadian roads contrasted with the narrow, winding country lanes familiar to the English. Similarly, to English eyes, North American cars of the fifties and sixties were huge. James Roland looked out his hotel room window at the cars in the parking lot and thought, "You could land a helicopter on the trunk; they were just so much larger than anything I had seen in England." Arthur Wood, a mechanic and garage owner from Nottingham, was favourably impressed by the American-made vehicles:

> I'm not a flashy person, but I did like the quality of the cars compared to the British cars of the day. They were more comfortable, more luxurious, and certainly the suspension and things like that were equal to the Rolls Royce, there's no doubt about it, they were so smooth and silent. That was a big plus, and to me it was just the size of the thing. I remember I bought a wheelbarrow and the girl said to me, "how are you going to get it home," and I said, "I'll put it in the trunk," and I opened the trunk and I put this two yard wheelbarrow into the trunk and closed the lid.

5. To English eyes North American cars were huge. A recently arrived English immigrant admires his Ford Mercury Marquis in 1976. Photo credit: By permission Rosemary Sloan.

Some interviewees also remembered being struck by differences in the built landscape. Houses, for example, varied in size, colour, and building material. As Barbara Trueman noticed, "There was a large difference in houses. In Britain you would get a street of all the same. They would be the same on the same street. Whereas here there was one small one, one big one, and a different style. And that was quite different from what we were used to." In addition, May Preston remarked that Canadian houses tended to be unfenced and more open to the road, increasing the sense of space, whereas English houses were more enclosed.

Food, shopping, and cooking

Those immigrants leaving austerity and rationing in England after the war were delighted, and almost overwhelmed, by the variety and abundance of food in Canada. Agnes Butcher thought the wide range of food and the way it was openly displayed in the stores was "wonderful." She was pleased that she no longer had to be nice to the butcher in order to get meat, or line up several times to get her oranges each week. John King went to the food counter at Woolworth's and thought, "I had never seen so much stuff in all my life, food that is." May Preston, living in a nurses' residence in Toronto, described the first time that she and another nurse went out to eat in a restaurant. It was definitely an occasion, because she had never eaten in a restaurant during the five years that she worked in London, although she had been to a Lyon's Corner House for tea. They sat at a booth with a "little thing at the end where you could put your money in and pick a tune" [a jukebox]. May remembered her astonishment when the meal arrived: "I couldn't believe it. I looked at this plate—I think I ordered liver and onions, mashed potatoes, I can't remember the vegetable—but I looked at this plate and thought, my God, this would feed my whole family. You know in the war that would be enough for the whole family and there it was just for me. I tell you, I ate it all and I thoroughly enjoyed it, and I think I even had dessert. Yes, everything was so different."

Pat Connor, however, did not appreciate her first restaurant meal in Canada. She ordered a hot chicken sandwich, thinking she would get hot chicken between two pieces of bread. She was not prepared for what arrived: "It looked a mess to me at the time. It was chunks of chicken with a piece of bread slapped on top and gravy over it. And I said, 'I didn't order this,' and [the waitress] said 'Yes,' and I said, 'No, I ordered a hot chicken sandwich,' and she said, 'This is a hot chicken sandwich.' Man, I'll watch carefully what I order next time." Pat thought that people were fed too much in restaurants: "First, they bring in a salad, and then they bring in this huge platter of food. What a waste!" Pat was undoubtedly irritated by the unsavoury appearance of a meal that was not what she had expected. Her attitude regarding waste, however, was typical of some who had known privation and were suddenly

6. English farm worker receives meal on arrival from farm wife. The Ontario government caption noted "Perhaps she (the farm wife) had heard that in common with many other English lads, Jim Pooley has not seen certain foods for some time and needs a little fattening." Photo credit: Archives of Ontario, RG 9-7-4-2-21, Ontario House Records.

transported to plenty; it was often difficult to accept what seemed lack of care in consuming resources that others did not have.

Our interviewees who migrated in the 1960s and '70s did not experience such a sharp contrast in the availability of food, but they still had to adapt to new methods of shopping and cooking. The greater prevalence of chain supermarkets such as A & P and Dominion stores meant more impersonal one-stop shopping, replacing frequent visits to the butcher, the baker, and the greengrocer. The much larger Canadian refrigerators facilitated such stocking up. When asked for his memories of settling in after his arrival in 1969, John Steven's first response was, "It's interesting that we'd go to the supermarket maybe once a week, once a fortnight or something like that, and buy mountains of stuff, where in the U.K. you'd go to the grocery store every day."

Women, who did most of the food preparation for families, had to learn how to use alternative ingredients when they could not find familiar name brands and products. They also had to adjust to a Canadian system that measured quantity with cups and spoons rather than measuring weight with scales. While they were learning, the results were sometimes hilarious but not always edible. Margaret Baldwin, an experienced cook, found many things that were slightly different; corn flour in England, for example, was called cornstarch in Canada. She figured out the differences by trial and error, or by consultation with English friends who had been in the same situation and shared their newly acquired knowledge. She remembered the first time that she tried to bake bread in Canada:

> I decided I would make some bread because, don't forget, I was
> going to do Home Ec stuff in England and I was much into cook-
> ing. It called for an ounce of yeast and it meant the wet yeast, the
> baker's yeast, and I couldn't find that anywhere, but all the dry
> yeast, yes. So I thought I'll just substitute dry yeast for wet yeast
> and I weighed it on my scales, an ounce of dry yeast, put it to rise
> and it rose nicely, put it in my oven to bake and I think I made the
> first ever pre-sliced loaf because when it came out of the oven it
> had risen right up through the rack above, so the rack had gone
> through it like slices. So that was a good learning experience.

Margaret's husband added that it was probably the tallest loaf that had ever been made.

Barbara Trueman had similar problems with Canadian ingredients but managed to bake the heaviest cake rather than the tallest one. The Truemans together described the result of her efforts:

Barbara: And I remember the first baking I did.
I bought some flour and baked a cake.

Roy: This is Canadian flour.

Barbara: Canadian flour. And I baked a cake. Well it would have held open the heaviest iron door you can imagine. Because it was plain flour, as opposed to self-rising flour, and I didn't know the difference. I just bought flour and baked a cake. And it was about this high and it was heavy...

Roy: I can tell you something funny about this. I filled the bathtub to see if it would float. And it sank.

Barbara: So that was my first excursion into cooking in Canada.

Food is a well-known signifier and component of ethnic identity. In recent years, historians interested in the acculturation of immigrants have given increasing attention to the "politics of food."[18] What immigrants ate could indicate their desire to maintain their traditional culture or their willingness to adopt Canadian ways. In addition, as cultural pluralism gained greater acceptance in postwar Canada, food was one aspect of culture that could be shared relatively easily. Canadian authorities involved with the reception of immigrants were most concerned about the eating habits of non-British immigrants, which often diverged significantly from the Canadian norm. The large groups of British war brides escorted to Canada at the end of World War II, however, also received their attention. Professional dietitians delivering orientation programs to war brides in England stressed the importance of acquiring Canadian ways and providing nutritional, well-balanced, meals. For example, the Red Cross officer in London told war brides "not to forget their own specialties such as scones and Yorkshire puddings," but she also urged them "to get busy and practise on pancakes and Canadian-style salads." To show "what Canadians like to eat," she demonstrated "a real apple pie, tea biscuits, a white cake with fudge icing, and several types of salads." The training of war brides continued at several centres in Canada and courses ended with the gift of a set of plastic measuring spoons.[19]

The invisible English immigrants whom we interviewed received no such instruction in adopting Canadian food ways. A number noted that they continued to eat items that they identified as British, such as roast beef and Yorkshire pudding or steak and kidney pie, but also incorporated new food into their diets. Isobel Sinclair remembered that baked beans on toast was an extremely popular, cheap food in England, but after arriving in Toronto she was happy to substitute the *very* Canadian double-decker sandwich with a toothpick in the middle and a dill pickle on the side. She also noted that seeing ketchup everywhere was new, as was tuna fish and broccoli, neither of which she had ever eaten before. Initially she avoided corned beef in Canada because she confused it with the "disgusting" tinned "bully beef"[20] that people in England tried to make edible with various recipes because it could be obtained off the ration. After taking a cooking class offered by the Consumer Gas Company in Toronto, Isobel and her roommate decided to host a Christmas dinner and bake a turkey in their apartment oven, which lacked a temperature gauge. Because it was the first time that she had seen a turkey, Sinclair did not know that there was a "bag of stuff [giblets] inside the turkey" until she tried to serve it, but, with much testing, she seemed to have got the turkey sufficiently baked. James Roland, also a single immigrant who learned to cook after coming to Canada, found Jell-O much more widely used in Canada and identified coleslaw as new to him. Tom Martin, who joined his brother in Toronto in the 1970s, noticed "a tremendous difference" in food: "When I came to Canada I had just the old standard English cooking—the meat and two veg." One example that stood out for him was the use of rice other than in the form of a rice pudding dessert:

> It was the first time, when I came to Toronto, that I would regularly
> have rice as a vegetable with a meat course or a fish course. I visited
> a couple of Indian restaurants when I lived in London, and we did
> have rice with our Indian meal, but that was extremely exotic and
> quite unusual, so to have rice as an everyday thing was wonderful. The
> other thing that I had never seen before was green and red peppers.
> I'd never seen those in England, and there were all sorts of little things
> like that. Your diet and your choice of meals was much, much wider.

As Tom realized, the variety of food that English immigrants found in Canada in part reflected contributions made by diverse immigrant groups to the country. In addition to coleslaw and the use of rice, other interviewees mentioned Italian food, and especially pizza, as being different for them. Although they had to learn new methods and products for cooking, English immigrants could choose the extent to which they wished to partake of the variety of food in Canada. No interviewee mentioned feeling deprived of traditional English fare.

The pub: Drinking and socializing

What many of the interviewees did miss were English pubs. It was not English beer that they missed; rather, it was the experience of neighbourhood or community that they associated with English pubs. Noel Taylor expressed the nostalgia for the institution he had left behind: "There are things I miss in England, and anybody will tell you what they are, mainly the pubs.... I miss the pub. We have pubs here but they are not the same, because they're inhabited by young people, and pubs to me in England are where all generations meet. You might see us [less youthful people] in a pub in the lunchtime crowd, but in the evenings you wouldn't go to a pub, an older person, you just wouldn't be part of the crowd in a pub." He noted that pubs in England had changed over the years—many were now more restaurants than pubs—but the warm feeling for the English pub that he had known remained with him. Peter Semple was one who frequented the pub opposite his Toronto workplace for lunch and sometimes also immediately after work at six o'clock, but even this regular attendance was not the same as taking the cat on his shoulder down the road to the pub for the evening. A pub could become a meeting place for English immigrants. Peter Robinson, the popular mystery writer who came to Toronto in 1974, recalled that in his early years in Toronto he felt culturally isolated, surrounded by Portuguese and Greek neighbourhoods. To compensate, he regularly drank at the Feathers' Pub, which was frequented by expats; their accents "provided a comfort zone" that made him feel English.

More often, the interviewees emphasized the contrast between Canadian drinking places and the English pub. Charles Hall had not gone to a pub regularly in England but liked to have pubs available as a place to go and have a few leisurely drinks; living in Montreal, he found that people who went to Canadian night clubs drank much more and finished the bottle.[21] Ron Inch had an even more negative opinion of Toronto beer parlours, which in no way could replace the English pubs that he missed:

"I hated what they called their 'beer parlours'. They were disgusting, I thought, so I would do anything to avoid going in them. But the British pub where you go in and take a pint and talk, or play darts, or some other card game or something, you'd spend all night drinking two pints."[22]

In 1950s Ontario, female English immigrants felt particularly excluded by the restrictions imposed on Ontario bars following the prohibition period of the earlier twentieth century.[23] Isobel Sinclair remembered:

> The first thing that struck me about Toronto were these strange
> drinking places because they didn't look like London pubs at all....
> We found a room in Summerhill and, next to the subway station,
> there was one of the places, and there were two doors and one said
> "Gentlemen" and the other said "women [sic] and escorts" [Ladies
> and escorts]. I used to think, "Oh, we go in there to rent an escort
> or something." We never went to those places, and somebody
> told me years after, women weren't supposed to go in the main
> door and they had to go to this side door. Very, very, peculiar.

When she experienced other rules imposed in the post-prohibition era, Norma Inch thought similarly: "The attitudes were *so* old-fashioned, the things you couldn't do!" She was amazed that "you couldn't stand up for a drink, you had to sit at a table. You had to have food with it, and you couldn't have more than one drink at a time."[24] Mary Irvine also recalled her astonishment regarding the "puritanical" culture surrounding alcohol in 1950s Ontario:

> When you used to buy anything from the Liquor Control Board you
> had to have a license and I've still got my license. It's a little booklet that
> they used to sign. It was so puritanical we couldn't believe it.... You
> weren't allowed to have it in the car; you had to have it in the trunk,
> and of course it could never be opened. It was the last thing that you
> bought when you were out shopping.... You picked up the bottle that
> you wanted and it was wrapped in a brown paper bag, and you put it in
> the trunk of your car and you had to go straight home. That amazed us.

Gradual modifications of Ontario's drinking laws eventually eased the restrictions, and such laws were never imposed in Quebec, but English immigrants continued to miss the English pub. Arriving in Ottawa in 1970, Arthur Wood, a mechanic from Nottingham, complained that the backyard barbecue in Canada replaced the community social life that the pub had helped to provide in England:

> I was very disappointed. I was a total stranger, but I like a social life. I like to socialize and the Canadian way to socialize is to have a barbecue in the back yard and that's it, but in England we went out, we got dressed, we went out and we went to the pub, to the dances, we went to the theatre, we went to the shows, and we did all kinds of things to socialize with our circle of friends.... When you're an immigrant, you don't have a circle of friends, so it's kind of restricted. That was one disappointment. The social life was a big, big adjustment to make.

Sensory perceptions[25]

The process of "settling in," of acquiring a sense of belonging in Canada, was personal and individual. Some of our interviewees felt at home quite quickly, while others took much longer to accept Canada as a familiar place where they belonged. Circumstances of family, employment, age, and place of residence made a difference, but so too did personal attitudes and emotions. As we noted in our examination of the English society that the migrants left behind, sensory perceptions are deeply embedded in an individual's response to the surrounding world. Historians are beginning to take more interest in the five senses and how they influence memories of the past; the number of observations made by our interviewees about the interrelationship between the experience of migration and sight, hearing, smell, taste, and touch justifies that interest.

The conscious or unconscious hearing of a language is one example, whether in personal conversation or in the media. Gordon Bulmer found that in Canada, "the radio was loud. It was full of advertising. I'd grown up with the BBC and no advertising." Similarly, Arthur Wood commented that everything seemed fast: "Even the advertising on the radio, things like that they push at you. They speak so fast, you can't even understand their rhetoric. The sports reporters, they tell you so fast what the score was... we're bamboozled with speed."

Sensory responses to the natural world had a major influence on how migrants adapted. English migrants to Canada were not as disoriented as those who chose Australia where, in the southern hemisphere, the seasons were reversed, the sky at night lacked the familiar stars, and even trees and flowers were strange and unknown. Nonetheless, English migrants settling in Canada had to adapt to new "sensual signposts of the natural world—colours, smells and sounds."[26] The extremes of the Canadian continental climate took English migrants' breath away. They knew that Canada was cold, but not that cold, and many did not realize how hot and humid central Canada could be in the summer. Their bodies felt assaulted, and some suffered from frostbite in winter and heat prostration in summer. For Hannah Marriot, who otherwise felt welcomed into the new society, "the new climate was perhaps one of the hardest things to get used to. At that point it was extreme heat and humidity." Similarly, Roy Trueman remembered his family's surprise and their problems: "We didn't know you got the heat, and this really took us by surprise. And it took us twelve years, twelve summers, for our bodies to learn to sweat, so that we could cope with the heat without feeling really sick and uncomfortable." Although the seasons followed the same northern hemisphere sequence as in England, they were significantly different in length. Winter in most of Canada was much longer and spring was both later and shorter. Arthur and Doreen Wood were not alone in finding a Canadian winter difficult to endure because, as Arthur recalled: "it lasts and it lasts and it lasts," and missing the signs of spring that characterized so many ideas of nature in England but were so ephemeral in Canada. The biting bugs that accompanied spring and summer in much of Canada were also an unwelcome new sensation. The Truemans, beginning with Roy, humorously described their introduction to blackflies when they went for a country walk on a nice sunny day in May:

Roy: We parked the car on the side of a farm track, and we went for a walk. Barbara was dressed in British garden clothes—a blouse and a skirt, voluminous petticoat beneath in the style of the time. We hadn't gone more than fifty yards down this track, and she starts swatting at her legs, lifts up her skirt and she was black fly right up her legs.

Barbara: I was covered.

Roy: Well this wasn't going to be a good day. We hadn't met black fly before.

Barbara: We didn't even know about black fly; nobody told
us about black fly. So we didn't do that again, did we?

Roy: No we didn't do that again.

Those interviewees who enjoyed the outdoors and outdoor sports often
felt quite quickly that they belonged in Canada—in spite of the bugs. Roger
MacKay thoroughly appreciated the outdoor life. He had adventures working in the Arctic with the Canadian Wildlife Service and living in a tent on
the tundra. With the friends that he made, he also took canoe trips in parks
where there was literally nobody around—an experience he could never have
in congested England: "One of the things which has always kept me in Canada
is the outdoor life. It's always been great, you know, to get outside. We've got
our mosquitoes to worry about here, but you know what, after a while they
don't really bother you that much, black flies a little bit in the spring, but
other than that no, not really, so that's probably why I like it so much here."
With his unconscious choice of words, "*we've* got *our* mosquitoes *here* [italics
added],"[27] MacKay reinforces his perception of himself as a fully accultur-
ated Canadian. Other interviewees, too, embraced the outdoors. Indeed, as
we have seen, the open spaces of Canada were one of the major attractions
of the country for migrants who were interested in hiking or camping. A
number even liked snow because they could ski regularly close to where they
lived instead of taking an occasional ski holiday. Opportunities for sailing
convinced others that Canada was an excellent place to live.

The very personal relationship with the sights, sounds, and smells of
a Canadian landscape had a deep impact on a migrant's sense of belonging. Vicky Williams knew that she liked Canada, that she wanted to live in
Canada, in part because of the "sheer beauty of the country":

New Brunswick is an outstandingly lovely province. It's got some lousy
weather, but it's a lovely province. I crossed Canada fairly early on
in the 1960s and sheer loveliness of the country struck me.... Going
down the St. John [River] in the fall when you've never seen the fall
before, and the hills between Edmonston and Fredericton are like
somebody throwing great bolts of brilliant cloths pinned down by the
evergreen trees. It's almost a kaleidoscope of colour—almost makes
you ill with its brilliance. It's a staggeringly full-on type of beauty.

She contrasted her appreciation of the vividly clear Canadian landscape with her continuing childhood memories of bomb damage and "a great deal of smoke in the cities." She never was nostalgic for the English countryside. With her socialist background, she could not see the English country landscape without seeing the huge impact of the social divisions that produced it. In the English cities, too, she had observed a tremendous gulf between the wealth and large detached houses in some hands and yet the building of "back to back housing that is also side to side" for others. For her, such a landscape was indicative of the condition of the people living in it: "You can stand in Victoria Station [in London], which was the station where the train went home for me, and you can see the difference between the working class and the upper class in the height and the general physique of the people going by."

Not all migrants were as critical of the England landscape that they had left. Most, like May Preston, perceived the English countryside as more manicured or domesticated and the Canadian landscape as more rugged. Some took much longer to appreciate the Canadian countryside and feel comfortable in it. Barbara Trueman, with interjections from her husband, explained their gradual adaptation:

Roy: We've finally, over the last five, six, seven, eight, years come to realize that there is beauty. There is beauty, yes. We've come to appreciate the beauty, just riding out of the city—the fields and the farm, and a silo.

Barbara: Well, they've entered your psyche recently.

Roy: Yes, and we feel comfortable with it.

Barbara: Whereas before, we'd go out for a ride, and we would be looking for things that looked English.

Roy: We'd look for the English fields and their little farmhouses.

Barbara: And for thirty years we'd been totally frustrated because we could never find it.

Roy: But we were in the Gatineau the other day, and oohing and ahing over the colours, and the lake, and the general landscape. So, yes, it is beautiful.

The spectacular fall colours, at least in eastern Canada, were an outstanding feature that drew praise from many English migrants, but, like the Truemans, migrants also had to become familiar with a Canadian reference system for understanding the day-to-day landscape around them. As Barbara Trueman noted, a new concept of beauty had to enter the psyche. Charles Hall believed that if he left Canada, he would not miss material things; "it's the landscape here that I'd miss more than anything." Sight, sound, and smell all entered into his relationship with the landscape. He would miss seeing and hearing the wild geese flying overhead in fall. He'd also miss the seasons, and the smell of the woodsmoke that he linked with going into the bush in winter, and the clicking of the wood sparks, all of which, he said, "gets to me occasionally; that is lovely."[28]

The $1,000 cure

While some interviewees learned to feel at home in Canada either quickly or gradually, others had to take "the $1,000 cure" before they could accept Canada as their new home. The cure was a product of the new era of commercial air flights that linked Britain and Canada. Migrants could return to England for a short visit without having to allot at least two weeks for an ocean voyage, as in the past. Regardless of the exact cost of a return trip, *the $1,000 cure* became the common evocative shorthand to describe overcoming intense feelings of homesickness by a return visit to England. The phrase indicated that the trip was expensive, because $1,000 was a large amount of money in the immediate postwar decades. Nonetheless, many English migrants who experienced the cure vowed that it was worth every cent. In a variation that showed the term's popularity, it was also applied to those unhappy migrants who actually moved back to England, only to discover in a short time that they preferred Canada and wanted to return. The proportion of English migrants to Canada who took the $1,000 cure is not known, but interviewees frequently observed its importance, whether they took it themselves or knew others who had done so.

The $1,000 cure is often associated with women, perhaps because British war brides, having left everything that was familiar to join their Canadian husbands, were prominent among the first migrants to take the cure. One English war bride, whose homesickness impelled her to return to England for a three-week visit with her family, thought maybe twenty persons on the plane were "girls like me."[29] As we have seen, some women were reluctant migrants because of family ties. In Canada, married women who were at home most of the day usually had more occasion for homesickness than did their husbands, who were busy at work. Mary Charles, who came from a close-knit family in London, had difficulty adjusting to her new community and the absence of extended family when her husband's work brought them to Canada:

> I cried and I whined and I wanted my Mum, and I didn't like it here, and the winter was long. So Jeremy said, "All right. We'll go back for Easter." Well, I think I was back in England at Easter for about five days before I said, "When are we going home?" That is what was called in those days the $1,000 cure.... So that's how much it cost to cure that "I-don't-like-it-here—I-want-to-go-home." It didn't take long there to realize what I'd left behind, and this was home. That was the turning point [when I knew] that I could hack it.

The "unhappy wife" also explained the moves back and forth across the Atlantic made by several English couples whom Robert and Margaret Baldwin knew. Robert learned about the $1,000 cure even before he migrated to Canada. A fellow worker at his English company had returned from Canada because his wife was homesick. "All of a sudden she found that England wasn't as she remembered it," said Robert, so the co-worker made arrangements to return to Canada. Robert determined that he would resist such upheaval and simply send his wife home for a visit if she should be unhappy in Canada.

Single women, too, sometimes needed the $1,000 cure before they felt satisfied in Canada. Norma Inch migrated to Canada in the 1960s in order to prove her independence, but as a single woman, she found making social contacts in Toronto much more difficult, she thought, than they would be for a man. Overcome by homesickness, after many aborted attempts, she finally took what she was advised was the $500 cure: "Once I came I was so homesick I must have booked my flight home I don't know how many times and cancelled it the next day. There was one time I even booked all my freight home, and I cancelled. And then people said to me, 'That's all right, you go for the $500 cure,' that was what they called it." Norma could take the advice because she had told her family when she left London that she was going to return in a year for her nephew's bar mitzvah, which would be the occasion for a large family festival. In advance of her visit she told everyone that she was going to return to Canada just long enough to make enough money to be able to stay in England for good. To her astonishment, "I wasn't home three days when I said to myself, 'I'm never coming home again.'"[30]

Although women were most frequently the central characters in stories of the $1,000 cure, men as well as women took the cure. Tom Walsh remembered the English people at his company "that came and went back and returned again." He thought about 30 percent of the recruits in his year went back to England and a number of those made the return move to Canada. In referring to how people changed because of the influence of their surroundings, he recalled several men he knew at work, who had benefited from the cure. Gordon Bulmer remembered a variation of the $1,000 cure that had a major impact on his own life. He believed that his return visit to England cured him, not of homesickness, but of his attitude of English superiority. Versions of the $1,000 cure became so important for many English migrants that best-selling mystery writer and unintentional English migrant, Peter Robinson, wrote about it in his Inspector Banks thriller, *The Hanging Valley*. Robinson found that for himself, returning to England helped him to renew his ties with the Yorkshire landscape and overcome his feelings of cultural isolation in his new Toronto home. For Robinson and others, the ability to return to a familiar landscape as needed aided acceptance of Canada. For most who spoke about the $1,000 cure, however, the return trip to England made them realize that they no longer fitted into England as they thought they would; either England had changed, they had changed, or their memories were selective.

Conclusions

Whether or not they initially intended to settle permanently, our interviewees all wanted to fit into Canada, to feel accepted by others and comfortable in the new environment. Of course those we interviewed did stay in Canada, so they may have been more predisposed to fitting in than some who decided to return to England. Understanding the personal and complex process of adaptation is not easy, but the thoughtful reflections of our interviewees provide important insights that often can be gained only from oral history. Because migration is a life-changing event, our interviewees remembered clearly the excitement of arrival and their first perceptions of what was new, different, and sometimes unexpectedly strange in Canada. They also recalled how they began to adapt and to feel familiar with what they had originally found foreign or different. They conveyed their individual emotions that accompanied the process, their enthusiasm, their humour, their frustrations, and sometimes their depression. Only when they were able to internalize a Canadian reference system as normal instead of making comparisons with England did they truly feel settled in Canada.

Coming to an English-speaking country, many of our interviewees were surprised when they had problems with communication. At first, differences in accent and vocabulary impeded the ability of some to be understood by Canadians or to understand what they were being told. As the interviewees' ears became attuned to the rhythms and sound of Canadian English, the problems of understanding quickly diminished. On the other hand, interviewees who came to Canada as adults never lost their English accent, although it might have been modified. As one remarked, they were audible as English immigrants even though otherwise they were invisible. The child migrants, by contrast, deliberately and successfully lost their accent quite quickly. Few interviewees recounted significant economic discrimination as a result of being identified as English. Only during the period of economic uncertainty immediately following the war did they meet strains of the traditional Canadian resentment of the English because of their assumptions of superiority.

Interviewees who lived in Montreal encountered distinct linguistic challenges. Their English accent became insignificant in comparison with their lack of fluency in French. As tensions escalated and drew sharper divisions between anglophones and francophones, they automatically became part of a larger anglophone community. Interviewees who arrived in Montreal in the more tranquil 1950s found their inability to speak French was not a problem. With the intensification of Québécois nationalism in the 1960s and 1970s, conditions changed dramatically. The varied responses of interviewees to the new priorities accorded to the French language in Quebec reveal deep personal and complex feelings regarding the significance of language, not simply for practical communication but also for a sense of belonging. The differing circumstances of the interviewees, and whether they felt or experienced discrimination as a result, also significantly affected their response to cultural change. In the end, these interviewees all left for Ontario—even though, as upcoming chapters will show, they had been actively involved in community and voluntary activities in Montreal.

Although language was a vital component of adaptation, so were many other aspects of daily life. Our interviewees had to adapt to new Canadian technology and products—from the large, North American cars that attracted the attention of men, to the new methods of cooking that produced hilarious results for women. Interviewees appreciated the abundance and variety of food in Canada, especially in contrast to English austerity in the 1950s, but many missed the English pub, and several women were astounded by puritanical Ontario drinking laws that imposed gender controls and other restrictions. Sensory perceptions—especially sight, sound, and smell—significantly influenced the response to the new environment. Interviewees recalled an almost overwhelming sense of space. They had to cope with the extremes of a climate to which their bodies only gradually adapted. They also had to learn about unfamiliar flora and fauna, and biting bugs. Many had to acquire a different concept of beauty in order to appreciate the Canadian landscape. Those who enjoyed outdoor activities soon appreciated Canadian opportunities. In contrast, many interviewees who experienced difficulty adjusting to Canada found the $1,000 cure—a return visit to England—necessary before they could settle into their new life. In the following chapters, we will examine how ties of work, home, family, and community increasingly bonded our interviewees to Canada, but also sometimes pulled them back toward England.

Chapter 5

EARNING A LIVING

Emigration is almost by definition an act of entrepreneurship.[1]

In the early 1960s, Kenneth Cecil was a hard-up engineer working for the British Aircraft Corporation in Lancashire. He was married with two children, and after paying his mortgage, buying food, and meeting other household expenses, he had less than twenty pounds in the bank. He recalled his family's situation:

> So we decided to look at alternatives. Was there any way we could improve our lot financially? At the time, there was a lot of emigration going on to places like South Africa, Australia, New Zealand, and Canada, so we got all the information we could get from all the embassies in London and Liverpool, and we got useful documents like Eaton's catalogues and things like that, looked at the lifestyles, found out about the different countries, and decided if we were going to move anywhere, it was going to be Canada. Australia and New Zealand—we considered them but decided they were too far to travel, we wouldn't be able to get back to see our families on a regular basis, and they wouldn't be able to see their grandchildren. Another important fact was that the engineering opportunities weren't nearly as great in those countries as they were in South Africa or Canada, and when I looked at the funding ratio—the cost of the house divided by the annual salary of an engineer—in Australia it was going to take me twenty-four years to buy a house, twenty-four years of salary; in Canada I could do it in six.

As we saw in Chapter 2, work was a critical consideration in a decision to emigrate. But, what do we mean by work? The answer is not as clear-cut as one might think. "The term 'work' generally is used to denote the exertion of effort toward some end; economically it refers to activities oriented toward producing goods and services for one's own use or for pay."[2] This definition, however, excludes unpaid housework and care work, as well as unpaid community work. In a recent large-scale survey on work and lifelong learning (WALL),[3] led by Toronto-based sociologists Margrit Eichler and Ann Matthews, four different categories of work emerged: activities that are paid for; unpaid activities like child care and housework; studying for self-improvement; and unpleasant but essential activities like snow clearance. During the postwar years when our interviewees came to Canada, unpaid work such as housework, caring, and volunteering in the community, was not considered work in the way it was in later years. The 1972 edition of the *International Encyclopedia of the Social Sciences* excluded unpaid housework from the North American labour force "because such work is outside the characteristic system of work organization of production."[4]

Attitudes to women in the workplace also changed during the second half of the twentieth century. Veronica Strong-Boag stressed that between the two world wars Canadians largely came to terms with the fact that many, if not most women, would spend a period in the labour market before marriage, and that they had a right to do so. From the end of World War II to the 1960s "Canadians confronted and debated the desirability of married middle-class women staying at home and/or returning to employment."[5] In some sections of society there was a stigma, felt by both men and women, attaching to married women undertaking paid employment. This issue was debated extensively in the popular press. Some newspaper commentators reflected the fears of the times. For example, in 1960 a male *Star Weekly* correspondent commented on the role of wives: "Their primary function is the bearing and raising of children. They do it better than anyone else and they do it best at home."[6] Also writing in the *Star Weekly*, psychologist Dr. Bruno Bettleheim asserted that the proper functioning of society depended on men remaining "breadwinners," "authorities," "protectors," and "moral influences"—roles that would be jeopardized by female wage earners.[7] In some quarters, however, it was acceptable for working-class wives to contribute to the family income by taking paid employment. From the 1960s through to the 1990s there was significant social change in the manner in which society viewed the role of women in the workplace. In the debate over the legitimacy of paid work for wives and mothers, Veronica Strong-Boag concluded that in the 1990s, much more than the 1950s, married women with children became an accepted part of the labour force. Their earnings continued to keep many Canadian families active consumers and out of poverty.[8]

This was the social climate in which our interviewee immigrants set about forging a new way of life in Canada. The patriarchal nature of the workplace was reinforced by the Canadian immigration authorities through the advertising they placed in English newspapers. References to Canada's excellent employment opportunities were mostly targeted at men.[9] Our interviewees' testimonies reflect this gender difference. Men tended to relate their life stories through work, and women through their families. Oral history pioneer Isabelle Bertaux-Wiame observed that, "men and women tell their stories differently because their lives follow differently shaped courses and these courses in turn depend on distinctive social—rather than sexual—positions." In her study of internal migration in France in the 1970s, she found that "men relate their search for work. For women the search is to establish the family context in which they can produce what society has defined as their proper product."[10] One exception to this rule occurred when we interviewed single women, who tended to relate their life histories to their work experience. This chapter, however, will not be exclusively about men and single women. Not surprisingly, we found that wives and mothers also engaged in paid employment. And, to overcome the problematic nature of defining work, this chapter will concentrate on the traditional view of work as paid employment. The next chapter will consider unpaid work, which manifests itself in various guises including housework, child rearing, caring, and voluntary community work.

As discussed in Chapter 2, one of the driving forces behind many postwar English people's decision to emigrate was their desire to improve their standard of living. The choice of Canada as their preferred destination was directly linked to perceptions of better-rewarded employment and enhanced career opportunities. The Canadian immigration authorities nurtured those perceptions; in their advertising, they generally stressed openings for employment, along with other benefits of living in Canada. Department of Citizenship and Immigration advertisements often took the form of tabular listings showing vacancies available in each province. For example, in what was headed a "partial list of employment opportunities forecast for 1960" the department listed sixty-five different job categories. The list included veterinarians, nurses, laboratory technicians, teachers, stenographers, salesmen, farmers, fitter-machinists, welders, dairy workers, cooks, launderers, and dry cleaners.[11]

What jobs did English-born immigrants do? How did they find employment? How did their careers progress through to retirement? Were they upwardly mobile? Did they face discrimination? To what degree did they suffer from insecurity, stress, redundancy, or unemployment? Did they achieve high levels of job satisfaction? These and other questions will be addressed in this chapter. We adopt a case history approach to allow the voices of immigrants to be heard. Their nuanced work stories reveal how work was a pivotal feature of the immigrant lives and how its reach interconnected and sometimes clashed with other elements of the immigrant experience. A number of significant themes, often related to gender, class, and age, emerge. The case studies look at the work experience of representative groups including: entrepreneurs, professionals, public sector workers, those who experienced discrimination, and working wives.

First, we attempt an overview. This is problematic because the employment statistics on English-born immigrants have been infrequently aggregated by official sources, including the various departments responsible for immigration, or by the national statistics agency, Statistics Canada. Even Duncan Sandys, British Secretary of State for Commonwealth Relations, when reviewing British emigration policy in 1961, complained of "statistical shortcomings" in the way Commonwealth governments published occupational statistics about their immigrants.[12] Notwithstanding, Sandys observed that Canada wanted "skilled workers and professional people, especially as there is a steady loss of such people from Canada to the United States."[13] He continued: "A significant change has taken place in recent years in the character of migration from this country. No longer are the majority of migrants unskilled labourers of the type who constituted an unemployment problem in Britain in the 1920s. The modern trend is toward professional and skilled workers, urgently sought by the white Commonwealth countries to develop their economies."[14]

The statistics largely corroborate this interpretation, although Sandys's criticism of Canadian statistics was not wholly justified (see Figure 3). According to the *Canada Year Books* for 1956 to 1961, less than 2 percent of

Figure 3 | PERCENT INTENDED OCCUPATION
ENGLISH-BORN IMMIGRANTS 1956–61

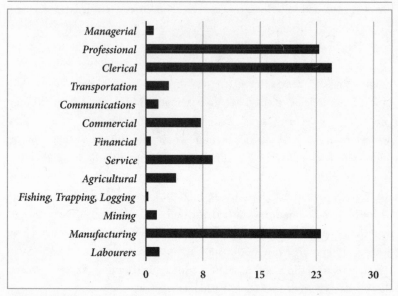

Source: Canada Year Books 1956–61

English immigrants were labourers, with some three quarters specifying professional, clerical, or manufacturing occupations. This pattern was mirrored by the employment histories revealed by our interviewee immigrants. While the majority of postwar English immigrants were in white-collar occupations, the occupational categories in Figure 3 embrace a wide range of job types. The first one in the list, managerial, includes entrepreneurs. While the phenomenon of migrating entrepreneurs was relatively rare, in a study using Statistics Canada's longitudinal immigration database, Peter Li found that male immigrants from the United Kingdom were more likely to engage in self-employment in the first five years after landing than were immigrants from South Europe, Africa, South Asia, Hong Kong, and South and Central America.[15] We now start our case histories by reviewing two entrepreneurial success stories.

The entrepreneurs

John Steven was an Oxbridge scholarship student who completed his PhD at Liverpool University. His first paid job was undertaking research in electricity and supply utilization. Wandering through the lab one day, he overheard one of the technicians saying he had got a job in Canada. As described in Chapter 2, John was disillusioned with the Labour government and the power of the unions, blaming both for England's decline. He therefore asked the technician how he got the Canadian job:

> He [the technician] said he'd been talking to his ex-boss who was a university professor, in Wales actually, and they were setting up this new program in Canada. So I called up this guy and went to chat to him and anyway, then I went home and then a week or two later I got this phone call from Canada and it was from this chap who was setting up this program there. This guy in Wales had talked to him and he'd said, "Oh this guy looks promising," so he phoned me and said, "Do you want a job?" So I said, "Oh, okay." and the next thing I know I'm employed in the space program over here. So that was kind of a bit of a bolt from the blue.

Opportunism and exploiting personal contacts brought Steven to Canada in 1969 as an employee of the new Canadian government Department of Communications, working on their Telsat space satellite program. The pay was poor and a second baby arrived in the winter of 1972: "We didn't have that much money so I had to buy this ancient 'cronker' car which of course kept breaking down every five minutes; it was a bit of a liability during the winter." Telsat's world-leading work, however, was attracting attention internationally: "A lot of people were sniffing around, so I and my buddies made this very formal presentation to management that we should sell this [our technology] internationally." After due consideration management said no. This led Steven and some of his close colleagues to quit and set up their own company, offering systems design and consulting work in the space business. The new company, Steven recalled:

> just kept growing and growing and growing. And, of course, it grew to a size where you couldn't carry on like that. We were borrowing millions of dollars from the bank and they started to get anti about that and we had to have more cash in hand, more investment.... If we'd been doing this twenty years later money would have been pouring in from investors but it was the wrong time, so eventually I

had a bit of a parting of the ways with my partners…. We eventually
managed to sell [the company], not for as much as I thought we
should have done, but we did manage to get out of there intact.

Many entrepreneurs have an exit strategy in order to maximize their
financial return from their company start-up. While Steven may have been
disappointed by the return he received from his twenty years in the space
business, he was not downhearted. He simply changed tack after the sale
and established a new business, this time in medical electronics. He sold the
business some ten years later to finance his retirement.

Roger MacKay, a hairdresser in Kent, came from a different social and
educational background. Nonetheless, in Canada he turned his passion
for flying into related employment and, eventually, ownership of his own
business. He came to Canada without a job, on the recommendation of
a friend who had emigrated to Canada earlier. The day after his arrival in
Toronto on 5 April 1968, Roger got a job in retail sales. He wasted no time
in contacting the King City Flying Club, based on Toronto Island: "I asked
if they were looking for anybody to work at the airport…and they said, 'Yeah
we could use you to do some work' so I stayed there for two years flying
and getting my licenses." During that time he "actually lived a year in the
control tower." Money was tight, and income from flying lessons had to be
supplemented with earnings from another job at a gas station. Next door to
the gas station was a company called Dominion Helicopters. Roger talked
his way into flying one of their airplanes to ferry maintenance engineers to
locations where helicopters were based. He quickly became attracted to flying helicopters, and took his endorsements to become a qualified helicopter
pilot. Dominion Helicopters sent him to the Arctic for about six months to
help conduct surveys for the National Research Centre and the Canadian
Wildlife Service: "About 1974 I decided there was enough interest for me to
buy a helicopter so I did. I bought one and based myself up in Sault Ste. Marie. I ran an ad hoc helicopter charter operation for about, oh maybe four or
five years, I guess. By that time we had about seven or eight helicopters, and
we got into the '80s, and the market started to collapse; my partner wanted
to change our method of business, so I sold him my company." Like John
Steven, when things got tough Roger sold his company and started again.
But, unlike Steven, Roger did not start another company. He became an
employee of Bell Helicopter as a salesman and demo pilot. His work was

based in Ottawa, but after a couple of years Roger heard that the company wanted to open an office in London, England. Roger talked his way into the post and returned to live in England, where he was responsible for sales in Northern Europe. Meanwhile Bell Helicopter was planning to open a new manufacturing operation in Montreal. Roger obtained a position in charge of manufacturing and marketing operations, and moved back to Canada, after having spent five years in England. His new job, however, was short-lived; Bell relocated the Montreal facility to Fort Worth, Texas, leaving Roger to run a small office in Ottawa, looking after the company's relationship with the Canadian government. He held this post for nine years before deciding to retire: "I took early retirement, not sure what I wanted to do, but needed to change because what I was doing had been the same for twenty years and I needed a change. So I opened up a small company which looks after aviation consultancy work, maintenance and flight training, and various things like that. It's been reasonably successful." Looking back on his career, Roger said that in his early twenties he had a goal to get into the aviation business. He attributed his success to the opportunities he found in Canada. Roger recalled that as a young man he had, not just the flying, "but being able to set up a business with what I came with, which was really nothing...I could never ever have done that in England."

The conventional image of an entrepreneur is that of a person who undertakes a commercial enterprise for profit, often at personal risk.[16] Both John Steven and Roger MacKay took risks and built up companies providing paid employment for others. Both men suffered when market conditions deteriorated. John sold his space business, though not on the terms he would have liked, and started another company. Roger was also forced to sell his helicopter business, but instead of starting another company he became an employee of a multinational corporation, before returning to self-employment.

"We couldn't be better off than we are here"

Many immigrants earned their living by working in multinationals or in smaller companies or professional partnerships. When Peter Semple came to Toronto with his wife and baby son in 1966, he intended to stay for only three years. Recently qualified as a chartered accountant at a time when English accountancy qualifications were fully recognized in Canada, Peter approached a number of accounting firms in Montreal and Toronto. He gained a position with Coopers & Lybrand for whom he did auditing work for around eighteen months. Then one of his clients offered him a more challenging and better-paid job at a small private company, which Peter would successfully help to go public through a Toronto Stock Exchange share issue:

> So I was there for two or three years and we got bought out by an American company, which was an interesting exercise. I was chief financial officer, did everything, and I had a bookkeeper who worked for me and stuff like that, dealt with everything. When we got bought out, the buyers decided they were going to merge us with a company they had down in Cambridge, southwest of Toronto. So, I commuted down there for a couple of weeks to do various things. Then, one day the boss said, "Well, I guess you will be finishing on Friday." I said, "Oh? Oh?"

Peter was fired. He went to a lawyer who won him a financial settlement that provided the Semples with sufficient capital to put down a deposit on a house. Around the same time, Peter picked up a job in downtown Toronto as a financial controller for a photofinishing company. Peter reported to the head office in Montreal and three years later his boss resigned to join a telecommunications company. Peter recalled:

> One day out of the blue, he [the ex-boss] called me and said, "Have you ever thought about coming to Montreal?" And I said, "Yeah, a decade ago, but I don't really have enough French." He said, "It doesn't matter. It doesn't matter." He said, "I just fired my chief financial guy and I've got to get somebody. Are you interested in coming?" I said, "Well, I can't afford to come to Montreal." "Oh," he said, "don't worry about money. We'll fix something up." And he did. Every time he called me it went up.

Peter joined the telecommunications business. This was a complex world of international finance, and multimillion dollar deals. It was also a time of rapid technological change. In his twenty years in the business, international communications traffic went from high-frequency radio, to analogue, to digital, and from cables with a sixty-call capacity to fibre optics with a 10,000-call capacity. Peter's role was a senior and multifaceted one that involved managing the intricacies of the Commonwealth

Telecommunications Agreement. This responsibility naturally required frequent business travel. From a family and work-life perspective, business travel was a double-edged sword. When in London, Peter would often catch a train to visit his parents in Oxford, only an hour's journey away. During the last two years of his parents' lives Peter commented that he thought he had seen more of them than did his sister who lived in England. The downside was being away from his family in Canada. One year, he was home only three weekends in the year, and he spent many other weekends either coming home from abroad or travelling away to another meeting. Peter recalled his ten-year-old daughter saying, "Daddy, when are you going away again?" He replied, "Not till next weekend, why?" She responded, "You upset things when you're here." Peter observed, "I guess I did do that, wander in, need to get clothes clean and all that sort of stuff, and back away again. In terms of being a parent, I wasn't much help." Peter's marriage also broke up. At the time of our interview, Peter was semi-retired, doing financial consultancy work on an increasingly part-time basis.

This brief resumé of Peter's career indicates that he was relatively mobile. He moved from job to job. After taking a junior position in an accountancy firm he was offered a better-paid position from a client. When this firm changed ownership he was fired. He then found another job, locally, in a photo-processing business. He was tempted away from this by his former boss to enter the world of telecommunications, an industry experiencing rapid growth and technological change. Here he held very senior positions in finance and had spells representing Canadian interests on international telecommunications regulatory bodies. Throughout his career, his income was on an upward curve, naturally falling upon retirement yet supplemented by part-time consultancy work secured through his experience, know-how, and contacts.

Kenneth Cecil, who was quoted earlier comparing Canadian and Australian house prices and salaries, had only two employers during his working life in Canada. Kenneth began work as a seventeen-year-old apprentice engineer in the aircraft industry in Blackpool in the northwest of England. This opportunity led to an engineering degree. He enjoyed his work on Canberra bombers and Lightning fighters but felt he did not have enough money to support his young family in the way he would have liked. Along with money worries, he faced the prospect of losing his job when Harold Wilson's government started talking about scrapping the TSR2, a new strike and reconnaissance aircraft. Around this time, recruitment executives from Boeing in Seattle and Canadair in Montreal sought to persuade qualified engineers to emigrate to North America. This activity coincided with a visit from an old friend who had been working in the West Indies and who now planned to go to Canada. Kenneth decided to go with him, even though neither had a job. He recalls their first days in Montreal:

> We got the *Montreal Star* and the *Montreal Gazette*, read them
> for job opportunities, and at that time, absolutely incredible, the
> engineering opportunities were so vast that we went round and
> interviewed employers and decided where we wanted to work.
> We both found jobs with Canadian Ingersoll Rand, and when we
> got the jobs, we found out that one of them was in Sherbrooke
> and one of them was in Montreal. And Barry said, "Well, you're
> married, you better stay in Montreal, I'll go to Sherbrooke." Janet
> had come over and joined me a month after I left England.

After only five or six weeks, Kenneth found another job with Trans-Canada Airlines doing work similar to what he had done in England. He remained employed by the airline for thirty years, rising to the level of chief engineer before he was made redundant and retired. Like Peter Semple, Kenneth used his expertise and contacts to establish a consultancy business in retirement. Indeed, he was so successful that after a year Kenneth claimed to have a higher gross income than he had earned on salary.

Kenneth's consultancy business was relatively short-lived, however, largely because of linguistic constraints. The Cecils had originally settled in Montreal, where Kenneth's first two jobs were based. Neither Kenneth nor his wife spoke French fluently. Janet "picked up" the language while shopping and by "learning through rote." The children went to bilingual schools. Kenneth had to learn the language for his job, so the airline sent him to classes where he became functionally bilingual.[17] He observed, however, that "there wasn't really a language problem. The language of aviation is English." The need to speak and write in French became a problem when he started his consultancy. The business was registered as a Quebec corporation. When he had clients only in Quebec, this form of registration was practical. When he found clients in Ontario, however, he was faced with a choice of registering in Ontario or federally. He chose the federal route. Kenneth explained:

7. Many professionally qualified English engineers were attracted to work in places like this drafting office in Montreal. Photo credit: Canada Department of Manpower and Immigration / Library and Archives Canada, e010982325.

"Abruptly all my correspondence with the Quebec government switched from English to French, and they just said, 'Sorry, we always deal with federal corporations in the French language.' Well, after thirty years in Quebec, I was functionally bilingual but the technical language of tax forms was absolutely beyond me, and they just said, 'Tough, get yourself a translator,' and I said, 'No, I've a better idea.'" The idea was to move to the rural suburbs of Ottawa. While recording his life story, Kenneth mused rhetorically whether they had been better off as a result of emigrating to Canada: "We couldn't be better off than we are here." In fact, of his TSR2 colleagues who had emigrated to Canada, "every one of them has done really well here." One of his friends, who planned to come with them, had his application for landed immigrant status turned down on medical grounds. That friend, at the time of interview some forty years later, was still working for the same English aerospace company and was still living in the same house. As Kenneth laconically observed, "So we know where we would have been."

Employment in the public sector

Not all English immigrants worked in business—whether for themselves, in a partnership, or in private or public companies. A significant number worked in the public sector as teachers, nurses, civil servants, academics, specialists such as meteorologists, military personnel, and a wide range of other roles. Like Kenneth Cecil, Tom Knight was an engineer. He chose to pursue his career in the Royal Canadian Navy. Tom was a wartime evacuee, coming to Canada with his mother as a baby and being left under the care of the Children's Aid Society. He returned to England at the end of the war. His father, a stonemason with poor employment prospects, decided to emigrate in 1951 with his family. Eleven-year-old Tom returned to Canada with the family and went to school in Hull, Quebec. When he finished high school, he felt his prospects of going to university were not good, so he applied to the Royal Military College in Kingston, where tuition was free. Tom was initially turned down, but he eventually satisfied RMC's rigorous selection process. He joined the Air Force, following in the footsteps of his father, who had been a navigator-bomber flying in Mosquitoes during the war. After two years of training, Tom had a dispute with one of his instructors. As a result, and because the Air Force was downsizing at the time, he was told, "We don't need you." This prompted Tom to talk to the Navy, which shortly afterward accepted him: "Well, what a difference—Navy training as opposed to Air Force training. In Navy training you get a few weeks of classroom training to prepare you for it, and then you get on a ship, and...you're going sixteen hours a day, just working, doing navigation, doing seamanship drills.... I loved it, and so I did fairly well, not the top of the class, but I did fairly well in the Navy and then when I graduated, after five years at RMC, I served at sea." While at sea, Tom continued with his training. One of his roles was that of onboard security officer, requiring him to become a Canadian citizen, which cost him "five bucks." According to Tom, the Navy was good to him. Academically, he was inclined toward engineering, with an interest in electronics and radio. He became an operations officer, a job that stimulated his interest in the equipment used for radar, navigation, and combat information systems. Early in his career, and newly married, he was based in Halifax, where he spent four years out of six at sea. Routine ongoing training, combined with Tom's interests, led him to complete an engineering degree. He gained a postgraduate qualification when he was posted, as a foreign sailor, to the U.S. Navy bases at Monterey, California, and Dam Neck, Virginia. While he was in the U.S., he also developed his interest in computers and programming. Tom eventually found himself back in Ottawa, working on command-and-control systems as a lieutenant commander. Unfortunately, he had a personality clash with his commander, whom Tom accused as having "more ego than Donald Trump." The outcome: "A couple of months later I took off the uniform, put on my civilian clothes and started working in another directorate," in the Department of National Defence. His work involved setting up a new software engineering support centre for the Navy's command and control systems on both the east and west coasts. After thirty-eight years of service, Tom was given what he called the "golden handshake" as part of the government's personnel reduction plan.

Tom's career had involved long trips at sea. During some exercises, he visited naval bases in England, including Portsmouth, Plymouth, and Chatham. On these occasions, he would "beg off a day and a half to go and see my grandmother, aunt, and uncle." Peter Semple, John Steven, Robert Baldwin, and others also used business trips as a means to visit family members left behind in England. On occasions these trips were rolled into holidays when wives and children came along too. Tom's career pattern was similar in another respect. Upon semi-retirement, Tom used his professional training, expertise, and contacts to do lucrative consultancy work. Among his clients was the Army, for whom he worked for eight years, undertaking process engineering to improve organizational efficiency. Tom finally retired a week before his sixty-fourth birthday, having served in the Air Force, Navy, Army, and Department of National Defence.

Elizabeth Summers trained as an occupational therapist. After completing her training and working for a couple of years in England, she emigrated to Australia, only to come back because she missed her family which was "a very long way away." Her return was tinged with regret. She had really enjoyed Australia and confessed she would have stayed if she had got married and had children. One of the things that she enjoyed about Australia was the wide open spaces. Back in England, she felt constricted by the density of the population. Compared with Australia she thought that, "living in England seemed to be like living in a lettuce.... I didn't want to go back to Australia, but I wanted somewhere else, so Canada was the obvious choice." In 1960 Canada was short of occupational therapists. At thirty years old she was hired, sight unseen, by the Montreal Children's Hospital. After a successful spell in Montreal, Elizabeth was invited to teach pediatrics at Queen's University in Kingston. Five years later, having missed working with patients, she took a senior role in the rehabilitation centre in what was then the Royal Ottawa Hospital, where she worked until retiring in 1990.

Abbi Andrews was a career librarian. Unlike Elizabeth Summers, Abbi was married. Her husband was in the timber business, and the couple had two sons. Abbi arrived in Canada as a teenager with her parents in 1947. She went to high school in Fredericton, where she was bullied because she was English. Having earned higher grades at her school in England than did her peer group in Canada, Abbi already had the qualifications to go to university, so she started an arts course at the University of New Brunswick, where she met her future husband. To help meet her student costs, she worked part-time in the library and for a year before her wedding she crossed the border to work in two libraries in Worcester, Massachusetts. Her new husband found work in Toronto and then in Ottawa, where Abbi had two sons and stayed at home as a full-time mother. The couple were not religious but wanted to expose their children to the Christian tradition. They joined a Unitarian church, where one particular sermon "had a tremendous impact" on the young mother. Abbi recalled the minister emphasizing that a woman, after raising her children, had twenty-five years of her life left to contribute to society. "So I decided that I would go to library school," Abbi recalled. "There was one at the University of Ottawa, and I went there part time so I was still at home for my children." She graduated four years later, in 1967.

Abbi then found a school librarian position whose schedule allowed her to look after her children. As the boys grew up and left home, Abbi moved on to full-time work. She soon gained a reputation as an innovative and effective librarian. A series of promotions and new jobs led to senior roles in leading national libraries, galleries, and museums. Her forte was the introduction of new methods to enhance efficiency and facilitate inter-library collaborations. Her reputation was such that she became involved in international projects, leading to her spending time in Europe. At the age of sixty she was "beginning to feel burnt out" from her heavy workload, so she retired. Her work, however, continued when she was invited to take up a consultancy appointment. The hours were equally long and onerous. With her parents now in their late eighties and living in a Florida retirement home, Abbi finally retired in 1992 so she and her husband could spend long spells with her parents and escape Ontario winters.

In December 1966, the cold, dark Ottawa winter came as a shock to young physics graduate James Roland, whom we last encountered in Chapter 3 as he was fast-tracked through his immigration application in London. He thought he had a job with Atomic Energy Canada but discovered that this was not the case. With the weather getting colder, and living in an ill-equipped rooming house, James got a job in Ogilvy's Department Store on Rideau Street for a few weeks in the pre-Christmas period. In the New Year he got a permanent job in the Meteorological Service of the Department of Transport. James takes up his story:

> They had a very forward-looking type of program where you could see a career advancement path that they had thought out. And, having a background in physics, that seemed like a good thing to do. And that led me on a merry chase around Canada, starting in Toronto..., then a few weeks here in Ottawa in July 1967—which was kind of nice to be here for the centennial celebrations and going down to Montreal for Expo 67—then back to Toronto for the second phase of what they called the Meteorological Officer course up to Christmas, and then another period in Trenton, Ontario, at the Air Force base there, training. It was interesting, too, because that was the time when the services were amalgamated, and there were a lot of sentimental Air Force people sorry to lose their status as a kind of an independent military force. Then it was off to Halifax for my first posting as a weather forecaster.

James did not stay there long. He had done well in his course, and his employers encouraged him to do a master's degree at McGill University. He then did a short assignment in Toronto before heading off to Winnipeg for eighteen months, doing serious forecasting on the Prairies. With his career on an upward trajectory, he got more educational leave, achieving a PhD in atmospheric science at Colorado State University. Next, he conducted research on air pollution in Toronto, after which he moved into management.

> I found I got more interested in what the science means for society
> rather than the science for its own sake, so I moved here to Ottawa
> and started working in a policy role. Probably the more interesting
> aspect for me in what I did…was [my role] as a negotiator on
> the Montreal Protocol on the ozone layer which involved some
> international work and feeling that you are making a difference,
> particularly since the Montreal Protocol is such a successful
> international environmental treaty.[18] And then in 1998, right after
> the ice storm,[19] the opportunity came up to get an early retirement.

Like others, before and after him, James arrived in Canada without a job. He found it relatively easy to find temporary employment before embarking on a planned career path that aligned with his interests, educational background, and aspirations. He recalled that his new life in Canada did not get off to "a propitious start." Initially he determined that for a year, he would not make any decision about whether coming to Canada had been wise. At the end of that year, once he had got into employment and training, he realized that he had made the right move.

Academics

One area of the public sector that attracted English immigrants was academia. A number of observers, including Howard C. Clark, a New Zealand immigrant who pursued a distinguished academic career in a number of Canadian universities, have commented that at the end of the war, universities were struggling to cope with the influx of veterans. Furthermore, demographic projections showed unambiguously that explosive growth in university enrollments would occur in the 1960s and 1970s. This led to a dramatic expansion of Canadian universities from the mid-1950s. A significant proportion of newly recruited academics came from England. Unfortunately, accurate figures are hard to obtain. In his autobiographical assessment, *Growth and Governance of Canadian Universities: An Insider's View*, Clark cites the composition of the chemistry department at the University of British Columbia in 1957. Of the nineteen faculty members, nine were Canadian, seven from the United Kingdom, and one each from the United States, Australia, and New Zealand. In 1964 the department had grown to a faculty of thirty-six, of which fifteen were Canadians, thirteen were from the U.K., three from the U.S., and two each from Australia and New Zealand. Clark observed that these proportions were similar to other departments.[20] Clark explains why so many academics from Commonwealth countries were attracted to Canadian universities:

> Canada was seen by all of us who migrated to it as a stable, rich, democratic country with a future of great promise yet very similar to our own native land, whether that be the UK, Australia, New Zealand, or South Africa. Clearly those similarities arose from the common British heritage we shared, even as that heritage was rapidly being discarded. In addition, while we did not know a great deal about Canadian universities, their histories, traditions, and academic standards were seen as comparable to those from which we came. Canada was attractive and the transition could be smooth and comfortable.[21]

The relative numbers of English-born academics declined, however, during the 1960s and thereafter, due partly to the increased number of Canadian PhD students coming on to the job market and partly to the growing influx from the U.S.

Canadian universities also attracted English students who came to study for higher degrees and remained to work in Canada. Two interviewees who fit into this group are Peter Robinson and Jeremy Plunkett. Peter Robinson came to Canada in 1974 to study for his master's in English and creative writing at the University of Windsor. He then gained a PhD from York University in Toronto. After teaching at a number of colleges and universities in eastern Ontario, he served as writer-in-residence at the University of Windsor in the early 1990s. Peter was attracted to Canada for a number of the reasons outlined earlier by Howard C. Clark. He strongly resented the class system in England and felt that the nature of society in Canada released him from its constraints. "Coming to Canada was a step towards freeing that baggage," he remarked. Peter had intended to stay for a short time, but once he had married a Canadian, he decided to remain. His work as an internationally best-selling crime writer takes him back to his native Yorkshire, where he owns a house, for around three months each year. He can thus reconnect with his Yorkshire roots while also conducting research and promotional work for his series of novels about Detective Chief Inspector Banks, an enigmatic Yorkshire cop. Robinson's novels occasionally allude to the lives of expat English immigrants. For example, as noted in the previous chapter, *Hanging Valley* has references to the $1,000 cure.

Jeremy Plunkett gained his master's in geophysics at Durham University. He turned down an opportunity to read for his doctorate at Cambridge in favour of going to the University of Western Ontario. After two years he ran out of money and got a job in Ottawa, as a labourer with the Geological Survey of Canada. He persuaded his employer to fund his courses at Carleton University, which prompted him to think:

> Maybe I should do something about restarting my PhD, but I didn't
> feel like going back to university.... I was doing a lot of research, busy,
> got a job, got a house and all the rest of it and I'd quite a lot, quite a big
> bibliography of scientific publications, and one day at a boozy party
> I got talking with a man who was at the Ottawa University Geology
> Department, and I described what I was doing and he said, "Well
> you know I'm sure if you approached the university and asked them
> if you could tie this research work up you could do it as a PhD."

This choice proved problematic. Still short of money, Jeremy started working for a British Petroleum subsidiary specializing in applied information systems and geophysics. Simultaneously the university allowed him to worked on his PhD *in absentia*. In this period he was promoted to the position of vice-president of the BP subsidiary. It took him six years to complete his thesis, only to have it rejected. Two years later, in 1984, he made a successful defence and was eventually awarded his doctorate.

Jeremy was attracted to Canada by its wide open spaces. Along with his Polish-born wife he enjoyed canoeing in the wilderness. One day the couple found a log cabin and a plot of land on an island in the Outaouais River in the wilds of Quebec. They spent time and energy on its restoration and development, and Jeremy readily admits that these interests, along with his love of the wilderness, hindered progress in gaining his PhD. Jeremy eventually left his job and worked for a number of leading consultancy firms. Eventually his last client decided to terminate his contract. Jeremy's response was, "Bugger this for a lark. I'm not working, I've got too much construction, too much gardening to do. That's the way it's been ever since, I've never looked back."

Difficulties in finding employment

Immigrants Need Not Apply was the title of a report published by the Ottawa-based Caledon Institute of Social Policy in 1999.[22] The report focused on problems facing immigrants in having their foreign qualifications and work experience recognized by a range of stakeholders, including federal and provincial governments, professional bodies, trade unions, and employers. According to the report, further hurdles in finding work, keeping jobs, and securing advancement arise from ethnic and gender prejudice and harassment. For many immigrants, language is also a problem. The employment experiences of immigrant groups from Japan, the West Indies, Poland, Italy, China, and the Middle East have been well documented elsewhere. What these groups have in common is not sharing English as a first language, and/or having an ethnicity other than Caucasian. English-born immigrants, with a few exceptions, are white and speak English, the common language of Canada outside of Quebec. In many respects the English are invisible, though audible (see Chapter 4).

The evidence in the testimonies recorded by our interviewees suggests that problems related to non-recognition of English qualifications or experience were relatively rare, as was discrimination or prejudice. There were some notable exceptions. Pat Connor, who was brought up in an orphanage in Cumbria where she was subjected to brutal beatings by the nuns, began her working life in the British Army. She wanted to be a driver, but when she achieved high test scores, the Army decided she was too intelligent to be a driver and transferred her into signals. She worked as a teleprinter operator, sending and receiving top secret information at Army headquarters in Aldershot. Ironically, she nearly failed the security vetting because she had a Polish uncle who lived in Ottawa; this was a time when there was deep suspicion of the eastern European Warsaw Pact countries. She met her husband at Aldershot, and because regulations prevented married couples serving at the same time, she took a job in London. Her army training had given her advanced skills and her new employment involved work on early computer systems for the University Central Council for Admissions (UCCA). After five years, UCCA was relocated to Cheltenham in the West of England. Pat did not want to move from London, opting for a generous financial settlement instead. After failing to get a job in computers, she decided to use the financial windfall to emigrate to Canada with her son, having previously separated from her husband. Pat recalled:

> I had discovered that, although I spent five years working on a computer, all of a sudden, I couldn't get a job on computers, because I didn't have a degree in math. And, I would say to them, "Well, why do I need a degree in math? You know, five years I spent working on a computer, I was a manager of the computer room, and never needed math, you know." Well, that's what they were looking for…so I said "well the hell with it." So I applied to immigrate to Canada. I had an aunt who lived in Ottawa, and her husband had a business there.

Pat's explanation about finding another job in England suggests that the reason potential employers rejected her was because she did not have a relevant degree; her experience did not count. A more likely explanation was because she was a woman. In the mid-1960s the embryonic field of computing was largely dominated by men.

It is also probable that Pat suffered gender discrimination at the hands of Canadian immigration officials as well. Pat applied to emigrate just after Canada had introduced the points system for immigrants.[23] Because computing was a new field, there was not a category for a computer operator; the immigration officials simply designated her as a typist, a distinctly low- status female occupation: "I said, 'At least you could put me down as a personal secretary or something, but a typist, I mean I'd worked at this job for five years.' And, when I did get a job I had to start as a junior operator, but I thought that was okay. I can understand that, I mean, why should I walk in there and be better than anyone else? You have to start at the bottom, and I worked my way up to manager." Once in Canada, Pat had a number of job applications rejected because of her gender. Pat explained, "Because the computers was [sic] shift work, they said that there was a law that if you [a woman] worked past midnight they had to pay for your taxi home, and a lot of companies wouldn't do that for women." To compound her feeling of mistreatment, Pat believed she suffered a different kind of discrimination when she lost a job because she was not bilingual.

Being out of work brought on a bout of depression which Pat described as "going down a dark, dark road." She remembered spending days in her housecoat and pyjamas because she had no reason to go out of the house. Pat also admitted contemplating suicide during her early days in Ottawa when she found it difficult to find work. She did not like the extreme cold, and she was frustrated when people could not understand her English accent. Also, in the background, there was her abusive childhood and more recent marital breakdown. Pat eventually found work with her uncle's accountant who ran a service bureau doing people's payrolls, general ledgers, and other administrative tasks. After she had worked there for nearly thirty years, this company went through a number of changes of ownership. Then, Pat recalled, "You know, I just walked in one day and they just said, 'Whoop, sorry, we don't need ya anymore, and you got fifteen minutes to get out.'"

The lack of recognition of foreign qualifications and work experience created a potential barrier for many immigrants in the professions and some trades. For example, there were legislative provisions requiring permission or licensure from relevant Canadian regulatory bodies to practise in a range of occupations, such as those of accountancy, medicine, or motor mechanics. Our interviewees, many of whom would have been caught by these types of requirements, were surprisingly silent on this issue. The most likely explanation is that either they felt achieving a Canadian "qualification" was entirely reasonable, or that it was a normal part of working in Canada. Or perhaps they did not consider the matter of qualifications to be significant enough to raise in the telling of their life stories. For many engineers, especially those in the aerospace industry, work in Canada was similar enough to the work they did in England that their English qualifications were, in fact, recognized. English-qualified engineer Robert Baldwin, who worked as an engineer in the Canadian aircraft industry, did not mention having to "qualify" as a Canadian engineer. His UK degrees were recognized by the Canadian engineering institutions. Years into his retirement, when he was interviewed, he still wore his Canadian iron ring on the little finger of his working hand. The ring was a symbol and reminder of the obligations and ethics associated with the profession in Canada. Robert and his Canadian-born son, also an engineer, had received their rings together, at the same ceremony, which Robert still finds moving.

Rare exceptions to the aforementioned silence in the testimonies came from Joan Martin, a nurse, and Arthur Wood, a mechanic. Joan qualified and worked as a State Registered Nurse in England. Her qualifications and experience were not recognized in Canada, when she immigrated in 1971.

She found this ironic, sarcastically observing that she had "only trained at the hospital where Florence Nightingale actually worked."[24] Joan had to go back to school. She went to the Wellesley Hospital School of Nursing in Toronto to do a year and three months of the two-year nursing program in order to pass the examination. She considered this requirement to be "ridiculous" but admitted, "I did learn a heck of a lot going round the second time. You pick up the things you didn't pick up the first time." After she graduated and qualified as a Canadian registered nurse, she worked for a year at Toronto Western Hospital in the intensive care unit, and then had her first child. Even after she started work, Joan found her English experience "didn't count, it didn't count for seniority, it didn't count for experience...my experience in England counted for nothing, big fat zero."

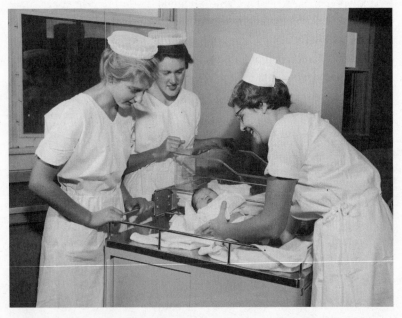

8. Like other English-qualified immigrants Joan Martin had to retrain to gain Canadian qualifications. Here two nurses in training are receiving instruction from a registered nurse in the maternity ward of a Toronto hospital. Photo credit: Gilbert A. Milne / Library and Archives Canada, e002504636.

Sarah Walsh was another English-qualified nurse and had worked as a ward sister in England. Like Joan Martin, she faced problems in securing registration, but for different reasons. Sarah first settled in Montreal with her husband and young family. "It was sort of reciprocal that nurses from

Britain got automatic registration in the province [Quebec]," she explained, "but unfortunately I wasn't bilingual and I couldn't become registered." In the years immediately following World War II, when Canada was experiencing an acute shortage of nurses, there were fewer restrictions regarding the recognition of qualifications. Indeed, immigration officials and the Department of Labour positively encouraged and facilitated the migration of nurses from Britain along with those from Switzerland, Belgium, Holland and Scandinavia "because they had the best nursing schools."[25] The Canadian Nurses Association (CNA) supported this initiative and as early as 1947 the Registered Nursing Association of Ontario even advised their provincial government that they would be prepared to accept European displaced nurses. By 1950, however, there were growing concerns about nursing standards, and the CNA began lobbying for a form of internship and the need to pass Canadian nursing exams.[26]

Arthur Wood, a car mechanic, accompanied by his new bride, came to Canada in 1970, without a job. He recalled, "As an immigrant I didn't have any credentials to qualify [certify] what I was capable of so the Department of Labour said, 'oh well in that case you'll have to write a trade test,' and I had to go to the Department of Labour and sit various tests in my automotive engineering field. I took two or three tests and they said, 'oh you're fine, you're fine'.... They gave me a certificate of authenticity and I got a job in a garage downtown in Ottawa."

Another area of comparative silence in the testimonies was the lack of reference to forms of anti-English discrimination or harassment in the workplace. Compared with other immigrant groups such as the Irish and Chinese, the English rarely experienced racism in the workplace. In the years immediately following World War II, when there were fears of immigrants and displaced persons taking jobs from Canadians, a few English immigrants did experience problems. We saw in the previous chapter that Ron Inch encountered the taunt of "Limeys go home." Emma Bulmer provided another example although her evidence was hearsay. Emma arrived in Canada in 1948 as a three-year-old with her family. She understandably admitted that she has no personal memories of her early years in Canada but referred to family stories. Her father went to Regina looking for a job. Emma testified that, "at that time the English were still not being very well received here [Regina]. The first few places he applied for a job he was told 'we don't want any English working here' and although it didn't directly affect me at the time it was part of what was happening to us." According to R.D. Francis et al., this form of discrimination was relatively common in the Canadian West in the late nineteenth and early twentieth centuries when newspaper advertisements often included the text, "No English Need Apply." The authors explained, "Canadians resented the haughty attitude of upper-class Englishmen in particular, many of whom refused to fit into Canadian society."[27] Other reasons for rejecting English workers also existed. According to Michael Hanson, in his privately published autobiography, anti-English attitudes were still prevalent when he arrived in Vancouver with his wife in 1968. In the first few days he "spent every minute trudging round looking for jobs" and found an apparent prejudice against English immigrants. According to him, a reason was that Canadian employers considered that the English were work shy and in thrall to rebellious trade union practices.[28] For most postwar English immigrants, however, their ethnicity was not a problem. Tom Martin, whose wife had a problem in having her nursing qualifications recognized, did not find his nationality a barrier to employment. He said that finding work through an agency was easy but was aware that his origins might be problematic. He commented:

> There didn't seem to be any reason why I would be barred from something because of being British. But the interesting thing is there was, I always refer to it as an "audible minority culture" in that you fit in perfectly until you open your mouth and begin to speak and then you become "other" and that was rather interesting.... I don't think having an English accent is any detriment anyway, I don't think so. Toronto is multicultural so it wouldn't be the kind of place you would experience that. If you were looking for a job somewhere outside in a more rural area, it may be, I don't know.

While latter-day Canada is often perceived as a liberal multicultural society with fewer problems arising from racism or ethnic conflicts than its neighbour to the south, it would be wrong to assume that English immigrants were totally free from discrimination or harassment in the workplace. Problems arose but to a much lesser degree than for other ethnic groups or, indeed, for English Poms in Australia.[29]

Working wives

During the second half of the twentieth century, the legitimacy of Canadian middle-class women entering the workplace was a constant source of controversy, contested and debated in both the popular press and scholarly journals. In simple terms, conservatives feared that working wives posed a threat to the psychological well-being of husbands and children. Furthermore, the morality of the entire community was believed to be in jeopardy. For those of a liberal persuasion, the expansion in the number of married women wage earners was part of progress and a guarantee of a good life. Liberals did not lament the loss of an older, patriarchal family economy so mourned by conservatives. It would be reasonable to conclude that liberal opinion largely prevailed.[30] At the heart of this debate was the recognition of the dilemma represented by women's dual responsibilities at home and in a discriminatory labour market.

We have already seen how Abbi Andrews juggled a full-time career and her domestic life and child care. Most of our interviewee wives, however, worked part-time to fit in with their children's needs or entered the workplace when their children were older or had left home. For many, the motivation was money. Joan Martin, who experienced problems in having her English nursing qualifications recognized, lived from hand to mouth with her student husband during their early days in Toronto. The couple were forced to use a local barter-exchange free store and walked to save twenty five cents on a bus fare. Joan was obliged to undertake evening work, sharing babysitting duties with friends in a similar situation. According to Joan, life was about "stretching the dollar as far as it would go." Joan's husband eventually qualified for a job, and they moved to Ottawa. Their income improved, though only marginally because Joan was pregnant again and could not work. Joan returned to work part-time, however, when her second baby was six months old, as her only income was her unemployment insurance benefit. She stopped work when she became pregnant a third time. Joan takes up the story: "After the baby was born I stayed home, a full time housewife for about two years. I did some day care, you know, in the neighbourhood. At that point women were really just starting to go out to work with the kids at school so I did a lot of after-school care or, if a couple of kids were in half day school, I'd look after them, that kind of thing." Joan eventually went back to work full-time. After the initial problems concerning her qualifications she found her experience of intensive

care nursing in demand. Nursing required that she work shifts, which created extra difficulties in managing child care. This problem was exacerbated
by her husband's frequent business trips overseas. Joan employed a nanny,
but found that she did not like live-in help. She gave up her hospital work
in 1986. Around this time she had started taking courses at Carleton University, supported by her part-time employment as a dental nurse and her
occasional work in daycare. In 1988, shortly after baby four was born, she
went back to casual work in daycare. In 1997 she gained a degree in social
work and, with her children older and more independent, worked full-time
in that field until she retired.

Family need drove Joan to undertake employment, especially during
her early years in Canada. In the years after World War II, the growth of
consumerism also created a demand for families to earn more money.
According to Veronica Strong-Boag, who was Director of the Centre for
Research in Women's Studies and Gender Relations at the University of
British Columbia, the growing acceptance of wives going out to work was
part of the general enthusiasm for a modern consumer society: "Wives'
income was understood as providing far more than frills for their fortunate
families. Long overdue improvements in housing, clothing, healthcare, and
education represented tangible benefits. Women's efforts helped to ensure
that at long last the promise of mass production…would be available to a
broad range of Canadians. Women's wages underpinned the enlarged community of consumers so celebrated after World War II."[31] New consumer
goods contributed to a reduction in back-breaking housework. Articles
in mass circulation magazines such as *Maclean's* and *Chatelaine* regularly
concluded that housework had become a "part-time job." Women were
being told that unless their children were of pre-nursery school age, they
could work, at least part-time, in the fields they were trained in before they
married.[32] Some later historians, however, have convincingly contested the
notion that advances in domestic technology have contributed significantly
to a reduction of time spent housekeeping.[33]

Meeting the needs of their children was a common theme among working mothers we interviewed. Barbara Trueman came to Canada with her
husband Roy, who had a two-year assignment with the National Research
Council. At first Barbara worked as a supply teacher before moving into a
full-time teaching position. At the end of the research assignment the couple
decided to stay in Canada, having been captivated by the Centennial and

Expo 67. Two years to the day after they arrived in Canada they adopted a two-month-old baby boy. Barbara became a stay-at-home mom. Two years later the couple adopted a baby girl, and sixteen months after that Barbara gave birth to another daughter. When the children grew older she secured part-time work teaching crafts in adult education. She then worked with the Weight Watchers organization. By then Barbara was in her mid-forties. Roy takes up the story in a segment of the interview that was accompanied by much laughter:

> She [Barbara] was getting a little bit plumpy. She decided she was not
> going to be a big woman, which my mother had forecast in one of
> her quiet confidences—"You know she will be a big woman." Which
> she hasn't turned out to be, you see. She was determined, so she
> went and joined Weight Watchers, and then she was the best thing
> for Weight Watchers since sliced bread. Because they made her a
> leader, they gave her an office job, they gave her an organizational
> thing for doing meetings, all around the country. So she got a work
> car, from Weight Watchers, and uh, she absolutely astounded me
> because she went down to wherever you buy maps, and she got a
> whole mess of maps of eastern Ontario. She learned how to read
> maps, which is something she didn't have a clue about. Am I right?

Although Barbara was a full-time mother during her children's early years, other wives and mothers combined part-time work with child rearing. Doreen Wood, wife of the aforementioned Arthur, came to Canada with her husband and cat in 1970. She soon found a job working for a multinational business machines company. She gave up work when she had her first two children, only to return to part-time employment when her first child was three and the second, two. Taking an evening job at a nearby supermarket meant that Arthur was able to look after the children. One day, Doreen's neighbour made a proposition.

> The lady next door, she's from Scotland, she was supervisor for
> market research work, so she asked me, she knew I was looking for
> work as my children were now in school. But I wanted to be here in
> the morning and I wanted to be here when they came home from
> school.... I said, "Yes I'd be really interested," so I started off then.

And then we did a lot of the surveys in shopping malls and Valerie next door would be working there too. She had two boys. So I would work until three and Valerie would stay later. Then I would come home and I would have my two and her two boys until she got home. And when I did other research work, which was not in the malls, I usually saved it for when Arthur came home and then I would leave and he would look after the children, so it worked out good and I still do it now. I've been doing it for twenty-seven years I guess.

Another working mother, Sue Jones, started a business when she was fifty-eight years old. In part, she was motivated by the need to find funds to support her adult son, who had Down's syndrome. Sue had had a varied working life since she first arrived in Canada. Initially motivated to earn money (see Chapter 1), she was later influenced by more altruistic motives. During the early years, she found a job working in a children's library for one evening a week. The family eventually moved to Ottawa, where Sue found odd jobs in stores. Then, making use of her higher education training, she started teaching evening art classes for adults and later, special classes in a community centre for adults with learning disabilities. Sue, who had a dyslexic son as well as the one with Down's syndrome, recalled, "This was when we started to realize what had happened, that people hadn't really been helped that much."

Sue's time caring for her Down's syndrome son contributed toward her sensitivity to the needs of other adults with learning disabilities. Although her son's disability did not prevent him from working in the library of a local newspaper and living semi-independently in a self-contained apartment in the family home, caring for him was onerous. At the time of the interview, the son was not working: "He had a heart operation, he had a pacemaker, he has arthritis, he's got sleep apnea, and if he gets sick he's sick for a long time." In 1979 Sue bought a plot of land and some cottages, and with the help of her eldest son, a wealthy doctor, funded a series of improvements to upgrade the properties. This investment produced a useful source of rental income, with the venture generating considerable repeat business. The lakeside property was also a godsend for her Down's syndrome son. Sue explained that her son "is venturesome and at the beginning he used to wander.... Everybody knew him around; you know you never need worry in the country, it's lovely living there. [*Long pause.*] So I've enjoyed it very much and I've got very much involved in what we want to do."

While finance was a motivational force for Sue, she had other reasons to seek paid employment, especially from middle age on. Her experience illustrates how money was not the only reason women with children went to work. Other motives included the need for self-fulfillment, independence, self-esteem, social interaction, achievement, the rewards of job satisfaction, a sense of being valued, and making use of earlier education and training. Margaret Baldwin, a mother of two, was married to Robert, an engineer who earned a good salary that funded a comfortable lifestyle in an upmarket district of Montreal. The family did not need a wife's income. Margaret, a passionate gardener, keen amateur artist, and Beaver (Cub Scout) leader, admitted to "being desperate to get out of the house." She tried to find satisfactory paid employment, but failed because she did not speak French.

Jenny Carter was another wife who had a high-earning husband, a senior naval officer. She too sought interest and company outside the family home. She was active in doing voluntary work and was a leading figure in promoting operatic and classical music. Jenny takes up her story:

> And I then went to my first paying job. I went to the prime minister's office, the correspondence division, on fourth October 1970, and a week later the world blew up in Montreal. Let me tell you there was a lot of brisk correspondence to be dealt with on Mr. Trudeau's behalf. And that was a marvellous experience, just terrific. And then I worked for the Canada Council after that, and then I worked for a thing called the Canadian Bureau for International Education, and then I had to stop working because my younger child was ill at that point. So that was the end of my brilliant career as a paid person but I've certainly done a lot of amateur, I suppose unpaid, work and I have thoroughly enjoyed it.

Conclusions

Was Canada a "land of milk and honey," as Mary Charles and Peter Whilesmith claimed in their interviews? The foregoing insights into individuals' working lives reveal a wide range of experiences, from the achievements of entrepreneurs like John Steven and engineer Kenneth Cecil, who reflected "we couldn't be better off than we are here," to Pat Connor's contemplation of suicide when she encountered difficulties in finding paid work. Overall, most of the interviewees recalled, with enthusiasm, their sense of achievement—often against the odds. Memories of work were vivid, especially from the men. For many, a sense of pride and enjoyment emerged in the telling of their stories. They talked at length about their technical skills, their career advancement, their friends at work, and in a few cases the limitations of their bosses. Some were fired or made redundant, while others experienced difficulties during economic downturns. Many demonstrated ambition and initiative as they exploited opportunities that came their way, made use of contacts, or undertook further education and training to enhance their employment prospects.

In many respects our interviewees faced similar challenges in the workplace as their Canadian-born neighbours. A significant difference was that the English, especially in the early years after their arrival, were working in an unknown and alien environment. Around one in five Canadian jobs required employees to hold a certificate of authentication, pass regulatory tests, or secure a licence to practice.[34] These requirements created a barrier for many of our interviewees, as they tended to work in professional and technical occupations. Evidence from the testimonies, however, indicates that these requirements created few problems. Ethnic prejudice or harassment was another potential barrier but, again with few exceptions, did not prove to be a significant issue for English immigrants.

A quiet, though sometimes noisy, revolution took place during the latter half of the twentieth century: changes in the relationship between women, especially middle-class women, and the workplace. The case studies demonstrate how English wives and mothers embraced the debates surrounding working women and how many went out to work, juggling those responsibilities with childcare and homemaking.

This conclusion would not be complete without a caveat: our interviewees do not form a statistically rigorous, representative sample of postwar English immigrants. In our defence, a representative sample would be difficult to structure. As we have shown, statistical evidence about the employment of English immigrants is not readily available. Where there is evidence, it suggests that the bulk of postwar English immigrants were professional and skilled workers. The case studies reflect this balance, illustrating a diversity of occupations. Additionally, the case studies concern work experiences from the east to west coasts. Interesting trends emerge. One is job mobility from junior, lower-paid work, to more senior positions offering higher incomes. Another is mobility from one location to another or from one employer to another. A number of interviewees travelled overseas on business or had spells working in the United States or back in England. Significantly, all of these travellers or sojourners used these opportunities to spend time with their parents and/or other members of their families they had left behind.

Work is closely linked to family life. It provides the financial foundation to exist, survive, and thrive—to experience "the good life" that is at the heart of most immigrants' aspirations. Work can also threaten family cohesion at times of unemployment or stress. The importance of work and family can be seen in the way in which many of the interviewees talked, with pride, about the educational and work achievements of their children. Even Peter Semple, who admitted that he was "not much of a Dad," boasted: "My daughter is now a cop. I went to her graduation in Vancouver the week before last. We have so much going for us and she is a good example.... She went to the police college and came out top of the class, and so now she is a fully paid-up cop with a gun and the whole bit. *Scary*. It is that kind of country, almost anybody can be almost anything they want to be, do anything they want to do."

Work is also fundamental to a person's sense of well-being, feelings of success and failure, self-esteem and identity. For many adult English immigrants, the workplace was one of the main channels through which they got to know Canada and Canadians. Employment is one of the central pillars of the immigrant experience. Work is connected in multi-faceted layers to important priorities such as housing, education, friendships, family, and community. It is to these that we turn in the next chapter.

Postscript

One unusual "job offer" came to light when interviewing Margaret and Robert Baldwin: they revealed that Robert was offered an assignment in counter-espionage as a spy. Robert Baldwin was an engineer in the airline business and one day in the 1970s he and Margaret attended a diplomatic function in Montreal, hosted by the Russian Embassy. There they met a young couple, Vladimir and Olga Oshkaderov, who had recently arrived from Soviet Russia. The two couples got on very well and a conversation about barbecues led Margaret to suggest that the Oshkaderovs should come

to one at their home some time. A couple of weeks later the Baldwins got
a phone call from the Oshkaderovs inviting them to go to dinner at their
home. Margaret admitted to having some doubts, but a "lovely evening"
of "fantastic caviar" and "fantastic vodka" was enjoyed by all. About three
months later, when Robert was abroad on business, two large men knocked
on the Baldwins' front door. Margaret takes up the story:

> They said they were from the RCMP and I must say I was quite
> surprised. I didn't ask for ID and I didn't know you needed a
> search warrant to go in and ask people questions. They said, "it's
> okay you haven't done anything wrong." So I said, "fine" and they
> came in the living room and questioned me about the last three
> months, since we had been to the Russian Embassy and since
> the dinner with the Oshkaderovs. So I said, "how do you know
> all this?" and they said, "well we've been following you."
>
> And, as it went on, I got more and more scared, as you can imagine.
> It was the sort of thing that happened in James Bond movies, but it
> doesn't happen to you, and so they sat, I guess they stayed for about
> an hour questioning me. And they said, "well, we aren't able to get into
> the Russian embassy; we can't get to these people, but we think that he
> is a spy." So I said, "Oh, really?" So what they wanted us to do was to
> carry on the friendship and feed the information to the RCMP about
> where they went, when they went. One of the questions had been
> about whether they ever went out of the city, and I said, "Yes, I think
> they've been to the border area," and so on and so forth. So they [the
> RCMP officers] left and I was in an absolute state when I realized they
> had basically been asking us to become spies. And, I thought, "This is
> the Mounties, the good guys." They don't do this sort of thing. I was in
> a state and didn't know what to do. Robert had gone away.... So after
> the boys [her sons] had come home and we'd had lunch, we had to
> go to the shops, and I'm driving along this quiet road and there's this
> big black limousine thing sitting on the side of the road, so I thought,
> "That's the Russians and they've been watching the Mounties."

When Robert got home, Margaret told him the whole story and about
how scared she had been. Robert phoned the RCMP and arranged for
an officer to meet him in his office. According to Robert, the RCMP said

basically the same thing, inviting the Baldwins to become "counter" spies. Robert said no, that he was not inclined to do this, as he was an engineer. This induced the RCMP officer to make menacing threats. Robert recalled the officer saying, "You do realize that if you decline we have the power to make it very difficult for your children when they grow up to get jobs in the civil service." Robert was intransigent. "I said, 'fine go ahead. We are not interested.' And that was the end of it."

Chapter 6

HOME, FAMILY, COMMUNITY

The family is one of nature's masterpieces.[1]

In 1952, Peter Whilesmith moved to Canada with his wife Rosemary and his two young children, largely as a result of frustration with the depressed atmosphere of postwar Britain. Although parting with parents was "tough," Peter wanted to live in a country with more "spirit of success," both for his own sake and for the welfare of his children. With his engineering experience, Peter had no trouble obtaining suitable work in Canada. Even before leaving England, he accepted a position in the aviation industry in Montreal, choosing from among several attractive job offers. As he later recognized, his transition to a new life in Canada was relatively smooth because he "went straight into work" in an expanding industry, and spent most of the day in a familiar work environment. Rosemary, a stay-at-home mother with two pre-school-age children, was more isolated and much more homesick. For Rosemary, and for Peter as family provider, obtaining a good house in which to raise a family marked a critical step toward putting down Canadian roots. Like thousands of young Canadian couples in the 1950s, they fulfilled their aspirations for home ownership by acquiring a new house in the suburbs.

The Whilesmiths arrived in Montreal on a cold, wet day in May. It was not an auspicious beginning, especially for Rosemary, who disliked the cold and had been reluctant to move to a cold country. Being housed in a little motel room while it rained did not brighten her mood. Many years later she recalled, "It was a very miserable situation and I looked around and

I thought, 'my goodness, what have I done? What a crazy thing to come over here!'" Rosemary could take some comfort in the knowledge that the motel was a temporary expedient while the Whilesmiths searched for better accommodation. Soon they moved to a "nice apartment" in town which nonetheless proved restrictive with two lively youngsters who were not accustomed to apartment living. Initially, the Whilesmiths had little furniture, so the children took great delight in running on the wood floor. As a result, Rosemary soon learned that the two elderly ladies who lived below them were much less delighted with the noise. Carpets and some furniture helped to make a difference, but Rosemary and Peter were happy to move to a house when the apartment rental expired at the end of three months. Although the Whilesmiths had been living in a new development in Bristol, Peter knew that the Canadian house was better than anything they could have obtained in England. In his words, "that was a gain right away," validating his decision to bring the family to Canada.

The new property was a typical middle-class suburban two-storey, three-bedroom house on a 10,000-square-foot lot on the West Island of Montreal. The lot was on the border of Beaconsfield and Pointe Claire, both predominantly English-speaking communities that were rapidly being developed in the 1950s as a suburban area. The Whilesmiths could afford the $12,500 property only because the government was offering a 2-percent mortgage reduction to encourage house building and home ownership. Peter and Rosemary remembered clearly how they were able to get a twenty-year mortgage for 3.25 percent instead of 5.25 percent. This government scheme enabled them to scrape by, although they had to postpone the purchase of a car for three years. To save money, they moved into the house before it was finished. Peter put a great deal of his own labour into the completion, including all the painting inside and outside and finishing all the nailheads. For both Peter and Rosemary, the house symbolized a commitment to a new community and to Canada. As Rosemary explained: "It made all the difference in the world. I don't know, you just felt that you were beginning to put down roots, you know. And it was more permanent. It was your own. And you were working on painting it, and doing things for it. And the garden had to be done. So I think it made a great difference."

Rosemary and Peter were pleased that moving to the house involved them immediately in a Canadian community. They wanted to make friends with Canadians and not solely with ex-Brits, although through common interests they did meet and socialize with plenty of ex-Brits. In the new suburb, most of their neighbours were Canadians, couples with young children like themselves, all moving in at the same time and all struggling financially with family budgets. Mutual need led to collaborative efforts. Neighbours sodded back yards together, shared lawnmowers, and babysat each other's children. The Whilesmiths had a third child in 1954, a couple of years after moving into the house, so Rosemary really appreciated the shared babysitting. With a next-door neighbour who became a good friend, Rosemary would keep a book of hours, recording the time spent babysitting each other's children. When enough hours had been accumulated, she could use them for an evening out or a day shopping. The two sets of children grew up together, and the other couple became known as the children's Canadian auntie and uncle. These surrogate relatives helped to compensate for the absence of family in Canada. As Rosemary noted, "Children are great things for making friends for us."

As the children grew up, Rosemary and Peter also became active with community organizations. Rosemary volunteered with the Girl Guides and later visited veterans in hospital. Peter was involved with the Scouts and was president of two Home and School Associations. As Peter observed, such volunteer activities "all made you fit in; you became part of the scene." When her youngest daughter was nine or ten, Rosemary stopped being a stay-at-home mother and began working as secretary for the school board, a job that she loved. Church was not central to the Whilesmiths' lives, but for a time it provided another community connection. Peter described himself as agnostic, although he had been quite a serious Anglican at one point. Nonetheless, the Whilesmiths took their children to church regularly while they were little because they believed they should have the opportunity to make up their own minds about religion. None of the children became a committed church member, but later all wanted to be married in church.

In addition to their neighbourhood and volunteer activities, Rosemary and Peter each had hobbies that were well suited to their Canadian life. These helped them adjust when, after more than thirty years in Montreal, they made the tough decision to leave Quebec and follow their children to Ontario—first to Kingston, and later to Ottawa. Rosemary had painted almost all her life and she joined painting groups in Kingston and in Ottawa. Peter's passion was sailing. The family's first location on the West Island was ideal for his interests. He started off in 1957 with a scow dinghy, then bought a twenty-two-foot wooden cruising boat, and in the 1960s progressed to a twenty-five-foot fibreglass boat made in Nova Scotia. He joined the historic Pointe Claire Yacht Club and began cruising-class racing.[2] Although the fibreglass boat had to be sold when the family needed money, Peter replaced it before long with a twenty-two-foot sailboat that he kept for more than thirty years. When the Whilesmiths moved to Kingston on Lake Ontario, Peter continued his sailing activities for as long as he was physically able.

The Whilesmiths' story highlights the importance of housing in the migrant experience. The Whilesmiths were not alone in gaining a sense of belonging and roots through home ownership. The speed with which they progressed from renting an apartment to buying a modern new house— only three months after arriving in Canada—would have made the While-smiths an ideal couple for Canadian immigration advertising in England. Nonetheless, they followed a common trajectory from a temporary stay in a hotel or with friends or relations, to rental accommodation, and finally to their own house. Similarly, the choice of a house in the suburbs was typical of English middle-class couples who came to Canadian cities in the postwar decades. Their dispersal among strangers in the suburbs contrasted with the concentration in ethnic neighbourhoods of postwar continental European migrants, such as the Italian immigrants who often brought extended families to Canada. As Canadian sociologist S.D. Clark observed in his 1966 book, *The Suburban Society*, recent immigrants who relied on ethnic attachments for support did not move to the suburbs. He found that the new suburban society was composed of "people with no position to protect, whose economic or social welfare was not dependent upon maintaining established ethnic or social ties."[3] Recent English migrants remained largely invisible in Clark's study but conformed to his description of the independent nuclear family that moved to the suburbs.

The availability of affordable houses that seemed well designed for raising a family drew young couples to the suburbs. Although spared the devastation that enemy bombs had created in Britain, Canada had emerged from years of depression and war with a housing shortage. The housing crisis, however, was short-lived. The Liberal government proved its conversion to Keynesian principles of stimulating the economy when, in order to avoid a postwar recession, it passed the National Housing Act in 1944, created the Central Mortgage and Housing Corporation (CMHC) in 1945, and subsidized lower mortgage interest rates. Low unemployment, the rising prosperity of the 1950s, easy credit terms, and the popularity of the automobile meant a wide range of middle-class families and indeed some working-class families could buy the detached houses with private yards that developers were hastily constructing on cheaper land, at a distance from the city centre. S.D. Clark calculated that most suburban homes were built for a mass market of people who could afford to pay a price ranging from $11,000 to $20,000.[4] The Whilesmiths, who struggled to pay for their $12,500 suburban Montreal house, fit into the lower range of this mass market.

The advantages and disadvantages of suburban living have generated considerable debate, but there is no disputing that life in the suburbs was a distinctly gendered experience.[5] Although Rosemary and Peter Whilesmith shared the decision to buy the house and cooperated in the work of making it into their own home, Rosemary had the constant responsibility of providing care for the family while Peter was at work in the city all day. The Whilesmiths' three young children formed part of the "baby boom" that resulted from the increased birth rate and larger families of the postwar years.[6] In both English and Canadian culture, middle-class women were expected to remain at home, at least while their children were young. Since she was caring for three children, it was not until after more than a decade in Canada that Rosemary undertook her first paid work. Therefore, during the first critical decade for migrant adaptation in a country, Rosemary faced challenges that were quite distinct from those of Peter.

Not all English migrants found homes in the suburbs, even though suburban living featured prominently in many of our interviews. Some of our interviewees lived in smaller communities located all the way from British Columbia to the Maritimes. Single migrants, in particular, had a lifestyle that differed significantly from that of married couples with children. The single migrants whom we interviewed did not come to Canada with "home dreams" in their head. Their accommodations ranged from boarding arrangements with Canadian families, to residence rooms, rented rooms with cooking facilities, or apartments that might be shared with English friends or with new acquaintances. Although we interviewed one who migrated as a farm labourer, most of the single migrants among our interviewees lived in larger cities, such as Toronto, Montreal, or Halifax. Single migrants accepted their accommodation as part of a transient phase in their lives—a time when they could be mobile if they wished, but a time that would end if they settled into permanent employment or married in Canada, as many did. Their living arrangements and their single status were isolating in some cases, but in other cases contributed to an active social life in the Canadian community.

In this chapter we shall examine how housing, family bonds, and community ties affected the lives and attitudes of our interviewees as they made the transition from early months or years in Canada to permanent residents. While some knew they wanted to stay in Canada from the time they arrived in the country, others for many years contemplated a return to England as a distinct possibility. Family responsibilities and emotional bonds with those left behind often pulled these migrants back toward England. At the same time, many were increasingly attached to Canada by children and grandchildren who knew Canada as their native land. Our interviewees also often became involved with Canadian communities through buying a house or by participating in sports and· outdoor recreation, music and art groups, educational and religious associations. Only a few chose to maintain a sense of English ethnicity or British heritage through specifically British clubs.

Buying a house

Obtaining a good place to live in Canada often formed a central component of migrant success stories. In addition, as the Whilesmith example illustrates, buying property generally symbolized a higher level of commitment to Canada and a new sense of belonging. The contrast between deprivation in postwar England and better housing opportunities in Canada was most pronounced in the 1950s, but the importance attached to a family home remained constant, regardless of when immigrants arrived.

Unlike the Whilesmiths, who expressed no strong dissatisfaction with their accommodation on the outskirts of Bristol, several of our interviewees were escaping from very unsatisfactory housing conditions in austerity England. Because they were mainly young couples with limited savings— and many spent much of that money on transport to Canada—their path to home ownership usually took longer than for the Whilesmiths, although the result was also a more dramatic change. Hugh Woods, a lower-middle-class shoe salesman whose territory covered the East End of London, lived with his wife and baby in a rat-infested basement apartment in Clapham Common.[7] As he stated bluntly, "There was no hope of getting a house." Intensely angry when he was informed that the shoe company that employed him was going to take over his account because he had done so well, Hugh immediately jumped into his little two-door black Ford car, drove to the

Canadian Pacific Steamship Lines office in Trafalgar Square, and bought three tickets to Canada. This sudden decision made in the heat of anger reflected a longer history of frustration with English austerity. Returning to the little rat-infested basement apartment to tell his wife, "We're going to Canada," Hugh undoubtedly had in mind the letters he had been receiving from Canada. Hugh's sister had moved to Canada two years earlier, had bought a house in Oakville (near Toronto), and was driving a large, shiny, white Chevy car. Although he was a successful salesman, Hugh was poorly compensated and had little money when the family left England in August 1956. As the boat sailed out of Merseyside, Hugh stood at the stern and thought, "What have I done? I've sold all my sticks of furniture and I have about $350 Canadian." After paying expenses en route, Hugh was down to $175 when his sister met the family in Toronto with her "gleaming white 1956 Chevrolet that looked like a Rolls Royce to us."

Hugh Woods knew that in Canada, unlike England, there was hope of buying a house, even though that prospect initially was out of his reach. Lacking funds, the Woods at first relied on the goodwill of Hugh's sister, with whom they lived for six months. By working double shifts, selling shoes wholesale during the day, and pumping gas at the local station at night, Hugh saved enough to move the family into a one-bedroom apartment in Mimico, a Toronto suburb. Years later, Hugh recalled their amazement at the brand new apartment with its modern appliances: "We'd never seen an apartment like it; you got a refrigerator and a stove and we didn't even know what a refrigerator looked like!" The Woods had no money for furniture, so they obtained the minimal necessities with the aid of Household Finance[8]—a bed, a cot for the baby, but no chairs. They sat on the floor and watched the black-and-white television that they bought with their remaining money because they could not afford other entertainment. Their next move was to a two-bedroom apartment a few blocks away. Then came the major move to a house, with almost as little seeming forethought as the decision to come to Canada: As Hugh recalled, "One morning we were going through the *Globe and Mail*, and I saw a house for sale. I had no intention of buying a house. I said, 'Let's go and look at it,' and so we bought this house in Port Credit for $16,500 with a NHA [National Housing Act] mortgage of 4½ percent."

Acquiring the house in a suburban development outside Toronto (now Mississauga) finally gave Woods the feeling of being settled in Canada.

Government mortgage assistance helped Hugh obtain the house, but he was "absolutely penniless" after the purchase. His entrepreneurial skills, however, soon made the house more affordable. Shortly after he bought the house in 1959, he rescued the Clark Shoe Company in Canada from failure, becoming manager and part owner of the company. Hugh replaced the British managers who, in his view, "had no idea of the Canadian market and Canadian marketing practices." The company's profits soon began to soar and Hugh's income increased accordingly. For Hugh, the highlight of his life story was his ability to create this turnaround. When leaving England, Hugh had tried to placate his wife, who was reluctant to leave her widowed mother, by promising her that she would never have to take paid employment again. He kept his promise. Struggling through difficult times and providing good accommodation for the family matched his pride in his Canadian business success.

Hugh was not alone in having to cope with difficult times upon arrival in Canada. Emma Bulmer, whose father encountered problems obtaining employment in 1947, remembered the "pretty cramped" conditions in which the family lived for their first seven years in Calgary. Their family of four rented the upstairs of a house—kitchen, living room, and one bedroom—and shared the bathroom with the people downstairs. Buying a house in the suburbs after they had saved enough money was "certainly a step up."

Among those motivated to migrate because of the housing shortage in England, Richard Nash and his wife Heather also temporarily experienced privation after they arrived in Montreal in 1953. They stayed for the first two weeks with a casual friend who had worked for the same company as they did in England. Indeed, because they knew no one else in Canada, the friend was a major reason why they chose to settle in Montreal. They thought they were fortunate because they brought £300 between them, a large amount compared to what many other English immigrants had, and around the maximum allowed by British currency restrictions. Nonetheless, they had to economize quite stringently when Richard was without work for six weeks and they had to rely solely on Heather's salary as a clerk for a British insurance company, a job that she found immediately.

The Nashes rented the lower apartment in a northeast Montreal duplex, a more common form of housing in Montreal than in other Canadian cities. Coping was "pretty horrendous," especially since they arrived in November, unprepared for the Canadian winter. They could afford to furnish and heat only one room. "It was tough," Richard recalls. "It really was tough. We had an apartment with one room with furniture, basically. We didn't even have a refrigerator. We used the windows in the spare bedroom as our refrigerator, 'cause it was so bloody cold in there!" For a time, Richard began to wonder what they had done, but conditions improved when he obtained a position in the shipping department of the Canadian Broadcasting Corporation, and then moved to the Ottawa headquarters. Within a few years his salary had reached a point "where we could begin to go outwards," and the family moved to a new suburban development in the west end of Ottawa.

Chance, initiative, and ingenuity, as well as resources, could affect English migrants' response to Canada. While the Nashes were freezing in Montreal, Frank and Agnes Butcher, who also had little money, were enjoying the warmth of the heated Toronto apartment that Frank had found to rent. Agnes described the apartment as "lovely" and "quite luxurious" in comparison to the old, cold rented house in London, which had been one of their motivations for migration. Their two boys could crawl on warm floors. The clanking refrigerator they bought for twenty-five dollars was only a minor irritant.

When Frank's work took them to Sarnia, Ontario, the Butchers initially rented a cottage on the shore of Lake Huron, but then decided to get "a place of our own." Housing costs were lower in Sarnia than in major urban centres like Toronto; nonetheless, the first house that the Butchers bought was old and not in good shape. Agnes remembered that she would not use the boys' bedrooms until she had painted the walls. Frank, however, managed to convert this first unsatisfactory purchase into a down payment on a much better house that he contracted to have built. The plot of land that they obtained from a builder only cost $100. Frank further cut costs by designing the house himself and employing a local foreman who built houses on the side. He chose the new split-level design that was popular in the 1950s, and included a full basement instead of the crawl space he originally contemplated. Agnes recalled her delight in the house, where they were to live for the next fifteen years: "We had a lovely playroom for the boys, and the boys used to come in and out with all their friends. There was a whole level where they could have their table tennis or whatever they wanted to do down there; they didn't have to come into the house which was up a few flights. There was a toilet down there and everything; that was one of the nice things about it... It was really a lovely, lovely situation we were in there."

Our interviewees who came to Canada in the 1960s and 1970s were less affected by inadequate English housing than the earlier postwar migrants, but they were equally interested in securing good affordable Canadian homes. We have seen how the Cecil family, who owned a house in Polton, in 1964 chose Canada over Australia. In part, they made this choice because Kenneth calculated that he could buy a house in Canada with his engineer's salary after six years whereas in Australia it would take twenty-four years. Kenneth flew to Montreal in advance of the family and rented a duplex apartment. He "got the basics of furniture, bedroom suite, living room suite, a fridge, a washing machine installed" and left the rest of the furnishing to Janet, who came by sea with the two children, eight tea chests stuffed full, and a big cabin trunk. After two years, they bought a house in the suburbs but soon moved to a larger house because they had a third daughter and needed extra space. "We had a wonderful time there, fifteen years," Janet commented; she felt they had been very lucky throughout their lives.

Similarly, Peter Semple, a chartered accountant whose work story is told in Chapter 5, sold a nice country house in the Leeds area when he and his wife migrated to Canada in 1966. Nonetheless, Peter had only a few hundred dollars in his pocket when he arrived in Toronto, where he had obtained a position. He rented an apartment on the lakeshore and managed to furnish it when his landlord guaranteed a bank loan to cover the cost of the basics—beds, living room set, kitchen table and chairs, and television. In the late sixties, Peter was fired without notice when the company for which he was working was bought out by another. Through a lawyer, he managed to obtain a settlement that became the deposit for the Semples' first house in Canada, a semi-detached in the Toronto suburb of North York.

Buying a house was often more than a financial proposition, an investment, a result of improved savings, or even a means of obtaining better accommodation for the family. For many English migrants like the Semples, who originally were unsure about staying in Canada, home ownership indicated greater permanency. Tom and Sarah Walsh, who migrated to Montreal in 1972, lived for one year in a rented townhouse on the south shore at St. Bruno. Many English and Scottish immigrants, often employed by the same company, seemed to be settled in the area. According to Tom, he and Sarah "decided that if we wanted to really settle we would soon think about buying property because we had property in Thornbury [north of Bristol], and we felt that the rented townhouse was almost an artificial environment. It wasn't really making a definite commitment." Sarah further explained, "We felt that to really make a decision about staying in Canada we would have to really integrate into the town and buy a piece of property, so we did."

Margaret and Robert Baldwin had the same response. They had intended to return to England after five years in Canada, but when the time came in 1971, Robert could not find a suitable English job. They were living in a sixth-floor apartment in a new high-rise just north of Montreal, and both enjoyed the rural area because they had grown up in a similar environment in England. With a second child on the way, however, they needed more space and decided it was time to buy "a house of our own." Purchasing a split-level suburban house on the west island of Montreal, they compensated for going over budget with the down payment by putting a considerable amount of their own work into the house before they moved. It was, as Margaret said, "a good move" and a "lovely house" in which they lived for the next thirty-three years. "When we bought the house," Robert added, "I felt we had put down roots." Thus, home ownership not only provided the space they needed but, as with the Whilesmiths, signified a new feeling of belonging, a commitment that was sealed by the time and effort they devoted to the property.

Little was said in the interviews regarding the decor, furnishing, or material culture of the interior of the house, even though Canadian household magazines of the period stressed the importance of decor in transforming a standard suburban house into a family home.[9] Barbara and Roy Trueman did address the issue, but mainly to express their puzzlement. The Truemans did not know why Canadian friends thought their house was "so English," especially since they had purchased maple furniture that was distinctively Canadian.[10] "You wouldn't find the like in Britain," they said; if they ever should return to England, they would certainly take it with them. They tried to make their house "warm and homey," in Roy's description, or "inviting and comfortable," according to Barbara, but they did not see those characteristics as particularly English, as opposed to Canadian. They agreed, though, that they certainly did not fit the immaculate model of show houses.

The Truemans, like many of our interviewees, had not had many possessions at the time they migrated to Canada and therefore had purchased their furnishings after arrival. In contrast, a few who already had well-established family homes in England brought numerous packing cases of belongings. Mary and Jeremy Charles, for example, who had owned a four-bedroom detached house, brought eighteen pieces of hand luggage and had the rest packed up and shipped. For Janet and Kenneth Cecil, who owned their house near Blackpool, the free transport of eight packing cases for a steamship passenger was an inducement to emigrate, helping Janet to choose boat travel over air. Janet filled one tea chest with pure woollen blankets that she purchased specially; in perusing the Eaton's catalogue Canadian officials had given her, she had discovered that woollen blankets were expensive in Canada. In the end, however, the Cecils never used the English blankets because Canadian heating made them unnecessary.

Charlotte Hinton, an artist, expressed the most distress at having to leave the English home that she had furnished. Flying to Canada with three children, she could only bring one brown suitcase with her. Her distress was compounded because the box of belongings that she had sent ahead was lost in transit for six weeks: "It was a box about four feet by four feet and that was my whole life. Five years of marriage was in that box. That was the most heartbreaking thing 'cause I had a home. I had it furnished you know and everything was all gone. Just in a box. And I still have a piece of the box downstairs; I made a bench out of a piece of it and my husband used pieces for building stuff. But that was hard." Nonetheless, Hinton did not look back. She started over with her Canadian home and did not make comparisons with the home she had previously furnished in England.

The single migrants

Single English migrants, on arrival in Canada, did not share the concerns of establishing a family home that preoccupied married couples with children. Their accommodation tended to be quite basic, often reflecting an expectation of transiency as well as limited resources. Still, their living arrangements could have a significant impact on their adaptation to Canada. For those in their twenties, as most were, migration coincided with a time in their lives when they wanted to expand their horizons, socialize, and meet new people. Their sojourn in Canada might have initially been seen as a temporary interlude, but for our interviewees it became a permanent commitment because of marriage or employment opportunities.

Choosing to share an apartment with others not only cut costs but also provided support for social activities. Communal living in the centre of major cities also meant that the single migrants often met other new immigrants of various ethnic backgrounds, even more than Canadians. Elizabeth Summers, the occupational therapist who came to Montreal in 1960, did not know anyone in Canada, but was a more experienced migrant than many of her peers because she had previously worked in Australia, where she had many relations. At first she stayed with her boss in her Sherbrooke Street apartment, but she soon moved into another apartment in the same building, sharing it with three others. She explained that they quickly got to know almost all the other residents, who were mainly other immigrants her own age—nurses, therapists, teachers:

> There were South Africans, there were Germans, there were Brits,
> there were some Canadians, fortunately, and we began to have a
> social life with those particular people. That's how it worked for
> me, and we were a group of people who went around together. We
> would ski in the winter.... I shared in a cottage across the border,
> actually in the States, with friends and we would go down every
> weekend, enjoy the weekend, and maybe have a week's holiday
> there, and it just all kind of fitted in. It suited me. It was fun. There
> were a lot of people who were on my wave length, I guess.

Roger MacKay, the flying enthusiast who came to Toronto in 1968, similarly shared an apartment with people whom he had not known previously. He responded to a newspaper advertisement placed by four men who were looking for a fifth to share a place on Davenport and Dupont Street. He got along well with them and stayed for two years. Consequently, he said, he had no problems adapting to life in Canada: "I was really fortunate...I ended up living in Toronto with those four other guys, three of them were from England, and they were a great bunch of guys.... We were accepted and had a great time. Quite honestly I wouldn't change it. I mean it was a fantastic time. I had an absolute ball.... People here were fine; Toronto is such a diverse city of mixed nations."

Some young women on a working holiday travelled from England with a friend in order to have someone with whom to share on arrival. Mary Irvine lived in the top-floor apartment of a vast old house in Toronto with her Torquay friend and another young English woman whom they had met on the boat. Mary remembered that, "breakfast used to be absolutely hilarious because we were telling each other what happened the night before and the dates we'd been on and various things." Initially, though, they did find difficulty in meeting people:

We wanted to get to know Canadians, but it was very difficult because at twenty-two most of the Canadian girls were getting married and they were involved with either their fiancés or their new situations as young marrieds and heavily involved with mortgages, etc. So really for the first little while, having said goodbye to all our English friends [from the boat], although having fun ourselves we didn't meet anybody.... Gradually we got to know people but mostly they were, funnily enough, English, Scottish, Norwegian a lot, you know people who had come out and were footloose and fancy-free as we were.

As we observed in Chapter 2, the friends with whom Mary shared her apartment decided to return to England after two years. Mary, however, travelled west to the Calgary Stampede because some South African friends in Toronto had given her the names of two Canadian girls with whom she could live. In Calgary, Mary continued her active social life: "From then on it was working hard all day and partying like mad every evening. In fact I used to have to wear dark glasses to work because of the bags under my eyes. It was fantastic; it was just fantastic. It was very much the place that all the young were going to. And it was a really international crowd, and we really met so many people." One of the people that Irvine met in the course of her activities—skiing, camping, playing tennis, as well as partying—was a British Olympic skier with whom she had "the most amazing romance," leading to marriage a couple of years later.

Isobel Sinclair (later Sinclair-Chang) and a friend from London, who also came to Canada on a working holiday in 1956, first stayed at the YWCA in Toronto and then lived together in what Isobel described as "this horrible apartment that didn't even have running water." They had to go downstairs to fetch all the water and cope with a "terrible" stove that did not have a gauge. Initially they socialized with other British immigrants; Isobel thought they must have antennae that somehow identified fellow ex-Brits. They partied together, and once a week they had a kind of social event. Isobel noted that, "everybody was sort of watching out for everybody else, so there was this sort of feeling that we all needed each other." While associating with other British immigrants helped to provide reassurance, there were significant disadvantages. Isobel found that "most of us ex-Brits all hung out together, so that wasn't particularly useful because we all had the same level of ignorance." She met her first Canadian friend when she changed jobs and went to work for a small Toronto firm. The new Canadian friend told her many things that she did not know about Canada. The friend became particularly excited when she learned that Isobel had wanted to be a teacher. She told her that Canada was so short of teachers that they were recruiting in the U.K. The friend also gave her phone numbers to obtain information about teacher training. As a result of this friendship, Isobel decided to end her travels and attend Toronto Teachers' College while her London companion, who had wanted to go to Vancouver, returned to England instead.

Isobel Sinclair soon knew many more Canadians. The students attending teachers' college were all Canadian. In addition, her first new Canadian friend introduced her to campus cooperatives that provided less expensive student housing than the University of Toronto residences. There were two women's houses and three men's houses, but one of the women's houses had the only table tennis table, so the men always came over and played table tennis. Isobel noted that one of the residents at the time was Ed Broadbent,[11] but more important for Sinclair was meeting the manager of one of the men's houses: a Chinese student from Hong Kong finishing his master of science at the University of Toronto on a student visa. Two years later, they were married. Both of their families were upset by the interracial marriage, but her husband's family had extra concerns. They were not rich and had saved all their money to send their oldest son to study in Canada as a financial investment for the family, whom he was then expected to assist. Isobel did not know how strongly they objected because she did not meet her husband's family until she went to Hong Kong in 1966. By that time, however, she had produced three sons and in the eyes of her parents-in-law could "do no wrong" and having a daughter was just "the icing on the cake."

Unlike the migrants who found a social life partly through shared apartment or residence accommodation, some single migrants lived in more isolating conditions. Norma Levy had never lived apart from her close-knit London family until she came to Toronto in 1966 in an act of rebellion against her father.[12] Her orthodox Jewish family had lived in England since her great-grandparents migrated there from Ukraine and Poland in the nineteenth century. She described her London home as upper-middle-class, a detached house with two garages and a big garden. In her late twenties, when she broke off an engagement shortly before she was to be married, Norma wanted to get her own place in London. Her father opposed the move, saying it would reflect adversely on the family but adding it would be all right if she were living abroad. Norma took up the challenge that her father unintentionally had given her. She decided to emigrate, at least for a couple of years, although she had never considered the possibility previously. She went to Toronto on her own, a "huge step" for her, especially since her only Canadian contact was an old family friend, a woman in her seventies whom she had met once. Norma found a furnished bachelor apartment and, after some unsatisfactory temporary work, obtained a good social work job at City Hall because there was a scarcity of social workers.

Not surprisingly, though, living on her own for the first time in a small apartment caused Norma to feel lonely and homesick for her "terrific social life" in London. The elderly family friend had promised that all her friends' granddaughters and grandsons would involve Norma in their social activities. Norma discovered differently: "Well, the granddaughters didn't want to know me because who wants to know another single girl? I mean, let's face it, they didn't know whether I was pretty or had a face like the back of the bus, but they didn't want to know. As far as the grandsons were concerned, I had a couple of blind dates, and I think they were the poor nerds that never got anybody to date at all; they got dragged out. So that was hopeless." At the time of the interview, Norma was happily married to another English migrant, and mother of a grown-up daughter, of whom she was proud. "Canada gave me a family and friends," she commented. Nonetheless, she remembered clearly that, "at the beginning it was very, very difficult, not being able to establish a social life." Norma wanted to go to a dance to meet people but was told that girls did not go to dances unescorted. She thought it was more difficult for a woman than a man, who could go into a bar on his own or to a party. She realized that her family's beliefs regarding how a nice Jewish girl should behave had been particularly restrictive: "I'd never been away from home on my own, so in some ways I was probably naive. But, no, I think it is hard, much harder for a woman on her own because there are certain areas that aren't available for you to get into social life."

James Roland could have told Norma that men on their own might also face difficulties establishing a social life. James, like Norma, migrated to Canada in 1966; at age twenty-one he wanted to see more of the world. His only contact in Canada was a brother of one of his father's colleagues who lived in Toronto. James was planning to stay in Canada, and had determined to wait at least a year before deciding whether it was a good move: "I had anticipated that I would go through a period of adjustment where I could feel quite miserable for a period, and that in fact turned out to be the case." James lived in a rooming house on Spadina Avenue. He had "pretty bare bones" cooking equipment but managed to cook for himself for the first time, having lived previously either at home or in university residences. Getting to know people while living on his own, however, was more difficult. In the early days, the friends that he picked up were mainly through work. He found there were barriers to making casual social contact in Canada: "It's not easy, being an immigrant, to make those initial friends even when you have the advantage of not having to deal with the linguistic problems. As someone coming from England you can't talk about hockey in the pub or how well the Rough Riders are doing and that sort of thing. You don't have the cultural background to do that."

For James Leonard, whom we met in Chapter 2, working on a farm in Canada left little time for any social life. After completing his national service in 1957, James had agreed to be a farm labourer as a means of emigrating to Canada. The Canadian National Railway, which was recruiting farm labour for Canada, placed him in Halton County, six miles from Milton in southwestern Ontario, on a farm owned by a mother and son. He liked his employers, who were themselves very hard-working, but found the constant demands of Canadian farm work quite isolating. His employers were devout Presbyterians, so Sunday was a day of rest except for chores. Yet Leonard was still up by six o'clock, did chores until nine, went to church, and then did afternoon chores until six or seven in the evening. He found that although he was immersed in a Canadian family, he had little chance to meet others. His best opportunity for socializing was after church, when he could talk to other farm people. Occasionally, he was able to get into town by driving the tractor six miles to Milton. He realized that he had no prospects on the farm.

One day, while reading the *Globe and Mail,* to which his employers subscribed, Leonard saw an advertisement recruiting people to join the military. He took a day off and signed up for the military in Toronto but agreed to remain on the farm until after harvest. Frequent movement with the military definitely gave James a different life than he would have had on the farm. Based in North Bay after training, James shared accommodation with Canadian recruits, who tried to help him sound more Canadian. After a couple of years he married a nurse, Ivy, whom he had first met in England. Coincidentally, Ivy had chosen to work at the same English hospital as

Leonard's twin sister, so she knew where to contact James when she decided to come to Canada.

Marriage is an important rite of passage, ordinarily celebrated not only by the bride and groom but also by their families, who are often closely associated with the arrangements. Postwar English migrants who decided to marry in Canada, however, faced being cut off by distance from family participation in this significant event in their lives. Those we interviewed responded to the separation in varying ways, depending on their personal and family circumstances. James Leonard and his bride, Ivy, who were both from England, went back to family in England just for the wedding and immediately returned to their duties in North Bay.

By contrast, Isobel Sinclair-Chang, who came from a working-class English family, and her husband from Hong Kong, were married on a weekend in Toronto. They had a church wedding because both were Roman Catholic, but the only member of either family able to attend was Isobel's husband's brother, who was also studying in Canada. Isobel described the wedding as "a very small affair" with a few friends present—"nothing very special." They went to a Chinese restaurant for a meal afterward. Although they had a good time, Isobel's language conveyed some regret at the absence of family to mark the occasion.

Mary Irvine also was married in Canada, but she first spent six months back in England during her romance with her future husband, the British Olympic skier. Her "marvellous" June wedding in Calgary was definitely not a small affair, although expenses were reduced because Mary and her friends did all the catering. An elderly friend lent his house, with a lovely garden stretching down to the river, for the reception. Mary was married in church, with a piper providing music; afterward, all the guests mingled and danced reels on the lawn. The honeymoon was a weekend at Emerald Lake, because they could not spare more time. The interview included no mention of missing family.

To a large extent, newly married couples usually found their lives shaped by family considerations, and they joined in the search for a family home. For example, Robin Lanson, who had migrated to Halifax in 1959, met his Nova Scotian wife at Scottish country dancing, an activity that attracted many who were not Scottish. As we saw in Chapter 2, Robin reneged on his promise to his mother to return to England in two years. Instead, the new couple found "a very small house, but a very nice little house" in Halifax.

Five years and two children later, Robin decided to take a government position in Ottawa. As he recalled, the family obtained one of the garden homes that had been built not too far from his work; "they were brand new, very nice with some sort of pioneer discount if you were the first people in." With another daughter and son being added to the family, the Lansons moved once more, and then, "life went on as a sort of suburban family for quite some time."

Family bonds

Creating a home and raising a family in Canada helped to attach English immigrants to their new country. At the same time, many of our interviewees missed the support of an extended family network or felt sadness and guilt because distance disrupted bonds with family left behind in England. These emotions became more acute at times of family change or need, such as the birth of a first child or illness and death. Most migrants potentially had to confront the problems of aging parents in England who needed assistance. The ties of family could continue to raise questions regarding the permanency of migration, even for some who seemed well settled in Canada. As migrants grew older and began to think more about the importance of children and grandchildren, they also recognized more fully how difficult their migration might have been for their own parents. Of course, not all migrants cherished close family relations. Some were not unhappy to put the Atlantic Ocean between themselves and their relatives. In reflecting on his situation, Tom Martin stated, "Maybe a reason for emigrating was to get away from a sort of fairly close and not all that pleasant family situation. Our family was okay, but you can take them [only] in small doses."

Our interviewees came to Canada mainly as nuclear families or single migrants. Ron Inch, who was not married when he emigrated in 1948 at age twenty-two, was unusual in bringing his parents with him.[13] They managed to overcome difficulties with Canadian immigration authorities who feared that his father, in his fifties, would not obtain employment. While several of the migrants appreciated temporary aid from siblings or other relatives who preceded them to Canada, they rarely considered themselves part of a family group. Peter Semple contrasted his interests as an English migrant with the chain family migration of Portuguese, Spanish, and Italian immigrants whom he observed in the Spadina area of Toronto: "You had one couple who'd come into the country and get jobs and buy a house, and they'd bring other members of the family in, and they'd all live in the same house, and they'd pay it off, and they'd buy another house, and so the clan expanded, and this is the sort of country you can do that.... Wasn't my thing. I had a brother-in-law living with me for months at one point. I didn't enjoy that very much."

Similarly, Jeremy Plunkett explained that he came to Canada because he was a very independent person. He got along fine with his family but he was not close to them. Others, however, would empathize with Janet Cecil, who had always lived near her parents, who owned a newsagent tobacconist shop in Blackpool; Janet had to really discuss emigration with her husband because "leaving family is hard to do." The discussion was centred on departing from family, not on including family in the emigration plans.

Isobel Sinclair-Chang was one migrant who felt the disruption of family bonds quite deeply. She found it was hard to overcome distance and communicate with her working-class London family in the 1950s and 1960s, when overseas phone calls were expensive and e-mail did not exist. Much of the time she was so busy she did not dwell on missing family. Nonetheless, she said, "Every so often I felt very cut off. I guess I felt more cut off when I got married and I had my first child because I had nobody to turn to. I was just so by myself and by that time I'd even left Toronto, where I had a bit of a network by that time. So I felt very isolated then, almost four years after I'd come." Isobel's isolation was exacerbated by her interracial marriage and by her family's subsequent move to what she described as the "narrow-minded and truly provincial" small city of Peterborough—away from the more multicultural milieu of Toronto, where she had developed a network of friends. The birth of her first child, however, was the occasion when Sinclair-Chang felt most alone, lacking the comforting presence and advice of her mother or other female relative.

Similarly, Mary Irvine felt the absence of family when she had her first baby a year after her marvellous Calgary wedding. Mary had many friends in Calgary, so she was not as isolated as Isobel Sinclair-Chang. Still, she reflected on "how lucky people are when they have their parents to help with these things; we didn't have anything." Mary missed the "joy of having parents around" to share in the important family event and to provide belongings that the couple required. Furniture that her parents no longer needed would have been useful to replace the orange boxes and second-hand dressers from a bargain basement store that were all that Mary and her husband could afford to buy then. Like Rosemary Whilesmith, whose suburban neighbours became surrogate relatives, Mary shortly acquired a "surrogate Mum in Canada" as a welcome substitute for her absent family in England. Although Mary and her husband had to curtail their partying after the birth of the baby, they still took camping holidays. A relative of her husband's had sent him an introduction to Ray and Veronica Milner, so they visited the Milners' luxurious house while camping on Vancouver Island. Mary and Veronica got along well, and Mary came to rely on the comfort of regular summer or Christmas visits to the Qualicum Beach house and Veronica's lovely garden.

While women felt most strongly the absence of family at the time of childbirth, male migrants also regretted having to raise children at such a distance from grandparents. John Steven, who came to Canada with his wife and three-month-old baby in 1969, remembered his father standing on the dock as they left England and realized their departure was "a wrench for the grandparents." Although John was able to return to England quite frequently because of his work, he nonetheless found isolation from family to be an issue: "It ended up being much more difficult raising a family here without having any grandparents around; you know, there's no one to mind the kids for a while." Thus, the separation adversely affected the family on both sides of the Atlantic.

Mary and Jeremy Charles had been married eleven years and had two children, age seven and five, when they migrated to Canada in 1974. They were living in a four-bedroom detached house in Chelmsford at the time of emigration, but Mary had grown up as an only child in a close-knit working-class family on the outskirts of London. Her grandmother lived around the corner and much of the family lived close together. Mary's father had died just before her first child was born. When Mary migrated to Canada, therefore, she left her widowed mother living alone in a bungalow. Mary's mother had adequate financial resources, but Mary and Jeremy still worried about her. After they had been in Canada for about a year and a half, they started to make arrangements to bring her to Canada, even completing most of the paperwork guaranteeing her support for the first six months before she would be eligible for provincial health insurance. Mary's mother thought about coming to Canada, but eventually said no, and continued to live in England until her death ten years later. Visits were made both ways across the Atlantic, and Mary took each child back separately to get to know the grandmother a little better. Nonetheless, Mary was left with sadness and regret at the family separation: "Knowing now that I can see my grandchildren when I want to, I think it was sad to take grandchildren away from a single grandparent. It is something that anybody that goes across the Atlantic, moves, emigrates, should think twice about before they do it."

Norma Levy similarly carried through her life in Canada sorrow at the outcome of her separation from her family in England.[14] After she had been employed as a social worker in Toronto for five years, Norma had to quit her job and return home because her mother became terminally ill with cancer. She was unable to ask for a leave of absence because she did not know how long she would need to be away. When her mother died, Norma stayed with her father for a while, concerned that the stress would affect his bad heart condition. For the next year, she flew back and forth frequently, using up almost all her savings because she could not take a permanent job. Then Norma was called back to London for her father's funeral. She did not get there in time, however, because the traditional Judaism of her family required that the deceased be buried the day after the death. Her "most horrible memory" was that her father was buried on her birthday and she had not been present for the final rites. In spite of the dispute that led to her emigration, Norma felt close to her father and adored him for his generosity of spirit in helping others. Although she had sacrificed her time, money, and energy to help him in the last year of his life, the distance separating them left her with a feeling that she had failed terribly.

Memories were one of the most important possessions uniting families across distance and generations. Fortunately, Norma Inch also had happy family memories that were reinforced by a treasured family heirloom, which she produced during her interview: the Sabbath candlesticks that her great-grandmother had carried from Poland to England in the nineteenth century. Her grandmother, who had silvered the brass candlesticks, gave them to Norma, who intended to pass them on to her own daughter. The candlesticks reminded Norma of the strong women in her family: her great-grandmother who had thrown overboard her head-covering on the way to England, saying, "I am going to a new life"; and her grandmother, a suffragette whose greatest memory was that she sat on the same platform with Mrs. Pankhurst. Her grandmother also sent her mother to chalk "Votes for Women" on the pavement, because she believed that the police would not arrest a little girl. Remembering her grandmother who fought so hard for female suffrage, Norma knew how important it was for her to vote in Canada.

Few of the other interviewees volunteered information about treasured family objects brought to Canada. Chapter 3 highlighted Anne Graves's story of her family's departure from England, which included giving to relatives "a lot of stuff" of sentimental value.[15] Her mother, a reluctant migrant who found settling in Canada difficult, later regretted not having brought more of the valuable family items, especially since some seemed to vanish as older family members died. Nobody knew what happened to the family Bible or to the picture of Anne's grandmother in a big old round frame, showing her when she was younger. Anne's mother was really angry when family ornaments were taken by cousins in England, and her children in Canada received nothing. Anne was the first to be married, so her mother was sure that she would receive something from the English house as a present, but she did not. Anne herself was less disturbed: "It didn't really bother me because by then I had figured things are things are things." It was a useful attitude for a migrant, especially one who did not leave England with crates of possessions.

More than household objects, letters provided the connection that linked families across the Atlantic. Indeed, a number of interviewees have bundles of letters that have been preserved and contain family memories. In keeping with tradition, it was the women who tended to be the family record keepers and took much of the responsibility for letter writing.[16] Charlotte Hinton explained that not only did she send letters and Christmas parcels to her own family but she kept in touch with her husband's family as well "because that's what women do. They are the ones that keep in touch." Similarly, Janet Cecil wrote to her mother and also to her husband's mother: "I wrote every ten days and mother wrote back. I wrote to the two mothers and we kept in touch. We had a phone, but my mother wouldn't have a phone, my mother and father wouldn't have a phone, so we just wrote to each other and I have many, many letters. She gave me them all back."

The exchange of photographs and sometimes tape recordings enhanced the communication, but the letters were basic. The impact of technological advances that dramatically affected letter-writing, phoning, and other means of family communication will be examined below.

Visits to England were more expensive than letters in maintaining family bonds, but the direct personal contact was especially valuable, and sometimes essential at times of family crisis or celebration. Many English migrants had chosen Canada over Australia because the distance from

9. A traditional English pub was often the first port of call when visiting family back in England. Photo credit: By permission Rosemary Sloan.

England was not "too far" for the time or expense of a return visit. Janet Cecil was lucky. Her husband began to work with Trans-Canada Airlines shortly after coming to Canada, so with his airline passes they usually went back to England every year: "I think that helped an awful lot that we were able to go back and visit them all. I think it would have been harder without that, much harder." Some who did not benefit from airline passes also returned frequently. The Cecils, who came to Canada in 1964, returned to England regularly to see family, the longest gap of five years occurring when they had to pay for a swimming pool. In one year in the '90s they visited England four times—for a birth, a couple of weddings, and a funeral. Elizabeth Summers and her mother kept in touch by writing regularly to each other, but she also visited England every two years and her sister came to Canada for holidays with her. Vicky Williams, like Norma Levy, returned to England frequently because of the needs of her parents, for whom she was the primary support: "I added it up at one point. I did something like sixteen transatlantic crossings between 1956 and when my father died in 1969." She preferred to go by sea because she enjoyed the ocean voyage and until the end of the sixties the fare was about half the price of an air ticket.

The list could continue, although some of our interviewees found a return visit too expensive or had other priorities. Charles Hall could not afford such visits; he did not return to England until 1973, twenty-six years after he came to Canada. His youngest daughter had become a flight attendant so he, like the Cecils, could take advantage of a free pass. Similarly, Anne Graves's father never returned to England. Her mother finally visited her English relatives when her husband died fifteen years after their move to Canada. The visit seemed to make her more satisfied with living in Canada.

The authors of *Ten pound Poms* found that "the complicated responsibilities, needs, desires and tensions of family relationships" were most important in explaining the return migration of postwar British migrants who took advantage of the ten-pound scheme to go to Australia.[17] Many of our interviewees had to deal with similar complicated responsibilities and tensions but decided to remain in Canada.[18] Families with children often became committed to Canada because of their children's interests and natural identity with the country in which they were born or grew up. An incident in Charlotte Hinton's life illustrates this. Charlotte recalled looking at a blue airmail letter that the letter carrier had just delivered and saying, "That's my mother. I wish I could call home." Her young son, who was at the house with her, laughed. "But Mummy, you are home," he said. As Charlotte explained, "That's when I knew I couldn't go back, because this was my children's home."

Two families did contemplate returning to England when their oldest child turned five because they believed that the English educational system was superior, but then rejected the idea as not feasible. More migrants thought about returning to England in retirement. They were restrained partly by the prohibitive cost of living in England, but usually even more by their attachment to children and grandchildren in Canada. By this time, bonds with the younger generations were most important. For example, Robert Baldwin inherited his father's house in England, and for some time he and his wife thought they would retire there. He explained why they changed their mind: "We woke up one day and realized that our two kids had married Ontario girls and were settled in Ontario and were probably going to stay settled in Ontario, and all our grandchildren would be in Ontario, and how stupid would it be to go back to live in England leaving all of them behind. So we put the house on the market [in England] and that was the end of that." May Preston, who came to Canada as a nurse but subsequently married and had three children, expressed the same view.

When her husband died, friends wondered if May would return to England, but she never considered such a move; while her roots were in England, her children and grandchildren were in Canada: "How could I leave three children and eight grandchildren to go and live there [in England]...What good would it do to live in a lovely place and be alone. People are more important to me than things. Here I can see my kids, I can see the children, you know the little ones, and that's more important to me." Even Anne Graves's mother was finally reconciled to life in Canada by the presence of her grandchildren. For a long time, Anne explained, her mother did not adjust to migration, and she feared being buried in Canada away from those dear to her in England. She slowly came around to accepting life in Canada, but "she never really, really settled until she had all her grandchildren."

Are the days of "gone forever" gone?
A revolution in family dynamics

Migrants coming to Canada in the eighteenth, nineteenth and early twentieth centuries would have known that there was a distinct likelihood that they would never see their family or friends again. Furthermore, communication would have been limited and infrequent if indeed there was any communication.

Separation was an accepted consequence of emigration. When she emigrated to Upper Canada in 1836, Barbara Argo Watt was instructed by her sister to "begin a letter to me as soon as you get this and write something in it every day when you have time and write very close so that I may have something in the form of definite correspondence with you, write anything, write everything and I will do the same.... I will expect a letter from you every six months, and oftener if anything particular happens."[19] Barbara thus makes a heartfelt plea not to lose contact, even though she expected only two letters a year.

Writing letters, or dictating letters if the immigrant was illiterate, was an expensive process for early settlers. A study of labourers' letters from Upper Canada in the 1830s found that because mail was charged by the sheet, the correspondent's message was crammed on to one side of a piece of paper, and the paper was folded over for the address. Mail services were slow, often taking as much as six months, with the average delivery to England taking between one and two months. Unreliability was a further problem, and many of these immigrants chose to send their letters to England via

New York. One of the immigrants from Petworth in Sussex, who settled in Guelph, found that he had to pay four separate postages to route a letter through New York. In addition, the recipient would have had to pay one shilling on receipt of the letter.[20] This was equivalent to half a day's pay for a well-paid labourer.

The cost of communicating by mail fell dramatically during World War II. By the time the first immigrants landed in Canada following World War II, they could benefit from the innovation of air mail. The Canadian postal authorities introduced lightweight grey air letter forms in 1942, offering free communication from Canada to Canadian, British, and Allied forces. Three years later these air letter forms were extended to communication with civilians in the U.K.[21] The British post office introduced lightweight, blue, pre-stamped air letters costing 4 pence in 1945. These air letters were also known as aerogrammes and like their Canadian grey equivalents had flaps cut for sticking over folds to avoid the extra weight of a separate envelope. Like the correspondents in the 1830s, space for correspondence was limited to three small pages in the English version and about 260 millimetres on the Canadian form. Communication by air letter was inexpensive, fast, and reliable. As a result, immigrants could communicate regularly, sometimes exchanging several letters a month.

The earlier Petworth immigrant letters were described as "a substitute for a conversation round the kitchen table."[22] Little changed in the intervening years; many of our interviewees related how air letters were a means of exchanging family gossip and news. Joan Martin recalled writing to her mother every week until baby number three arrived, after which writing became less frequent. Her letters were handwritten before she acquired a typewriter to make writing easier. Joan recalled that she, her mother, and her grandmother "tended to write letters like we spoke. I would write a letter and I'd be telling my mother something about the kids as if she was there." Emma Bulmer, comparing herself with her mother, sister, grandmother, and uncle, admitted she was "not a good letter writer." Yet, regardless of her letter-writing abilities, she stressed the importance of letters for keeping in touch. Emma, like Joan and a number of other immigrants, kept her old letters. Janet Cecil said she exchanged letters with her mother every ten days and on one occasion sent a tape recording of her children to their grandparents. Sarah Walsh communicated less frequently, around eight times a year.

Elizabeth Summers's testimony demonstrates that, other than letter writing, there were alternative ways to stay in touch:

> I'm the youngest of four—the next sibling is nine years older than
> me—so when I left, I had nieces by that time, so that was a lot of family
> to keep in touch with. And in those days, in the '60s, you wrote letters,
> you didn't pick up the telephone.... My mother wrote regularly to me
> and I to her and that was how I kept in touch. I very, very seldom used
> the telephone to keep in touch with my family but…in those days I
> would visit England probably every two years I think, yes I would,
> and my sister would come out and we would have holidays and my
> other sister and her husband came…. That was how we kept in touch
> and, well, we keep in touch all the time. I've just had a note from one
> of my great, great nieces just this week to thank me for her birthday
> present. You know we're in great touch really, we're in strong, strong
> touch…and now of course I telephone. You know, it's no problem.

From the 1960s, the use of jet aircraft revolutionized long-distance family relationships. By 1964 more immigrants arrived in Canada by air than by sea, and this trend continued and accelerated.[23] Air travel was also beneficial for landed immigrants and their families in England; short trips and vacations became feasible and affordable. Britain's national carrier, BOAC, introduced the first scheduled Boeing 707 service from England to Canada in 1960. By the early 1970s these trailblazing aircraft had been replaced by Boeing 747 jumbo jets. These aircraft dramatically increased the number and availability of seats. Inevitably the airlines came under economic pressure to fill these seats and, with the deregulation of International Air Transport Association (IATA) controls, prices fell in real terms. New forms of air travel also emerged to put further pricing pressure on scheduled carriers. On 1 April 1973 the Advanced Booking Charter was introduced. This permitted Laker Airways to introduce a competitively priced service between Manchester and Toronto the following day. Other charter and low-cost carriers like Wardair, Canadair, and Zoom followed. John Derbyshire, who came to Canada in 1957 and spent forty years in the computing industry, recalled how he circumvented IATA regulations through a local immigrant organization: "The cost of air travel improved considerably with the introduction of charter airlines such as Wardair. [Earlier, however,] my mother and father were able to fly out for a month-long vacation in 1963 by virtue of having a relative on the prairies and [their] becoming members of the Prairie Relatives Association—cost $10.00."

All but one of our interviewees had returned to England on a trip for one purpose or another, as many of their stories here and in Chapter 5 illustrate. Most had been more than once, and many went every couple of years or so. Additionally, family who lived in England visited their immigrant relatives in Canada. In the early days of jet travel there was often a compelling family reason to make the trip, such as illness, death, or a wedding. As air travel became more common, people went for holidays or to get together with friends and family.

In addition to letters and air travel, Elizabeth Summers mentioned the telephone. Although transatlantic telephone services were inaugurated in 1927, the cost of making calls was still prohibitively expensive after World War II. In her early days in Canada, Elizabeth did not use the phone often to call England. She found "the lines were impossible, there was no good connection, you were cut off, and it was vastly expensive." Calls had to be booked and placed through an operator, and when a connection was made, often the callers had to shout to make themselves heard. There was another problem: even in the 1960s fewer than half the households in England had a telephone. This was the issue for Joan Martin. In order to speak to her mother at Christmas, Joan had to phone her brother, who had a telephone.

Expense was the main reason for avoiding the telephone. When John Derbyshire arrived in Canada in 1957, he was shocked to discover that a five-minute transatlantic call cost him seventy-five dollars. A similar call in his retirement would be no more than a few cents using a phone card or any one of a number of discounted phone services. The fall in the cost of telephone calls, combined with improvements in direct dialling and line quality led to significant increases in the number of calls between families in England and Canada. In addition, the introduction of cellular phones in the 1990s and smart phones a decade or so later made calling easier. The latter also provided other means of communication, notably texting and the sending of still and video images. Elizabeth Summers, who had found phoning impossible, soon changed her habits when "the cable under the Atlantic started to improve" and the cost of calls went down. Her habits changed again with the arrival of the Internet. Along with her trips to England and phone calls, she sent and received e-mails. "That's even cheaper than phoning," she said.

In their study of postwar migration to Australia, Hammerton and Thomson found that "the transformation of transport and communications technologies—from ocean liners and aerogrammes to jumbo jets and e-mail—changed the ways in which migrants moved from one country to another, and altered relationships within extended families that straddled the globe."[24] Hammerton and Thomson's study, whose findings largely parallel our own in this area, was completed before the explosive growth of the Internet, social media, and new forms of digital communication further transformed the way in which migrants and their extended families bonded and related to each other.

Suburban living and community ties

In *The Suburban Society*, S.D. Clark defined community simply as "a place where people know each other."[25] Although place can be an important basis for community, subsequent scholarship has rejected a straightforward equation of place with community.[26] Instead, scholars have examined community as a social process predicated on relationships that may or may not be bounded by a particular physical space. Thus, extrapolating from the insights of Benedict Anderson, a sense of community can extend to an imagined reality with others not directly known.[27] In addition, people within the same geographical space may be included or excluded from community belonging. In an examination of community as a socio-cultural process, institutions and public spaces such as churches, schools, and sites of leisure, therefore, can be important signifiers of meaning. In the following sections we will examine the involvement of our interviewees in community activities, how they were included or excluded, and how they perceived the significance of these relationships.

One of the most important community spaces for English migrants was the neighbourhood in which they lived. When our interviewees bought a house in the suburbs, as many did, they were also acquiring a way of life. Like the Whilesmiths, whose migrant story introduced this chapter, the Baldwins found that they were immediately involved in Canadian community life when they moved to a suburban house instead of returning to England in 1971. Robert Baldwin described their experience:

When we lived in apartments before we bought the house...almost
all of our friends were immigrants like ourselves. We had very
few Canadian friends if any, actually, but when we moved into the
house, the first full day we were in the house, the fellow from across
the street came and said, "Hi, and by the way there's a community
dance in a couple of weeks. We'd like it if you'd join our party," and
we did. In that evening we met more Canadians than we had met
in five years previously. The great thing about that was that practically all the people that lived [in the community]—there were 800
houses—were Canadians. A lot of them had kids the ages of our
kids or close to that, and there was a thriving community spirit,
and for me that was when we really put down Canadian roots.

Women had more continuous immersion in suburban living than did
men, but the experiences of women also varied according to their family income level and resources. The Baldwins both participated actively in
community activities, but Margaret, like Rosemary Whilesmith, spent her
days in the suburban society while Robert departed for work. Margaret was
restricted from obtaining the kind of work she might have liked in Montreal because of her lack of fluency in French, so she stayed home with the
children. When the children were at school, she played tennis twice a week
for many years with a group of friends; she found the sport to be a "good
social thing because I wasn't out working."

Charlotte Hinton similarly did not take paid employment while her
children were growing up in a Montreal suburb. When she emigrated,
Charlotte had three children aged four, two, and nine months and was
pregnant with the fourth child, so she was fully occupied for many years
caring for the family. "My job was to look after my husband and look after
my children," she said, "and that was all I did." While she accepted looking
after the family as her full-time work, she also observed somewhat regret-
fully that she did not have the option of taking paid employment: "I couldn't
get a job because my husband was on overtime all the time. I couldn't afford
babysitting for four children. So it wasn't a question of whether you wanted
to or not. I did do some freelance artwork sometimes, but not often. I didn't
have time." Charlotte emphasized how her draftsman husband worked a
seven-day week—twelve hours a day, except Friday, when he was allowed
to come home at four o'clock. She looked forward to Fridays because that

10. Suburban backyard potlucks helped English immigrants integrate into the community. Photo credit: By permission Rosemary Sloan.

was when her husband took her shopping. He would look after two of the children while she kept the other two with her: "The nicest part about Canada was Friday.... I went shopping and filled up the fridge with marvellous food and I'd think, Wow! Just great! Sometimes it's been pretty hard but the food's always been good." Charlotte did all the cooking for the family; the Hintons could not afford to go out much and never ate in restaurants.

Analysts of postwar suburban society have noted the self-sacrifice of families in purchasing their homes. This denial affected women more severely, as their needs were deemed less important than those of the male breadwinners.[28] English migrants seem no different from Canadians in this respect; luxuries such as babysitters were often not possible. On the other hand, the need for extra income led to the expansion of some part-time activities that were compatible with child care. The door-to-door selling in the community of products such as Avon was one such activity in which Agnes Butcher engaged.[29] Agnes believed strongly that women who have children should be mothers and not dump their children while they go back to work. Being an Avon lady, however, was quite acceptable because she could do the work while her older son was at part-time school and the younger was still at home and could accompany her: "We used to have to go to the door and say—and of course I was all dressed up in my red velvet coat and hat—'I'm your Avon representative. May I step inside? I have a gift for you.' It was a little sample lipstick. That's what I did and I did really well. I became the 'Queen of Avon' and I got a crown."

More women became involved with the community through volunteer activities, especially those affecting their children, than through door-to-door selling. Thus, as Veronica Strong-Boag concluded, although suburban life could be isolating for women confined at home with young children and no car, the suburbs also offered women the opportunity for leadership in developing schools, hospitals, churches, and libraries.[30] Such activities were particularly important for integrating our interviewees into a Canadian community, even as they contributed to its development. Sarah Walsh serves as one example. Sarah and her husband Tom, as we saw earlier, bought property in order to become part of a Canadian community. In England, Sarah had worked as a nurse at the local hospital, but when her daughter was born, she and her husband decided "it would be easier for us to manage with me staying at home." With a second daughter born shortly after they moved into their first Canadian house, Sarah, who had a certificate in early childhood education as well as her nursing qualifications, became involved with the community cooperative nursery school. Like many parents, she helped with the programs, but because of her background, she also became assistant director of the school. When Tom's work led them to settle in a small community outside Ottawa five years later, Sarah continued her volunteer activities: "I decided to focus just on raising the girls because it just didn't make sense with no family, immediate family, in the area, and with their dad travelling, it really didn't make sense for me to leave them to pursue a career. There was no need, we had everything we wanted, and I think the children benefited—well, they did benefit quite a lot. I got actively involved again, involved in their schooling as a volunteer and helped in the primary schools and the nursery schools and their figure skating, and got immersed really in volunteer work." Sarah also taught a nursing program for the Red Cross and volunteered with the Cancer Society for ten years. As she concluded, "There was a lot to keep me actively involved, both in the community and with the children." Similarly, Charlotte Hinton, in spite of her full-time family responsibilities, also became a school volunteer when her children started school. Others, such as Rosemary Whilesmith and Margaret Baldwin, volunteered with youth organizations; Rosemary helped with Girl Guides, and Margaret with Beavers for younger boys.

Although most attention in studies of suburban living has been given to women's roles, our interviews reveal that fathers as well as mothers were often involved in community volunteer activities relating to their children. Peter Whilesmith enjoyed feeling part of the community when he assisted with the Scouts and became president of two Home and School Associations. Most youth groups were gender specific, so men were organizers with boys' activities, although women might assist with the younger boys, as Margaret Baldwin did with Beavers. Robert Baldwin joined his wife by taking on the older boys in the Scouting movement. He started by assisting with Cubs, the stage above Beavers, and then progressed to become a Scout leader. In addition, Robert became active in coaching the sports in which his sons participated: "I coached soccer, which was quite a thing for a guy who went through a rugby school in England. If you play rugby at school you don't play soccer and if you play soccer you don't play rugby; that's changed now by the way. So I had to learn how to play soccer and then how to coach little boys, and I started into that when Mark was six, I think, and then it was hockey, and so I had to learn how to skate." Through his coaching activities, he got to meet a "huge amount of the community." Indeed, if he went to the shopping centre, he would meet so many people he knew that he would spend two hours talking and one hour shopping. He found the experience "an invigorating part of our time here" because he and Margaret developed such a wide circle of good solid acquaintances.

Suburbs varied in character and composition.[31] As we saw in Chapter 4, Charlotte Hinton and her family unwittingly moved into a francophone suburb of Montreal at a time of rising Québécois nationalism. Hence Charlotte was not active with local youth organizations. Suburbs were nevertheless child-centred, and Charlotte's four children connected the family with the neighbourhood apart from formal organizations. Charlotte would often find many children in her living room, none of whom were necessarily her own. The house was well situated, with a forest at the back where the children played in the summer and skated in the winter. In summer there were also neighbourhood movies on a big screen that everyone could watch sitting on their deck chairs.

While most suburban neighbourhoods drew English migrants into contact with a predominantly Canadian community, Richard Nash had a different experience when he and his family moved outwards in Ottawa in the mid-1960s.[32] They moved to a brand-new community, he said, and "a great influx of Brits" arrived about a year later. Computer firms such as Northern Telecom and government organizations like Atomic Energy brought to Ottawa large numbers of British immigrants, many of whom settled in the newly developing community of Kanata not far from their work. "We had this influx of people, all highly skilled, intelligent people," Richard remembered, "and it was absolutely marvellous! We had a wonderful time and we met the most wonderful people and our kids grew up in this environment. We had a club-house there and we learned to do everything and had social activities. We formed a British social group."

The British community group organized social evenings with "some music and somebody playing guitar, or then a bit of dancing and drinks, and it was great." Richard judged the activities "successful, because we had a lot of people to draw on." He believed that the concept of a "social evening" was quite British, deriving from the old British idea of organizing a social group get-together. The posters that advertised "Social Evening" were eventually changed, however, for fear that Canadians would misinterpret the event as a political gathering. The evenings did little to overcome British lack of knowledge of Canadian society, but they did forge strong links among the participants, links that endured for Richard even after he moved to Vancouver Island in retirement.

When Rob Watson arranged a transfer to Canada through his British computer firm in the mid-1970s, he too settled in Kanata with his wife and two children. He noted the village atmosphere of the community, but what he found quite amazing was that "the first time we went to put our daughter on the bus to go to camp for Guides, everyone talked like us!" Rob did not mention British social evenings, but he did note that parents were active in starting youth organizations: "There was a Scout association with a couple of Cub packs and Scout troops. Same thing for Girl Guides. Somebody started a ballet or dancing school. Obviously there was kids' hockey and all of that sort of thing. And it was very, very much organized by the parents of the kids." It is striking that the iconic Canadian sport of ice hockey was accepted as inevitable, even in a community with many British immigrants.

Personal interests and organizational activities

Like the Whilesmiths, English migrants had a range of personal interests that not only gave them pleasure but also led to involvement with a wider group or community of people sharing the same interests. Our interviewees included gardening, music, art, and sports among this type of leisure recreation. A number also belonged to women's organizations or joined churches and ethnic associations.

A love of attractive gardens was part of the cultural baggage of some English migrants who valued the flowering displays around small houses in English villages, as well as the more formal gardens on larger estates. From the nineteenth century in England, women had been particularly associated with the cultivation of flowers, whereas men often tended vegetable gardens.[33] May Preston, who married in Canada shortly after she migrated as a nurse, was enthusiastic about her flower garden. "I think a lot of my garden," she said. "I think a lot of English women do." She remembered the lovely gardens in England where "everybody has roses," and beautiful flowers that smelled fragrant. Unfortunately, in eastern Ontario May found her soil was not suitable for roses, so the plants would grow but never produce a flower. Nonetheless, May continued to cherish her flower garden, although she was having to scale back a little at the time of the interview because of her age.

Mary Charles similarly brought a love of gardening from England. Her main instructions to her husband, who preceded her to Montreal, were that any house he obtained must have a garden and a tree. Mary had learned a great deal about gardening in England from her next-door neighbour, who was an avid gardener. In Canada, she had to take another route for instruction. She quickly observed that her neighbours were not gardeners "so I joined the local gardening club, and that got me over the hurdle, and I made lots of friends there." Mary had to learn how to garden again because "it's different here; there's things that you want to grow here and you can't. Well you try and you give up because of the weather." With the aid of the various horticultural societies to which she belonged, Mary not only met the challenge of adapting to Canadian conditions but also made many new friendships. After moving to Ontario with her husband, she was elected to the board of the Ontario Horticultural Association, a volunteer commitment that demanded time and travel but was rewarding and fun. Mary combined her interest in gardening with an enjoyment of art and painting, so she also was involved with art associations. Reflecting on the friendships that she developed over the years through these volunteer activities, Mary concluded, "with all my garden clubs probably half of them [the members] are British, [in] the art association half are British, and you tend to keep your friendships among the Brits." Interestingly, with the influx of postwar

British migrants, some clubs and associations that were expected to promote integration simultaneously reinforced British (but not necessarily
English) ethnic ties.

Gardens could be a gift to be shared with friends and community as well
as a source of personal pleasure. Such was the case with Veronica Milner's
garden, which Mary Irvine so enjoyed while visiting on Vancouver Island.
Mary found that when her life in Calgary was busy with child care, "it was
always great to go out to Veronica's garden and be there in the summer." The
house at Qualicum Beach on Vancouver Island was the Milners' own re-
treat from Alberta, where Ray Milner was a founding director of Canadian
Utilities and an influential businessman. Originally built in 1931, the house
contained features of a Sri Lankan tea plantation dwelling, including many
screened doors leading into the garden. It was Veronica's artistic vision and
her horticultural knowledge that developed the space into a garden that
would be described by *Canadian Geographic Travel* as "one of the ten best
gardens in Canada." Veronica, who had been born in London, England, was
a member of the British aristocracy; her mother was a cousin of Winston
Churchill, so she also was descended from the Duke of Marlborough. During her first marriage, Veronica helped to create a spectacular garden at
her Irish castle estate near Limerick. These skills she transferred to British
Columbia when, as a widow, she immigrated to Canada in 1954 to become
the second wife of Ray Milner. The relatively mild climate of Vancouver
Island allowed Veronica to bring plants from temperate zones around the
world to her garden, including a large collection of rhododendrons. The ten
acres of garden surrounding the heritage house were set off by sixty acres
of British Columbia woodland. The view near a bluff overlooking the water
was spectacular. As an artist, Veronica also added a painting studio from
which she could view the landscape. "Veronica's Garden" continues to be
enjoyed by many visitors. Veronica Milner died in 1998, but she bequeathed
her garden to the care of Vancouver Island University.[34]

The joy of music and singing brought other of our interviewees into
social groups and volunteer activities, sometimes across what might appear
to be ethnic boundaries. After first coming to Canada with her school in
wartime, Jenny Carter led an international lifestyle, returning to England
to help with the war effort and then resuming studies at Bryn Mawr in the
United States. Eventually she married a Canadian naval officer, whom she
had met during the war, and settled in Canada. Jenny may have inherited

her interest in music; her mother had been concert mistress of the orchestra at her private girls' school in England. This interest in music, however acquired, gave her an opportunity to participate in Canadian culture and arts. Living in Kingston for a year, she joined the choral society, "which was lovely because that got me meeting Canadians again, Canadians with whom I had something in common." When she moved to Halifax with her husband, her music interests helped to offset what she described as an "awful house," in a new subdivision. In the United States, Jenny had been involved in a system, initiated by the famous violinist Isaac Stern, which brought music into schools. With this experience, she similarly helped with music for children in Halifax and later in Ottawa: "Halifax had a lot of music, in a curious way. They had a conference while I was there and this was the first High School Orchestra in Nova Scotia ever, I think, and it had a woman conductor, and Wilfred Pelletier came as the [guest] conductor, and I have never forgotten it. The tears were just pouring down his face, and he said, 'This is how you have to go; this is a torch you will have to carry'—and they did, and it was just wonderful, just terrific. So that got me started." Jenny soon became active with CAMMAC (Canadian Amateur Musicians / Musiciens amateurs du Canada). She took Nova Scotian children to a music camp in the Laurentians, where "it was okay for a boy to play a violin" and after moving to Ottawa, she used her organizational talents to start a branch of CAMMAC there. She also transmitted her passion for music to her own children, two of whom sing in choirs.

Barbara and Roy Trueman also found that their enthusiasm for singing smoothed their transition to Canadian life when they migrated to Ottawa in 1964, and thereafter remained an important community activity for them. "We've always sung." Barbara explained. "We've sung all our lives." Roger had been a choirboy as a child, so the Truemans joined Ottawa's Christ Church Cathedral, where Roger became a member of the cathedral's internationally known men's and boys' choir. The Truemans both sang with the Ottawa Choral Society for many years. When they retired from it, Barbara took up barber-shop singing, which she discovered "I absolutely love."

Barbara and Roy also joined the Ottawa Welsh Choral Society after accidentally learning about it from a neighbour who was a member. The Truemans had lived for a few years in Wales immediately before coming to Canada, so, although they were not Welsh, involvement in the Choral Society was important in helping them to overcome their severe homesickness. They

206 | INVISIBLE IMMIGRANTS

gained a sense of community in Canada from the Society, which welcomed them and actively organized various activities, including New Year's fancy dress parties and November "Faggots and Peas" events with Welsh-style food. The choir also attended international music festivals in Wales, providing opportunities for return visits, which eased feelings of being cut off from their past. While explaining their participation in the Welsh Coral Society, the Truemans made a point of denying any interest in more general British ethnic associations. Roger noted, "There was a U.K. Society but we never bothered with it," and Barbara simultaneously concurred, "No, we never, ever did that." Although the Truemans did not analyze further, they seemed attracted to the Welsh society because of the combination of a music that they loved, and a welcoming community that both openly accepted them and provided links to their immediate past in Britain.

Chapter 2 related how a number of our interviewees were attracted to Canada because they valued outdoor activities and sports. Peter Whilesmith was not the only migrant to find personal enjoyment, a sense of accomplishment, and a social network through his passion for sailing. Badminton and tennis were other favourite sports that provided links to social groups or clubs. Family camping in parks, hiking, or canoeing on lakes and rivers provided an inexpensive way of enjoying nature either away from others or as part of a social group. Some of our interviewees, like Robert Baldwin and Mary Irvine, found delight in downhill skiing, which was so much more accessible in Canada than in England. Others were less enthusiastic. Barbara Trueman and Margaret Baldwin had difficulty managing the ski lift and quickly abandoned the sport. Peter Semple expressed his aversion to skiing because of his strong dislike of the cold: "I hate the climate. I don't like the cold. I last went skiing in about 1968 or so. I got frostbite. I lost all the skin off my fingers—got it very bad. I couldn't lift a pencil for two weeks. That's the joy of frostbite. And I decided at that point that skiing was not something that I wanted to do."

The popular Canadian winter pastime of skating similarly was not a skill easily acquired by an adult immigrant. Few English migrants came to Canada as good skaters, and not many of our interviewees learned to skate with much proficiency. Charlotte Hinton was proud of learning to skate at age forty, but sailing on the Ottawa River in the summer was a much more significant family recreational activity for her. In general, skating was most popular with the children, who grew up playing on backyard ice rinks and participating in youth hockey teams.

Organizations designed to draw together people of similar background and interests for mutual benefit, service to the community, or the preservation and promotion of particular values also appealed to some of our interviewees. From the nineteenth century a number of middle-class women's organizations had developed in Canada, reflecting women's separate place in society as well as their interest in community social outreach and national values. Mary Irvine in Calgary joined the Junior League, which she described as "a wonderful women's organization," started in New York in the early twentieth century by a group of debutantes who wanted to do something for people rather than spending all their time socializing. Like many service clubs, the League raised money for community projects, particularly those directed at women and girls. As Mary explained, "For the first year you were a provisional member, and you learned everything you needed to know about your community, and you got a taste of all the various projects." Her placement one year was to teach cooking in the girls' club that the League organized. Many of the girls were from single parent families, so she taught them simple menus they could go home and prepare. It was fun, both for herself and for the girls who queued at the door for the classes. Mary also became the Junior League representative attending the public school board meetings, and so was quite busy as a volunteer.

In Ottawa, May Preston belonged to a group which more specifically drew together British migrant women for mutual support and charitable activities: the Overseas Women's Organization. She joined because her mother belonged to the parent group in England—the Canada & United States Parents Association (CANUSPA). Initially, the Ottawa group had been started by British war brides, but by the time May moved to Ottawa in 1962 the organization had changed its name to Overseas Women so that anyone could join who had been born outside Canada. Nonetheless, almost all the members were from the United Kingdom—English, Scottish or Welsh; the only exception that May remembered was one French woman. Many joined partly out of self-interest because, at a time when air fares were expensive, they could obtain cheaper fares on BOAC as a member of the group. The Overseas Women's Organization, however, also raised funds for cystic fibrosis during the years that May was a member.

Overseas Women, however, was not the only organization with which May was involved. When she joined, she was already an active community volunteer in relation to her children's interests: "While I was a stay-at-home mum, I was a Cubs leader; I was on the executive of the Guides and Brownies 'cause I had a daughter." She went every week to the Cubs, but Guides and Brownies was once a month, when she helped arrange bake sales and teas, mother-daughter banquets, and other such events. In addition to the children's clubs, she also served on the executive of the Home and School Association.

Religious and ethnic associations

Organized religion traditionally had been a major force that assumed responsibility for the moral values of Canadian society, linked spiritual and social life, and actively endeavoured to shape the character of an evolving Canadian nationalism. In the increasingly secular society of both Canada and England in the postwar era, the institutional leadership of the church was declining, but religious faith was still significant in the lives of many individuals. Although the majority of postwar English migrants were at least nominally Protestant, the religious affiliation of English migrants was more diverse and less central in defining a group identity than was the case for members of several other ethnic groups migrating to postwar Canada. Church membership nonetheless remained important for some of our interviewees as they adapted to Canadian life, even though many others did not mention religion in recounting their life stories. The Whilesmiths, as we have seen, were among those who transferred an inherited religious allegiance from the established Church of England to its Canadian descendant, the Anglican Church of Canada. The Whilesmiths were not alone in wanting their children to have exposure to religious values and the opportunity to decide about religious commitment. For several other interviewees, the role of the church in providing a social as well as a spiritual community was important. The Cecils, for example, played badminton with an Anglican church group in Montreal.

James Leonard similarly emphasized the community social role of the church. Coming from a small English village in East Sussex where the Church of England was the only church, James was often astounded to find five or six churches in a small Canadian community. He explained changing attitudes toward religion in his family by recounting how his mother was more upset when his older sister married a Roman Catholic than when he decided to emigrate to Canada. But, he added, "That's changed a lot!" James, like his sister, was tolerant of religious differences and he had no objection when one of his daughters married a Roman Catholic in Canada. As a farm labourer when he first came to Canada, he liked going to the rural Presbyterian church with his employers. He found the service was quite different from the Anglican form of worship, however; communion involved little squares of ordinary bread and grape juice rather than the wafers and wine of the Anglicans. James believed that local churches provided an excellent way to get to know the community, whether initially the Ontario farm families with whom he socialized after the Presbyterian church service or later during his military career, the northern Alberta rural community around Bonnyville that attended the Anglican church. When asked during the interview whether he belonged to clubs, he replied, "No clubs, just the Anglican church."

A supportive religious faith could be instrumental in overcoming isolation and aiding the transition to a new country. Isobel Sinclair-Chang, from a working-class London background, felt that she was sustained by her Roman Catholic faith. "For me," she said, "the centre of my social life has always been my parish church." Through the Roman Catholic church in Toronto she began meeting people, initially other British Isles people and then a wider group. She and her Chinese husband-to-be became involved with Newman Chapel, a student Catholic organization on the University of Toronto campus, as well as with a nearby Catholic church. Religion acted as "a kind of refuge, because you sort of feel that if there's nowhere else that you can go, they ought to be nice to you there."

A personal religious commitment, however, could not overcome the isolation that Jennifer Short felt on emigrating to Canada.[35] In communicating her migration story, Jennifer identified religion as a major part of her life. Although she was baptized in the Church of England, she grew up attending the Methodist chapel and Sunday school in a working-class Sheffield neighbourhood. Neither her father, a labourer in the steel mills, nor her mother participated much in organized religion, but Jennifer went regularly with a close neighbourhood friend to the Methodist services. She persisted, even though her commitment created a rift with her father, whose heavy smoking and drinking contravened Methodist precepts for behaviour. Jennifer's life changed dramatically in 1968 when, in her mid-twenties, she married a member of the Canadian military whom she met while on holiday in Austria. Coincidentally, her husband, who was considerably older than Jennifer, was originally from Sheffield but had migrated to Canada after the war. Her husband's military service took Jennifer first to Germany for a couple of years but then to northeastern Alberta, near the military base at Cold Lake. Jennifer was excited about the move but she was not prepared for the culture shock of rural northern Alberta. "I didn't settle down well," she recalled. "I missed the Sheffield Playhouse and I missed my church. I missed my family and I missed things in Germany, like the guest houses and the nice wines." Living briefly in the village of Bonnyville, Jennifer was able to attend the United Church of Canada, which had absorbed most of the Methodist churches in Canada during church union in the 1920s. Soon the Shorts moved six miles down the highway to Fort Kent, an even smaller place, where Jennifer described her existence as "a prisoner in my home." With young children and no car, and not even knowing how to drive, she lacked any means of escape. Although she did not make the comment, obviously the church did not go to her as it might have tried to do in earlier days, so she was not even able to obtain solace from a sense of religious belonging. When the Shorts moved to the larger centre of Prince George, British Columbia, Jennifer was able to resume a life within a church community and greatly enjoyed all the things she did with "the ladies from church." Her church affiliation, however, became almost as transient as her life as a military wife. She became disillusioned with the United Church and moved to the Presbyterian Church, which she loved until too many grey heads appeared in the congregation, reminding her of the English TV program *Waiting for God*. Settled in Nanaimo on Vancouver Island, she transferred to the more evangelical Alliance Church, with its missionary focus.

Charles Hall, who came to Montreal in 1947, was another interviewee who changed his church affiliation but in his case as part of a family compromise.[36] Charles was Anglican but had married a Scottish land army lass at the end of the war, so the Hall family belonged to the United Church in Montreal. The Hall children attended church regularly, and Charles took a leadership role in the church by becoming a steward. His responsibilities included calling on members of the congregation on Sunday afternoons, talking to them, finding out if the church could help them in any way, and soliciting donations. He carefully carried out these responsibilities for several years. Then a senior church person, while reviewing with Charles the list of members to visit, instructed him not to bother with one family because they were unable to donate to the church. Charles was deeply offended by such monetary priorities, especially since he knew the family was suffering serious illness. Although the perspective of one individual did not constitute church policy, for Charles it was sufficiently indicative of a failure in the basic understanding of church community that he left the church, never to return.

Organized religion thus did not always provide a sense of belonging even for those English migrants who sought a religious commitment. English migrants also might be affected by the deep historical divisions between Protestants and Catholics that in Canada were often intertwined with the conflict between anglophone and francophone cultures. Mary Charles encountered the continuing impact of religious segregation in the Quebec school system. As she recounted:

> There were kids all over the place [in the Charles's Montreal subdivision]. But they were divided into four: English Catholic, French Catholic, English Protestant, French Protestant, so of course there wasn't the school there. They all got bused off in four directions. The kids tended to stand at the same green square round the corner, and they all hated each other. There were snowball fights, Catholic versus Protestant, French versus English. It wasn't particularly violent but it was definitely there. That was a bit of a horror to me.

In spite of instances in which religious affiliation failed to provide support or indeed functioned to increase tension, several of our interviewees found that church membership and associated social activities assisted their own adaptation and contributed toward raising their children. In contrast, few belonged to patriotic or ethnic associations specifically designed to foster an English or British ethnic identity. A couple of interviewees knew of such societies in Canada but emphatically declared that they would not belong to them. As we have seen, the Truemans, who joined the Welsh music group in Ottawa, had no interest in a general U.K. society. Similarly, Charles Hall was invited to one meeting of a British association in Montreal but refused to return. Since he went only once, he no longer was sure of the name of the society, but thought it was a British monarchist league:

"They went a bit too far. I like Britain, but I don't want Canada to be hurt as a result of what I've said or done." He explained that the problem was not that they were negative about Canada but rather too positive about Britain. For Robin Lanson, a major advantage of his national service in England was that he qualified for membership in the Victory Services Club and the Union Jack Club, both clubs for present and past members of Her Majesty's armed forces. In spite of the patriotic-sounding names, Lanson's reason for joining was practical, rather than nationalistic. Based in London, the clubs provided cheap accommodation for his return visits to England.

English ethnic societies, which had existed in Canada since the nineteenth century, declined in membership or disappeared after World War II. The Sons of England, started in 1874 as a mutual benefit society, disbanded in 1971 after the introduction of government medical insurance. The even older St. George's Societies, established in Toronto and Montreal in 1834 as charitable and fraternal societies, were created to aid needy English immigrants.[37] After World War II, the St. George's Society of Toronto gradually loosened its membership criteria and expanded its social activities in order to continue functioning in the changing multicultural environment. In the 1950s, the Society helped Scottish and Irish as well as English immigrants find employment in Canada.[38] As English immigration dropped off in the 1970s, membership in the Society also declined. Gail Rayment, who as a new bride migrated to Canada from London in 1968, was finishing her term as president of the Toronto St. George's Society when Jim Hammerton interviewed her in 2000.[39] Rayment described how in the 1990s the Society changed its bylaws to extend membership not only to those born in England or of English descent, but also to anyone interested in things English. In addition, while the Society continued its charitable function by awarding bursaries to University of Toronto students doing English studies, it expanded its social activities from the traditional Christmas dinner and Rose Ball to croquet, Gilbert and Sullivan performances, pub nights, and trips to Stratford. From a nadir in the 1980s, the Society resurrected itself, attracting younger members who were mainly interested in the social events. Rayment explained that people attracted by the Society did not want to go back to England—"just dabble in Britishness every now and then." Reflecting on her own identity, she said that she took out Canadian citizenship as soon as she could; she believed that, "if you come to a country, you owe transferring some of your allegiance, at least." She regretted that the Society had few "blue-collar members," but understood that the blue-collar generation of British immigrants was dying out. Now, in the early twenty-first century, the Toronto St. George's Society functions mainly as a social club for professionals with some interest in vaguely British activities rather than as an organization designed to promote the retention of English ethnic identity.

Other exceptions to our interviewees' general lack of interest in English ethnic organizations were two British—not English—social clubs with which a few were actively involved. As we saw earlier, Richard Nash forged firm friendships through participation in the social evenings of a British club that formed in an Ottawa suburb as a result of the influx of educated British immigrants.[40] Richard, in retirement, and two other interviewees were actively engaged in "The Nanaimo British Club" that developed in another community of significant British settlement. Anne Graves founded the Nanaimo British Club in the 1980s[41] because, "I wanted Britain to be *recognized* on Canada Day, because it wasn't at that time. Every other culture would do their dances and the whole bit, and we did; we started a British tea-room. And they meet once a month and organize things" (italics added).

Anne was influenced by what McGill philosopher Charles Taylor has analyzed as "the modern preoccupation with identity and recognition" that underlay much of the impulse for multiculturalism in Canada from the 1970s.[42] As Taylor explained, in modern society, recognition by others had become increasingly important for the authentication of both individual uniqueness and the culture-bearing group to which the individual belonged. Anne would not have been familiar with Taylor's academic philosophy, but she definitely wanted the British to cease being invisible and to be recognized equally with other ethnic groups. The British coal-mining heritage of Nanaimo was important personally for Anne, whose father had been a coal miner in Newcastle-upon-Tyne in England. She described Nanaimo as a "British town, because the first people here were British. They were coal miners and they came from the north of England. There's lots of streets up here; there's Newcastle Avenue and Blyth and Sunderland." While Anne may have overlooked the Aboriginal people who were displaced by British settlement, she was acutely aware of the large multicultural centre in the community and the recognition being given at times of national celebration, such as Canada Day, to other ethnic groups such as the Chinese, East Indians, Dutch, and more recent Vietnamese immigrants in Nanaimo.

Unlike her mother, who had been a reluctant migrant when the family moved to the small community of Port Alberni near Nanaimo in 1956, Anne at age seventeen had been an enthusiastic immigrant who quickly found work in Canada. Three years later, she married another English migrant, whom she met after she moved to Victoria. After her husband left the army, the family bought a small house in Nanaimo, where Anne raised four children with a dog and a cat. For twenty-five years, Anne also worked as coordinator for the senior citizens' program of Nanaimo Parks and Recreation, a position that honed organizational skills that she would use in starting the Nanaimo British Club. Precisely because she was well integrated into a Canadian community that she considered to be home, Anne wanted her family and ethnic heritage to be recognized as an important part of the community and national heritage.[43]

The Nanaimo British Club simultaneously functioned as a source of publicity for the British in Nanaimo and as a social centre for group activities. Jennifer Short, whose many moves as a military wife ended in Nanaimo, felt less at home in the community than did Anne.[44] Therefore she appreciated being able to get together with a group of people who understood her Sheffield accent, shared her British sense of humour, and accepted her English ways of doing things. "It was good to go," she said, "and I loved their sense of humour, and to be able to bounce it off other people and they'd have a comeback and they wouldn't be excusing themselves or apologizing. You know we were all Brits together." Short found that her British sense of humour made her different from many people; even her daughter, as she grew older, complained about the family's English ways of doing things. Unfortunately, Jennifer did not explain the rather vague reference to "English ways." They seemed to include a greater sense of privacy, which might reflect her having grown up in close-knit terraced Sheffield housing, with net curtains to prevent the neighbours knowing everything that happened inside.

In the Nanaimo British Club, *British* was not a synonym for *English*. Anne Graves stated clearly that the club was intended for British people. Those that came were mostly English, but there were one or two from Scotland, and also Wales and Ireland. She did not explain the decision to create a British social club rather than an English social club. Was the need to be inclusive and attract more people part of the reason? Did ethnic differences that might be important within the United Kingdom diminish in significance in Canada when Britishness was defined against other non-British ethnic groups? Was she influenced by the existence of British rather than English clubs in other communities? Or was the conflation of English with British so automatic that it was simply assumed that a club that was for the English would be called British? The question of who was eligible for membership arose in the 1990s, when Richard Nash was president. The issue revolved around how the term *British* might be interpreted, although it had no connection to the identification of *English* with *British*. At a time when membership was declining for lack of recent British immigrants, a member asked whether a friend who was not from the United Kingdom could belong to the club. Nash consulted a committee member of the British club at Duncan, a short distance away, which was similarly losing members. He was told, "We took the easy way out and we decided to change the name of the club to the British-Canadian Club, and that would open the doors to anyone and everyone." In contrast, some Nanaimo members were not willing to dilute the Britishness of their club, and sufficient new recruits were found to sustain the status quo. Richard Nash, however, believed that the ambiguous wording of the bylaws permitting membership to those of "British heritage" could be interpreted, if necessary, to open their doors more widely. The Nanaimo British club thus provides an interesting case study of some aspects of English identity that will be examined in greater detail in the following chapter.

Conclusions

Home and living conditions, along with connections to family, friends, and community were as important as employment for English migrants' integration into Canadian society. The majority of our interviewees, like most postwar English migrants, settled in larger urban centres, particularly Toronto and Montreal. Whether married or single, most lived initially in rented accommodation in the more central districts of the cities where they frequently associated with other recent immigrants, sometimes British and sometimes from a variety of ethnic backgrounds. Buying a suburban home not only represented the better standard of living that many English migrants hoped to achieve in Canada—it also symbolized a more permanent commitment to Canada and brought a feeling of belonging. As one interviewee commented, "You just felt that you were beginning to put down roots." In the suburbs, English migrants were generally surrounded by Canadian neighbours and thus drawn into a Canadian community; but there were a few exceptions, as in the Ottawa suburb of Kanata with its greater concentration of English immigrants, or one francophone suburb of Montreal where English migrants were less welcome. Nonetheless, establishing friends and community in Canada could take time, especially since English migrants typically came as individuals or nuclear families and not with larger family or community groups. Among our interviewees, some single migrants initially felt quite isolated in the midst of a bustling city, and a few married women in rural areas felt cut off from social support.

Family bonds pulled English migrants in opposite directions—back to parents and other relatives in England, and increasingly, as time passed, to the attachments of children and grandchildren in Canada. For many of our interviewees, leaving family was difficult, even if they thought that they would be returning to England after a few years of experience or adventure in Canada. Important family events, such as the birth of a first child, or crises such as illness and death, made the distance across the Atlantic seem far. Women usually were the letter writers who kept families in touch, especially in the immediate postwar decades when phone calls were expensive and e-mail did not exist. Visits to England were important for renewing personal contact or providing more direct aid for aging parents, but working-class migrants in particular could not always afford the airfare for such visits. Although some interviewees remarked that their siblings in England had little more contact with their parents than they did, nonetheless family separation resulting from migration created continuing burdens of sadness and guilt for some. For interviewees with children, these family ties to England were offset by the even deeper attachments to the younger generations in Canada. Many realized that it made no sense to return to England when their grandchildren were in Canada. Toward the end of the twentieth century, the Internet created a new means for families to keep in touch and in a number of ways helped to revolutionize the immigrant experience.

Active participation in community activities was important in integrating English migrants into Canadian society. Many of our interviewees engaged in volunteer work, both in their local neighbourhoods and with charitable or other organizations that brought together people with similar interests. Many assumed leadership roles in youth and educational associations relating to their children, such as Girl Guides, Scouts, and Home and School Associations. They also gave leadership in broader community organizations such as the Horticultural Society or the Junior League. It is striking, not only that they were willing to undertake the work, but also that Canadians accepted them in these positions of leadership. The general lack of barriers to their participation is highlighted by the contrasting racial discrimination encountered by Isobel Sinclair-Chang when she and her husband lived in Peterborough: "Because my husband was Chinese, we did experience prejudice from the population. He ran for the city council and we got hate calls and unpleasant things like that, and when my children went to school, there were children that called them niggers.... At one point we had to call the police, but they could not do anything."

Religion and ethnicity seldom defined a group identity for the English migrants whom we interviewed. Church membership remained a major part of life for some interviewees but religious affiliation varied from the Anglican church, which was most directly associated with England, to the United Church of Canada and other Protestant denominations, to the Roman Catholic church, or the Jewish community. Similarly, most interviewees did not become involved with ethnic associations, even though they were aware of their existence. The few who did lived in communities settled by British immigrants and, interestingly, formed British clubs rather than specifically English societies. The intriguing questions of identity raised by issues of Britishness or Englishness in relation to both personal interests and an evolving Canadian nationalism are the subject of the following chapter.

Chapter 7

NATIONAL IDENTITY

An Englishman, a Canadian, and an American were
captured by terrorists. The terrorist leader said, "Before we shoot you, you
will be allowed to say some last words."

The Englishman said, "I wish to speak about loyalty
and service to the crown."

The Canadian said, "Since you are involved in a question
of national purpose, national identity, and secession, I want to talk
about the constitutional process in Canada, special status, distinct society,
and uniqueness in diversity."

The American said, "Just shoot me before the
Canadian starts talking!"[1]

On 1 January 1947, after a rough crossing, Abbi Andrews disembarked
from a small banana boat, called the *Cavina,* and landed on Canadian soil
as a new immigrant. This particular New Year's Day was also a watershed in
Canadian history, and its significance was etched on Abbi's memory. "We
arrived in Canada...when the new Canadian Citizenship Act took effect on
midnight and so I was not automatically a Canadian citizen as any British
subject was before."[2] The Act created a new form of national status, that of
Canadian citizenship separate from British nationality. A few years later
Abbi became a Canadian citizen. She recalled, "All I had to do was to go to
the Town Hall in Toronto and become one; it was simple. It was not like it
is now." Sixty years later, sitting in her Ottawa apartment overlooking the

Canadian War Museum, she was comfortable and confident about being a Canadian: "I'm Canadian now. At first, yes, I was conscious of my British heritage... There are certain British things that I keep, you know, I mean my specialty is steak and kidney pie.... We still keep some of those British traditions, I guess, in the way we do things, but I really think of myself as Canadian. After all, I've been here since I was sixteen, I've lived most of my life here. I still have relatives in England, but I don't have that much in common with them."

This chapter explores how national identity was constructed, deconstructed, and reconstructed in the minds and lives of English-born immigrants who chose to settle in Canada in the years after World War II. National identity is a complex, slippery, and much contested topic. Identity formation, whether in private or public spheres,[3] is not limited to national identity. Ask the question *Who am I?* and answers will likely incorporate thoughts about personal identity, gender identity, age identity, workplace identity, family identity, and community identity, as well as national identity. To a greater or lesser degree all these forms of identity tend to be interrelated, as has been evidenced in previous chapters. It is now time to take a closer look at national identity. Did all English immigrants see themselves as Canadian, with occasional spells of English nostalgia, like Abbi Andrews, or were other patterns more common?

Before seeking answers to this question, we must acknowledge that not all of our interviewees volunteered comment on their sense of national identity, or more precisely, their sense of national identities. Many had to be prompted by questions toward the end of the interviews. Interviewees tended to talk more about everyday realities, such as the reasons they came to Canada, their families, their work, their social lives, and their leisure time. Their narratives are extremely complex, with many aspects of their lives intersecting with each other—and it is from these that we draw our evidence from which to investigate national identity.

What is national identity?

The question "What is national identity?" plunges us into a maelstrom of academic debate and controversy that intensified in the closing decades of the twentieth century. Assessing how postwar English immigrants in Canada perceived their sense of national identity is also problematic, as perceptions changed over time, dependent upon individual, social, cultural, economic and political change. The sociologist Frank Bechhofer argued that "a complex process forms a person's national identity whereby individuals make identity claims, be they explicit or tentative, in differing contexts over time, and…these claims are received in different ways, and in turn modified by their reception."[4] As we noted in earlier chapters, the experience of migration is a life-changing event, a process that itself challenges and re-forms an individual's sense of identity and sense of place. Beyond daily life experiences of earning a living, falling in and out of love, bringing up a family, illness, and death, the interviewees were subjected to a barrage of change in the public sphere. Significantly, these external changes occurred on both sides of the Atlantic, with consequential impact upon their perceptions of identity. Out of this complexity it is possible to structure explanations about the feelings of national identity of English immigrants living in Canada. A number of themes emerge from the testimonies.

Within a labyrinth of theoretical concepts, a number of useful tools can be used to assess national identity at a personal, community, and national level. The tools we shall use come from the work of Anthony Smith, Benedict Anderson, and Linda Colley. Smith provided a useful model to define what he called *ethnie*, in which he defined five elements: a common name; a shared myth of descent; a common history; a distinctive shared culture; and links to common territory.[5] Anderson introduced the useful concept of imagination in his definition of a nation as an "imagined political community."[6] Identity was imagined because people did not know everyone in the nation or community, and yet they felt a deep horizontal comradeship with others in the nation or community because of shared symbols, values, and so on. As an example, Anderson cited the symbolic value of national anthems, as exemplified by the singing of "O Canada," and in earlier years "God Save the Queen," before NHL hockey games: "No matter how banal the words and mediocre the tune, there is this singing, an experience of simultaneity. At precisely such moments, people wholly unknown to each other utter the same verses to the same melody. The image: unisonance… [provides] occasions for unisonality, for the echoed physical realization of the imagined community [the nation or national identity]."[7]

In his book *Thinking English Canada*, Philip Resnick identified several ways in which anglophone Canada might be "imagined."[8] They include the defining characteristic of language; the immensity of geographic space and the intensity of climate; a spirit of multicultural tolerance; regional and political cultural diversity; and a multilateral international orientation.[9] Intriguingly, a number of these themes emerge from the interviewees' testimonies.

Linda Colley, drawing upon the insights of Edward Said, stressed the concept of "other" in relation to Britishness.[10] Colley wrote that national, ethnic, and communal identity were conditional, relational, and defined by social and territorial boundaries.[11] In other words, a Scot is a Scot because he or she is not English, a Catalan is a Catalan because he or she is not Spanish, and a Canadian is a Canadian because he or she is not an American. Throughout the period we are studying, the steamroller advance of U.S.-led global capitalism meant that important economic decisions for both Canada and England were being made elsewhere. This economic power and influence was also accompanied by U.S. cultural hegemony. The influence of the United States over Canada was encapsulated in Pierre Trudeau's metaphor of a mouse sleeping with an elephant. Interestingly, a number of the interviewees commented on the nature of this relationship. Jenny Carter, who went to the U.S. as a university student, took out American citizenship before she left London in 1946, only to renounce it in 1951. After half a century living in Canada she said, with no little emotion, "I just love North America, I think it's great. I have become a fierce Canadian as opposed to an American." Peter Semple, when musing about his sense of identity, said, "I start off being very anti-American." When he was in the telecommunications industry, he had found that Americans were aggressive in business. Peter also referred to his mother, who lived in Norfolk during World War II. She complained that the American military was "over-paid, over-sexed, and over here." As English immigrants, Jenny and Peter were constructing their feelings of national identity in relation to a significant other. Perhaps, in Colley's sense, they were truly Canadian.

James Leonard, after he arrived in Canada, joined the military and became a technician in the Royal Canadian Air Force. In the interview he said that Canada was his home, emphasizing that he was not a "nationalist": "I'm not a flag waver, for any country. To me nationalism is one of the worst things; it causes more war and more problems." He went on:

> I always remember. We were lined up for something in Lahr [an Air
> Force base] in Germany, and there was some Americans there too...
> and they fly the American and the Canadian flag, and this American
> guy came by and somebody made a joke about the American

flag, and oh God, the guy went berserk! I just don't understand
that nonsense! To me, a flag's a flag. I know it means something
and to be proud of it, but there's a difference between being proud
and getting hostile with everybody, when they don't necessarily
agree what that flag stands for. No, I'm not a nationalist at all.

This extract provides a different example of Americans being treated as
the other. Additionally, it presents two other issues that merit comment.
The first is the strength of feeling about flags, to which we shall return later.
The second is Leonard's use of the word *nationalist*. We need to take care to
differentiate between nationalism and patriotism in a discussion about national identity. Nationalism describes political movements that seek either
national unity, independence, preservation of national interests, and/or
domination over other nations. George Orwell made an important distinction between patriotism and nationalism; patriotism is about love of your
surroundings, with their culture and environment, whereas nationalism is
actually believing your country is superior.[12]

In light of this background, difficulties arise when defining the terms
Canadian and *English*, with the latter often being conflated with the word
British. Canadian scholars, journalists, and commentators struggle to define
what it means to be Canadian, given a colonial past and a multicultural
present.[13] As a result, we are faced with a bewildering and much-contested
complexity. Are we talking about anglophone or francophone Canada?
Aboriginal Canada, or multicultural Canada? Furthermore, attitudes have
changed since our interviewees settled in Canada. In the 1940s and 1950s,
many anglophones essentially perceived their sense of national identity as
rooted in British heritage or a romanticized Anglo-Saxonism. José Igartua
conducted a detailed study of daily editorial columns about national identity
and reviewed the nuanced changes in the teaching of Canadian history. He
argued that English Canada shed its definition of itself as British in the 1960s.
In a short time, Canada adopted a new stance as a civic nation without ethnic
particularities.[14] Since the 1960s, "Canada has witnessed the symbolic dimin-
ishment of the English Canadian national community through biculturalism,
multiculturalism, and encroaching Americanization."[15] Contributing to these
changes were Québécois nationalism, diverse ethnic immigration, North
American free trade, U.S. economic dominance and the reach of American
popular culture. The Canadian state was also active in promoting Canadian

civic nationalism. Five examples of this include: Canada's first Citizenship Act (1947), the Canadian Bill of Rights (1960), The Royal Commission on Bilingualism and Biculturalism (1963), the inauguration of the Canadian maple leaf flag (1965), and the development of social programs like medicare (1966), which highlight the assertiveness of the federal government in creating a pan-Canadian identity. These activities led Jeffrey Ayres to argue that "since the postwar era, the Canadian state has played an active role in crafting social and economic policies with the intent of developing a shared national identity."[16] It was not only from Ottawa, however, that governments played an influential role; for example, Quebec and Washington DC also played their part. Debates still continue about the changing nature of Canadian identities. It is not our purpose to review these here but to emphasize what Ayres referred to as "the dizzying effect [of change] upon English Canadians' sense of anchorage and place in Canada."[17]

11. Prime Minister Lester B. Pearson at a 1964 press conference showing the design for the new maple leaf flag to replace the red ensign. Photo credit: Duncan Cameron / Library and Archives Canada, PA-136153.

In comparison to Canadians reflecting on their identity, English scholars were not so obsessed with attempting to explain or articulate what it meant to be English, although following the establishment of the devolved Welsh Assembly and new Scottish Parliament in 1999 there have been vexed debates about the construct of "Englishness."[18] Jeremy Paxman, a pundit known for his ruthless interrogation of politicians on television, began his book about the English with the observation: "Once upon a time the English knew who they were."[19] He went on to ask the question, What does being English mean? Three hundred or so pages later, he had not really answered the question. In Paxman's defence, perhaps he was overwhelmed by the confusion that surrounds the concept of Englishness, and the conundrum of when to use *English* instead of *British* and vice versa. Evidence of this confusion was apparent throughout our testimonies, with interviewees often using the words *English* and *Brit* interchangeably, and sometimes saying one when they meant the other. For example, Robert Baldwin, when asked what he did in Canada to remember his Englishness, replied that he went to the Glengarry Highland Games, a quintessentially Scottish occasion. Here Baldwin was confusing Englishness with Britishness.

At the end of World War II in both England and Canada, there was a great sense of patriotic pride in victory, as demonstrated by the intense feelings expressed by Sue Jones at the beginning of Chapter 1. In the post-war years, as we have seen, the Canadian state actively sought to develop Canadian civic national consciousness. The British state—and we do mean British, as there is no form of specifically English government—was less proactive. Nonetheless, there were combinations of events and influences that contributed toward changing perceptions of what it meant to be English. Andrew Marr in *The Day Britain Died* highlighted four key factors. These were the demise of the British Empire, the emergence of the European Community, the impact of the globalized economy, and Celtic nationalism and devolution.[20] Alan Thoms commented on some of these influences when he was explaining why he emigrated to Canada: "In the 1950s, there was a certain stagnation in all of Europe.... There was definitely a malaise. It was the end of the colonial era. We just had, in 1954, the defeat of the French in Indochina. Egypt had come along, caused all kinds of trouble.... India and Pakistan had gone in 1948. You had African countries agitating, and various troubles."

There are other contemporary factors that we could add to the mix: fear of the atomic bomb, persistent relative economic decline, loss of respect for the royal family, the secularization of society, and so on. Given the possibility for confusion about what being English means, what being Canadian means, and what identity in general means, we must let the interviewees speak for themselves and leave you, the reader, to determine, with occasional guidance from ourselves, how best to employ the tools suggested earlier in this chapter.

Becoming a Canadian citizen

One way to approach the complexity of identity is to explore our immigrant interviewees' attitudes to taking out Canadian citizenship and acquiring Canadian passports (the latter being a separate transaction). Both activities provide an outward and visible sign of an individual's sense of belonging, loyalty, and patriotism. Nearly all our interviewees had taken out Canadian citizenship; some acted soon after arrival when, for those arriving in the 1940s and '50s, becoming a citizen was a relatively mundane and near-automatic process for British subjects; others waited a number of years, by which time becoming a citizen involved taking citizenship tests and participating in elaborate loyalty-swearing ceremonies. Nearly nine out of ten of our interviewees held Canadian passports, with the remainder having only British passports.[21]

At first sight these figures would appear to indicate that this group of immigrants had an overwhelming desire to be seen as Canadian; it would be reasonable to assert that they felt Canadian and were proud to be Canadian. This hypothesis receives further corroboration when we find that two of the interviewees, even though they held only British passports, were both sworn Canadian citizens. There is, however, evidence to contradict the hypothesis. Of the large percentage who held Canadian passports, more than half also held British passports. What do these joint passport holders tell us about their sense of national identity?

Close scrutiny of the testimonies reveals that, for many, taking out citizenship and deciding which passport or passports one held was not a big issue, and for some it was primarily a matter of convenience or necessity. Tom Johnston was obliged to become a Canadian citizen when he became a security officer in the Royal Canadian Navy (see Chapter 4). Isobel Sinclair-Chang admitted to never really thinking about citizenship until her

Chinese-born husband thought of standing for political office in Peterborough. It was a legal requirement that candidates for public office be Canadian citizens. Similarly, only Canadian citizens, after Trudeau's reforms, had the vote. It was for these reasons that the Changs became Canadian citizens. Isobel noticeably failed to answer her own rhetorical question, "Where is your allegiance?" Her cavalier and pragmatic attitude to identity was reinforced later in her testimony when she talked about passports:

> I would never pay for two passports. I'm so stingy, and the British one was expensive, so if I had to buy the Canadian one, I did not think I'll buy the British one, but I've all kinds of friends who run around with two.... I've had funny experiences travelling back to the UK. I've been scolded: "You're British, why are you in this Canadian line?" I said, "I've got a Canadian passport." "You were born in Britain, you're always British, you should be in the Brit line".... Another time, I go in, they stamp my passport: "You can stay for six months, but you can't work."

A number of interviewees commented on the convenience of holding two passports, especially being able to choose the shortest line at immigration and border controls. Noel Taylor provided a bizarre example of the potential problems of having only one passport. The Taylors originally emigrated to Canada with one child, who became a landed immigrant. They had a second child in Ontario, who was Canadian, and when in England for an extended stay, they had a third child, who was English. On arrival at Canadian immigration they were faced with three queues—for Canadians, landed immigrants, and others. Noel's wife spent an anxious time rushing between the queues looking after her children. Doreen and Arthur Wood were regular travellers back to England and went on vacations to the Caribbean and the United States. Being holders of only British passports, they feared they might not be allowed back into Canada. They also began experiencing difficulties on crossing the Canadian-American border, where they were questioned by U.S. customs officials:

> Doreen: The last time when we went to the States we were having problems with our British passports, they wanted to know why we lived in Canada.

> Arthur: They were questioning, the customs people were questioning...

Doreen: Yes it got more difficult

Arthur: "How come you're Canadian citizens when you're travelling on British passports?"

Doreen: So they wouldn't even go by the passport half the time; they would go by this [citizenship card]. It was getting more difficult, so we decided we would get the Canadian passport. So we have both now and I don't know whether that's legal or what, I don't know, but anyway we have both.

Border officials were also instrumental in Hannah Marriot's decisions about citizenship and passports. Before she and her French husband started a family, they travelled extensively throughout North America and the Caribbean. Hannah's husband first encountered problems as a result of having a French passport. According to Hannah, American officials gave her husband a hard time because of his French nationality and because they did not like General de Gaulle, who was the president of France at the time. The solution was the acquisition of a Canadian passport. Hannah, however, did not follow her husband's example nor did she become a Canadian citizen. "There didn't seem to be any point as far as I could see," she said, "except that I couldn't stand for office, public office of any kind, and I couldn't vote, but I didn't really care about that much either, in those days." Hannah was shamed into changing her mind some years later by a well-meaning Canadian immigration officer:

It got to the point, when the immigration officers, when I was coming back into Canada, were remarking on this rather tatty piece of paper [confirming her landed immigrant status] that I was producing and saying, "Oh my goodness, you've been here since … and you're still not a Canadian." And so I thought, "Oh well, I should do this." And it was only, I suppose, about fifteen or seventeen years ago that I applied and took the test and got my Canadian citizenship. And so we now have both Canadian and European passports, which we keep up, but…to me it hasn't really made much difference. I do vote now, take my civic duties seriously [laughs].

Attitudes varied regarding the significance of taking out citizenship or acquiring a Canadian passport. The step was not always a deeply meaningful experience, or one that created new and emotive bonds with the immigrants' new homeland. Peter Whilesmith had an ambivalent attitude. He took out Canadian citizenship at the first possible opportunity because he worked in Canada and felt a sense of belonging. Otherwise citizenship was of no great significance, and both he and his wife felt that "a piece of paper doesn't really make any difference." Avril Cranston recalled, "We had become Canadians quite soon after we got married just because we thought we should; we're Canadian, we live here, we like the country, we're not going back to England to become British, we liked what Canadians stood for." Canada was not warlike, Avril said, as were the U.S. and Britain. Canada stood for peacekeeping; it was a polite, community-oriented society, and so on. Tom and Sarah Walsh were also reflective as they explained how they felt. They both held Canadian citizenship and passports. They had positive feelings for both England and Canada. Sarah summed up the immigrant experience, as she saw it, in the words of a story a Polish immigrant friend had told her: "He said something that stayed with me, and it's going to stay with me. He said, 'I love Canada as I love my wife and I love Poland as I love my mother, and you can love your wife without being disloyal to your mother.'" By way of contrast, Pat Connor, who arrived in Canada in 1968 as a thirty-year-old mother of one, felt that she would be disloyal to her mother if she became a Canadian citizen. Such a step would be a rejection of her English and British identity, and was one step too far. Pat steadfastly refused to become a Canadian citizen and held only a British passport. It took forty years of living in Canada and the death of her mother for Pat to begin to think whether she should be a Canadian citizen as were all her children and grandchildren. Pat recalled the changes in the legislation on voting, under Pierre Trudeau:

> When I first came I could vote, and then he changed something,
> I don't know what it was he changed, but at first he lowered the
> residence years from five to three for immigrants and allowed them
> to apply for citizenship. And, this is how he ended up getting a lot of
> the immigrant votes. And, uh, but before he did that I had voted a
> couple of times and then all of a sudden I couldn't because I wasn't a
> Canadian citizen…I wonder if I'd pass it [the citizenship test] now?

You get to a point where you, you know, as you get older you don't
retain a lot of things, you know, so I would really have to study hard,
you know. I mean, I know who's in, I know who the Prime Minister is,
but it changes so often these days, you know, sometimes they're only
in for a short period of time and then it's somebody new, you know.

Embracing Canada

Myths, traditions, and icons are all crucial components in the construction
of national, group, and individual identities. How did our English immigrants adapt and respond to these components in either forming a Canadian identity or clinging on to their Englishness? Many of the interviewees
commented on the vastness of Canadian space and its wilderness, comparing them to the compact green English countryside, the small houses, the
fenced-in gardens, the density of the population, and the narrow, winding
roads. Embracing the Canadian outdoor experience was, for some, a psychological demonstration of their enthusiastic acceptance of their new life.

This pattern of behaviour included a penchant for cottage life in the
summer. While living in Toronto, Abbi Andrews and her husband had a
cottage on an island north of Peterborough. Going for the weekend involved
at least a three-hour drive, and then they had to trans-ship to the island. But
in Abbi's words, "We just loved it there." When the Andrews later moved to
Ottawa, they wanted their children to experience what it was like to be at a
cottage, so they bought one beside the Rideau River within an hour's commute of Ottawa. At age two and three, the children had been too young to
appreciate the first cottage, and at age fourteen and fifteen were rather too
old to like the second, especially since there were no young people nearby.
The sons, however, were eventually given joint ownership of the cottage in
the hope that they would enjoy it later in life.

Janet and Kenneth Cecil similarly considered acquiring a cottage, but
they did not like the idea of commuting. Instead, they installed a swimming
pool in the backyard. When they moved to a bigger house, however, they
did not miss the swimming pool or the hordes of neighbourhood children
who came every day to swim in it. Mary Irvine in Calgary was close to
mountains, rather than to cottage country. She and her husband built a log
cabin on land he had bought fifty miles from Calgary, with an amazing
view of forest and mountains, and English neighbours nearby. Although

12. Picnic in Rockies: The extensive Canadian wilderness appealed to many English immigrants. Photo credit: By permission Rosemary Sloan.

Mary and her husband enjoyed great days at the cabin, they eventually sold the property to the president of the University of Calgary, after receiving a serious scare when their young son wandered off into bear country. Mary's story resonates with the lives of Canada's early pioneering settlers and is worth repeating in full. Putting her tale in context, recall that Mary had arrived in Toronto as a twenty-two-year-old looking for adventure and eventually married a British Olympic skier in Calgary. They were delighted to receive a gift of $1,000 from the groom's mother:

> We had this eighty acres of land at a place called Water Valley in Alberta, and we built a two-storey log cabin. We'd started before my daughter was born because I can remember helping peel a mile and a quarter of

logs when I was pregnant [laughs]. My husband built it and put it up
with the help of this wonderful cockney family that lived in the middle
of the foothills. They'd come out to Canada after the war and they were
called Dave and Vi Wilson, and they were absolutely wonderful. They
came to our wedding because we got to know them. We had bought
this land before we were married and, um, they existed in their little
wooden house, it was always warm. Vi was always cheerful. We used
to go [there], when we went up to look at our land and start building.
We always stopped off and had a cup of tea with them and learned
about all their excitement when they had immigrated to Canada
from the East End of London. It was amazing; what a transition.

Anyway, they had two children I think. We had bear and we had
cougar and all sorts of things, none of which did we ever see
but there were certainly signs of it all the time.... I mean it had
the most amazing view; you looked across twenty-seven miles
of forest and you saw the mountains, and there was of course
nothing in between.... I can remember an eclipse of the sun, and
I can remember so many people coming to visit us there and just
staying and looking, and being with us for picnics and things....

Another great friend of mine, Sally Roberts...she and her husband
Michael were in the hotel business, and Sally was English.... She and
I took our children—this was when we each had two children—up
to the foothills to pick raspberries, wild raspberries, and my
eighteen-month-old son Christopher disappeared into the forest,
and...I sort of went practically hysterical rushing through the forest
calling out his name. We had just taken delivery of a bull terrier
from England and...I had forgotten that Duffus was with us, and
do you know that dog stayed with Christopher, and I went through
the forest calling out Christopher's name, and suddenly the dog
barked, and that was, oh, what a relief. In actual fact he hadn't left
the path; he'd gone round, but we had a sort of curved driveway to
go in from the road allowance to the cabin... and it was, you know,
he could have been snatched by a bear or a cougar at any time...

But I've jumped ahead just to finish that story....Um, the Trans-
Canada Highway across the mountains, across the Rogers Pass, was
not completed until 1962 and we went on various trips on the July

weekends, two years in a row, in our little Volkswagen with Sarah who was in a carry cot in the back seat—no seat belts, nothing. And we would take off round the Big Bend, which was the only way of getting around, and that was only available to go through in the summer and it would follow the Columbia River round and come down. We used to camp by the side of the road and I used to wash her diapers in the streams [laughs]. I hope nobody was downstream collecting up the water to drink [laughs]. Anyway, it was wonderful eating all those cherries in the Okanagan, we'd do it in a weekend and think nothing of it. And...I can remember when we went on one occasion across the Monashees; ... you saw sixty miles to somewhere and you thought, oh that'll take us an hour but of course it took four hours.

The early years of Mary's marriage saw her and her family engaging with and accepting a number of stereotypical traditions, myths, and icons that contribute toward forming a Canadian national identity, including: log cabins, the Rockies, forests, wildlife, camping, picnicking, and skiing. Paradoxically, Robin Lanson, who married a Canadian after he landed in Nova Scotia in 1959, used the outdoors in England to cling to his sense of being English. Robin was a keen hiker, a hobby he had come to love when he was a boy scout and national serviceman during his youth in Croydon and Catterick. He had kept up the close friendships he forged with the fellow hikers of his youth. On his sixty-fifth birthday in 1998, he arranged a reunion with his old mates and went hiking across Dartmoor. For the next ten years he returned to England to go hiking in Cornwall, Yorkshire, and Pembrokeshire[22] among other places. It would be incorrect, however, to assume that Robin saw himself primarily as an Englishman. When asked how he perceived his national identity, he answered:

Well I'm a Brit, culturally I'm still a Brit, I think, but as far as anything else I'm Canadian. I got my citizenship in 1967 as part of a centennial project if you like and...I've got a Canadian wife, I've got four Canadian children, two Canadian grandchildren, so in that way I'm Canadian, you know, but sort of. Well, I mean I still have a soft spot for England or for the U.K. I'd never go back there to live but I do like to visit and particularly the hiking, because here I do not like hiking in the woods, because I can't see any point in it. I've been to New Hampshire to the White

Mountains, and you do, after two or three hours of flogging up through the woods, you do actually come out to where you can see something, but it doesn't compare in any way to the Lake District or to North Wales, or to anything like that so I tend to do most of my hiking over there.

Robin thus exhibited a sense of dual or multiple identities—a topic we shall examine in more depth later in the chapter.

Sport is another outlet for expressions of national identity. Colin Howell in his book *Blood, Sweat, Cheers: Sport and the Making of Modern Canada*, pointed out that some sports historians argue that, "sport is a form of 'social capital' that encourages civic improvement and loyalty to the community, and inculcates notions of fair play and social peace."[23] International sporting events offer opportunities to display national feelings. The Olympic and Winter Olympic games are occasions when national feelings peak, as evidenced by extensive media coverage and the upsurge of retail sales of Canadian sporting memorabilia, replica garments, and flags. The Montreal Olympics in 1976 offered immigrants the opportunity to display their colours. Charlotte Hinton realized that was the first time she felt Canadian: she found herself "cheering for the Canadians. That's when I knew."

Different feelings about nationality manifested themselves when Robert and Margaret Baldwin watched the London 2012 Olympic Games on television. They admitted they wore metaphoric Union Jacks—and that was forty-six years after they originally landed in Canada. Robert Baldwin also confessed to wearing a metaphoric maple leaf when Canadian athlete Simon Whitfield won gold in Sydney and bronze in Beijing. Baldwin observed, "We are confused puppies."

In sporting terms Canada is substantially different from other parts of the British Commonwealth where English immigrants also settled. Canada has an essentially North American sporting tradition. North American football, ice hockey, basketball, and curling are all popular in Canada, but they are minority sports, if played at all, in places like Australia, New Zealand, South Africa, and Scotland. In those countries there is an English sporting heritage where games like soccer, rugby, and cricket are more popular. This means that English immigrants to Canada cannot use sport, in the same way, to mediate their sense of national identity. We saw in Chapter 6 how families, especially through their children, engaged in traditional Canadian sporting activities like hockey, skating, and other winter sports. Whether we can ascribe this to their becoming Canadian or because the typically English sports were not available is difficult to say. As we saw, Robert Baldwin learned how to coach soccer for his Canadian-born sons. He can also be seen regularly in the Heart and Crown pub in Ottawa's Byward Market, alongside other expats wearing replica English jerseys and cheering on the English rugby team during the Six Nations tournament.[24]

In countries where there is an English sporting tradition, it is easier for immigrants to use sport as an expression of their new national identity. In New Zealand an immigrating English coal miner found it took only two years to become "a committed NZer even cheering for the All Blacks [the New Zealand rugby team] against the Poms."[25] Similarly, a middle-aged English woman who migrated to Scotland demonstrated her transfer of allegiance when she painted her face with a Saltire [the Scottish flag] when she supported the Scottish rugby team at Murrayfield in Edinburgh.[26]

As noted at the beginning of this chapter, Anthony Smith considered that a shared myth of descent, a common history, and a distinctive shared culture were key elements in national identity formation. Being part of the British Empire in the past and now the British Commonwealth, the Canadian nation has much in common with England. Both England and Canada share similar parliamentary and legal institutions, and the same head of state in the shape of Elizabeth II, and George VI before her. Strangely, our testimonies were surprisingly silent when it came to references to the Royal Family. This is almost certainly because royalty was not considered to be important by the interviewees in the telling of their life stories. One of the rare mentions was by Peter Semple, who recalled the time when he became a Canadian citizen. When asked to swear allegiance to the Queen of Canada, he refused because he had been "allieged" [sic] to her since he had been born. A tolerant Canadian official said, "Okay forget it," and Semple became a citizen. The interviews of English immigrants conducted by Jim Hammerton were more directed than the free-flowing nature we adopted in our interviews. Hammerton always asked questions about royalty, usually toward the end of the interview. Anne Graves admitted to being patriotically royalist when she lived in England, keeping detailed scrapbooks and "sitting glued to the radio the day Prince Charles was born." When she lived in Canada, she admitted that her loyalty to the Queen "wasn't a big thing" and "it wasn't something they talked about."[27] A number of interviewees recalled going to see the Queen when she visited Canada, but this was more of an exciting day out rather than a statement about being English, British, or Canadian. Hugh Woods said that Canada did not feel like a foreign country because, when he went to a movie theatre in the 1950s, everybody stood to attention and sang "God Save the Queen" while images were projected of Her Majesty "mounted on a horse outside Buckingham Palace."[28] Overall, even with different interviewing techniques, the role of the monarch as a shared head of state appeared to be of little consequence in the formation or reaffirmation of national identity.

Can the same be said of the flag, another iconic identity symbol? The adoption of the maple leaf flag that replaced the Red Ensign was a topic of heated debates, aired with regularity by politicians, journalists, and commentators from the late 1940s to the 1960s, and culminating in the great flag debate in 1964. Much has been written about this episode elsewhere, and there is no need for us to go over that ground again. On 15 February 1965 the Red Ensign, with its Union Flag overtones of colonialism, was lowered on Ottawa's Parliament Hill and the new maple leaf flag run up in its place. February 15 has remained "flag day" ever since. Given the iconic significance of the new flag, feelings about the flag formed another area of relative silence in the interviewees' testimonies. Noel Taylor was an exception. He recalled, "If I'm travelling in Europe or wherever, I sometimes wear a maple leaf, and people look at it, and immediately there's a warmth there. It really is amazing how well regarded Canadians are, as opposed to Americans [laughs]." Here Noel is using his flag pin to let everyone know he is Canadian. Providing further evidence of his new sense of identity he has also used the concept of "other"; he is a Canadian because he is not an American.

Francophone Canada, English immigrants and issues of Canadian identity

No assessment of national identity in Canada would be complete without considering francophone Canada—particularly Quebec, whose linguistic, cultural, and historical distinctiveness made it stand out from the rest of Canada.[29] Many of our interviewees settled in Quebec or other parts of francophone Canada. Some stayed, and others moved on. In addition, Québécois nationalism had a major impact on the construction of Canadian national identity in the postwar era, thus potentially affecting all English immigrants whether or not they lived in Quebec. Our interviewees'

testimonies make an interesting contribution to the complex study of anglophone and francophone relationships.

In the two decades after World War II, Quebec caught up with the rest of
Canada economically, demographically, and socially. According to historian
J.M. Bumsted, Quebecers were no longer the "simple, priest-ridden, rural
folk of the old Anglo myth."[30] As *Le Devoir* pointed out in 1954, the "socioeconomic change that was taking place in Quebec was literally unparalleled
in any other industrialized society."[31] It was against this background that
a profoundly anti-clerical nationalism emerged. As in other nationalist
movements, such as those in Northern Ireland, Kenya, and Wales, there
were groups bent on violence and extremism in pursuit of their ends. During the 1960s Quebec experienced mailbox bombings culminating in the
October Crisis in 1970, when the federal government declared a "state of
apprehended insurrection" under the War Measures Act. Political terrorism
and violence arrived in Canada when the Front de Libération du Québec
(FLQ) kidnapped James Cross, a senior trade commissioner at the British
Trade Commission in Montreal. The FLQ referred to Cross as a "representative of the ancient racist and colonial British system." The kidnapping was
followed, less than a week later, by the abduction and subsequent assassina-
tion of Pierre Laporte, Quebec's deputy premier and minister of labour. The
FLQ referred to him as the minister for unemployment and assimilation.

The tense atmosphere of the October Crisis deeply affected Vicky Williams, who came to Canada in the 1950s. Although she had not become a
Canadian citizen, she shared the fears of many Canadians that their country
was on the brink of disaster and soon to be torn apart. Realizing how closely
she identified with the fate of the Canadian nation led Vicky to apply for
citizenship at this unpropitious time. As she recalled:

> I was in Quebec City with some francophones when Laporte was
> kidnapped. I also remember vividly the third of September 1939
> when war was declared, and the atmosphere on those two days was
> incredibly similar, incredibly similar, and I remember standing on
> the steps of the Chateau crying, with the news, the news of Laporte's
> kidnapping, and I remember thinking that if you care that much for
> this country, you get in. And I had the right because I came over in
> '66 before the citizenship thing came in. If you had a U.K. background
> there was no real difficulty, and I'd become a landed immigrant in

Fredericton in 1957.... I remember taking the citizenship oath and
I was the only person that day and the Judge said to me, "You're
joining us now"? [laughs] and I said, "Yes I'm joining you now."

Vicky was somewhat unusual among our interviewees in linking her personal identity so immediately with national identity. Having lived in New
Brunswick and Ontario and been accepted by both francophone and anglophone communities, she hoped she had something to contribute to Canada.

Elizabeth Summers also had experience of Canada's "two nations." In
her case it was the sharp contrast that she perceived between " French
Montreal" and " Anglo Kingston." Elizabeth became aware that "something
was brewing" after she landed in Montreal in 1960 to pursue her career as
an occupational therapist:

> We had students from the University of Montreal and McGill working
> with me in the department of occupational therapy at the Montreal
> Children's Hospital, and even before I'd heard the term "the Quiet
> Revolution" I would worry because the francophone students, I can
> only describe it as I just felt all the time, they had this chip on their
> shoulder, and it worried me. You know they were keen to learn...
> everybody was fine. But there was just something about those girls,
> as most of them were female...that didn't quite click, you know, there
> was something about it. Of course in Montreal there was the Montreal
> Children's Hospital and then St Justine's Hospital for Children, it was
> a French/English sort of division. In the children's hospitals there were
> teachers for the children; there were French Protestants, there were
> French Catholics, English Protestant, English Catholic you know,
> everything went by religion. What the religion of the child was, that
> [determined] what teacher they would have in the hospital.... That
> was new to me, that education and religion went hand in hand....
> French people were tired of being trodden on by the English because
> in those days in 1960 English was the predominant language for
> business...although medicine and law and certainly religion were very
> much in the francophone hands as well. So in a way when the Quiet
> Revolution [happened], which was of course when Pierre Laporte was
> captive.... I wasn't in Montreal at the time, but it really didn't surprise
> me because I had felt there was something brewing when I was there.

Elizabeth was not surprised by the crisis in Quebec but neither was she as profoundly affected by it as Vicky. Although Elizabeth related the evolution of Canadian nationalism to the Quiet Revolution, she attached even more importance to Expo 1967 in Montreal as a turning point.[32] Held at the centennial of Canadian confederation, Expo 67 gave Canadians a chance to demonstrate to the world what they had achieved as a nation. Having lived in Australia as well as England and Canada, Elizabeth linked Canadian national identity to the decline of the British Empire in particular and imperialism in general in the postwar world. In her words:

> I think in a way what has changed and certainly, certainly for the good, [is] that this "Brit" business has just become secondary and that Canada, if you like, is for Canadians, and you know Expo really did that …. I'm one of those people that think Expo 67 put Canada on the map because it just showed, you know, what we could do…. Canada is proud of itself, I'm very proud of it as you can hear, and thank goodness you know, it is no longer British dominated but that has happened all over the world. I mean that was no different because that was happening everywhere at that time.

Elizabeth enthusiastically embraced a Canadian national identity, becoming a Canadian citizen in the early 1970s; being a proud Canadian accorded with her personal values and aspirations. She believed that Canada gave her greater freedom, equality, and opportunities to grow both personally and professionally than she could ever have achieved in England.

The October Crisis and Quebec nationalism later intruded in an unexpected way into the citizenship decision of one of our interviewees. Charles Hall, who lived continuously in Montreal since migrating to Canada in 1947, finally succumbed to the pressure of his wife and others and agreed to become a Canadian citizen in the early 1980s. He attributed his delay not to the situation in Quebec, but to his deep sense of English identity. Influenced by his English school and the Royal Navy, he always felt as soon as he stepped off the plane on English soil that he was "home again." The acquisition of Canadian citizenship was possible for him only because he could also keep his British citizenship. The preparation for Canadian citizenship, however, was made more memorable because the woman who guided him through the process was Mme Laporte, widow of the assassinated Quebec minister. While Charles's identification with the Canadian nation may have been somewhat tenuous, he was nonetheless strongly opposed to the breaking up of the country.[33]

The turmoil in Quebec affected some prospective English migrants as well as those already residing in Canada. When Tom and Sarah Walsh began considering migration to Montreal in 1971, they were conscious of all the news reports on the October Crisis and the FLQ. They came to terms with the possibility of violence by comparing Canada and Britain. As Tom explained: "My thoughts were that moving into that environment, moving into Quebec at that time, didn't appear any more threatening than having the troubles in Northern Ireland being relatively close. I mean, living and working in the West Country it's not exactly on your doorstep, but on the other hand, it's close."

Sarah agreed: "What I remember more was the activities in Britain with the IRA and leaving Heathrow with all the army trucks and the soldiers that were out at the airport." From her perspective as the mother of a sixteen-month-old baby, however, the welfare of the family was more significant than the political situation. "When we arrived in Montreal, I was more concerned about…getting settled…. I think as a young family you are more focused on your personal situation." The Walshes' ability to compare the Canadian political situation favourably to Britain, as well as a focus on family, assisted both Tom and Sarah to feel Canadian and at home in Canada within a few years. On their return trips to England, Tom felt like an outsider, whereas Sarah felt like she was simply revisiting a different stage in her life.

While the violence surrounding the October Crisis made a dramatic political impact across Canada, legislation passed by the Quebec government to reinforce the French language and culture in Quebec had a more sustained effect on the lives of English immigrants in the province. The social and economic tensions surrounding the increasingly restrictive language legislation have already been explored in Chapter 4, but some attention needs to be given here to the implications for national identity. Québécois nationalists considered the French language to be vital for the preservation of their distinct society. The French language in the nineteenth and early twentieth centuries had been valued as the guardian of the Roman Catholic faith in Quebec. By the latter twentieth century, it had become the means of preserving a distinct francophone identity against the pervasive inroads of North American mass popular culture and advertising.

For Québécois nationalists, however, the French language was much more than a protective barrier or even a necessary tool that they wanted to have accepted for employment. The French language was integrally intertwined with the culture; their cultural and national identity could not exist without the language that expressed it. Hence the urgent need to defend the French language, in part against increasing numbers of immigrants who were choosing to identify with anglophone society.

Those among our interviewees who felt most oppressed by the language legislation drew upon different concepts of national identity in articulating their position. They used the discourse of citizenship and rights, not of culture. As discussed in Chapter 4, Margaret Baldwin described being made to feel like "second-class citizens" as a result of the subordination of the English language, and Charlotte Hinton objected that "slowly, slowly, they ate away at all our rights." Margaret and Charlotte believed strongly that their democratic rights as British subjects in a British country were being abrogated. In the terms of Benedict Anderson, they also felt discrimination and rejection; rather than being invited into the imagined national community, they were being excluded from it. Not all English immigrants in Quebec felt so excluded and only some more extreme Québécois nationalists were unaccepting of immigrants, but the different concepts of national identity were nonetheless significant. The language legislation was followed by two Quebec referendums, in 1980 and 1995, on the issue of sovereignty for Quebec. Surgeon Reggie Allen found himself "spooked" by the closeness of the 1995 referendum in which the No side (opposed to Quebec sovereignty) won by the narrow majority of 50.58 percent. Allen, with his family, moved to Toronto after having lived and worked in Montreal for seventeen years.

In response to the challenge of Quebec nationalism, the federal government took action to promote greater equality for francophones across Canada. In 1963 Pearson's Liberal government appointed a Royal Commission on Bilingualism and Biculturalism, with instructions to recommend ways of managing Canada's cultural dualism. The reporting and implementation of the recommendations mainly occurred while Pierre Trudeau was prime minister (1968–79 and 1980–84), so implementation was associated with the Trudeau administration. A central feature of Trudeau's new federalism was the Official Languages Act of 1969, which declared English and French to be official languages with equal status in all institutions under federal jurisdiction.

A number of our interviewees commented on changes to Canada's iden-tity during the Trudeau era. John Steven found Canada still quite English when he arrived in 1969 as an employee of the federal government. Then, he recalled, "it gradually changed, particularly when Trudeau was in power. It all gradually changed over a period of five to ten years, slowly so that you didn't quite notice, but then, you know, bilingualism came in." John and his family adjusted without major difficulties to the change. His two oldest children "ended up in French immersion [schools], so they ended up being bilingual so they are doing quite nicely in the government." Similarly, Jeremy Plunkett, who was also working for the federal government, had to take the government's French course in order to comply with the bilingual-ism quota in the Geological Survey of Canada office. He did extremely well in the course and now finds his knowledge of French to be a valuable asset when travelling in France. His fluent bilingualism makes him feel Canadian and, he added, also European. Thus, for these professional immigrants, the adjustment to the new language culture in the federal government did not pose the same identity issues as did the legislative changes that affected daily life in Quebec.

"The England I had left was no longer there"

In John Osborne's much acclaimed and controversial play, *Look Back in Anger*, Colonel Redfern returns to England in 1956, after having been away since Edwardian times. He comments: "The England I had left was no longer there."[34] Our interviewees, contemplating their identities in the early twenty-first century, also recognized that the England they had left behind up to sixty years before had changed. Some used the old England they had left behind to mediate their identities, while others used the England that had changed, or at least how they perceived it had changed.

Margaret Bell, who came as a newlywed to Alberta in 1968, considered herself "a pretty analytical sort of person," who reread her diaries before her interview. She also reads, weekly on the Internet, her old local newspaper from Brighton. Her first impression of Canada was the space: "Calgary in '68 was enormous, it was spread out over a huge area." She and her husband en-joyed an active social life as well as camping in Banff National Park. Margaret admitted to "feeling Canadian quite soon." She also admitted to thinking often about going back to England, once during her thirties when she confessed to going through a "mid-life crisis," and then after her parents died in Brighton in 2000 and 2001. She was a frequent traveller to England both before and after her parents died. The interview gave Margaret an ideal opportunity to ponder her identity, and this was the dominant theme of the interview.

Occasionally contradictory, always thoughtful, Margaret negotiated her past in attempting to affirm her identity. She became a Canadian citizen in 1973 and spent twenty-four happy years working for the federal government in the Department of Indian Affairs and Elections Canada. Her work took her all over the country. She felt able to call Canada home, but with a "reservation." "Brighton—my roots are definitely there, and when I go back, I feel, when I get there, I feel like this is where I belong." Regardless of this pull, Margaret chooses to remain in Canada. She objected to overpopulation in England:

> What struck me, only in the last couple of years, is the sense of there being so much pressure on the landscape and on the infrastructure, you know the roads, the houses...I have always been aware of the open spaces over here versus the southeast of England, the smallness and everything close together and the density of population. And I think, as I have gotten older, I've realized there are actually some unpleasant things happening over in Britain, and one of them, I think, has a lot to do with this pressure that I feel that there's just too many people.

The unpleasant things she referred to were social problems and crime, "the terrible, terrible things people do to each other." Her final reason for staying in Canada: "I think the bottom line now is financial, you know the [lower] cost of meals, the cost of housing, the cost of living in general."

Doreen Wood was another interviewee who mentioned social problems in England. In a visit back to her home town of Nottingham in 1999, she felt that social conditions had "really deteriorated, there seemed to be a lot of single mums, young single mums pushing strollers everywhere." "And a lot of crime," added her husband Arthur. Regardless of the drawbacks, the Woods conceded that they would go back to England if they did not have family in Canada. "The English way of life is, at least to my memory, is much, much slower pace, a much easier-going pace," Arthur said. "Here... you're in the fast lane and it's all statistics and it's all money and it's all impressionists [sic] and all this sort of thing whereas the village life in England, it's much more docile. I love that feeling. I suppose in retirement it's one of those things." In a self-deprecatory put-down, Arthur explained his attitude in the words of his children: "Dad you're old-fashioned."

After an unsettling first year in Canada, Jeremy and Mary Charles returned to England, taking the "$1,000 cure" (see Chapter 4). After a short time back in England Mary realized, "I don't like it here. I want to go home." This was a turning point in their lives, when their memories of England became less positive. Mary observed, "I go back to England and I don't find it's England anymore because it's so full of foreigners." Her husband interrupted with, "Tsk, tsk, racist, racist." So ended that strand of the discussion. Similar attitudes, however, were not uncommon among our interviewees. This was surprising, since many of the interviewees were sympathetic to Canadian ideals of multiculturalism, and some were empathetic to the plight of the First Nations. Kenneth Cecil found that, "Canada was very British when we first landed in 1964, to the point where about the second Sunday I was in Canada, early May, I went to a cricket match and watched the Canadair cricket team play the Montreal Motor Works cricket team." Today, he felt that British identity has diminished, even back home:

> There's been a lot of changes in England since we left and I don't
> think people who lived there for the last forty years notice them as
> much as someone who's come away, stayed away, and then went back
> would. There's a lot of changes in Bradford but there are more Muslim
> mosques than there are churches of all Christian denominations put
> together, and that's something that you can't help but notice. I was
> extremely irritated one year when the Immigration Officer in London's
> Heathrow Airport who happened to be a gentleman of Pakistani
> descent, asked me all the usual questions and when he'd finished,
> welcomed me to his country. That was not the right thing to say.

Another of the interviewees offered similarly intolerant sentiments in his reminiscences:

> When I go to the pubs now in England, most of them are restaurants
> not pubs [laughs] and…if you go into a pub now and order a beer
> and some sandwiches you are shown into a restaurant right away. I
> lose [miss] the pub. We have pubs here, but they are not the same,
> because they're inhabited by young people, and pubs to me in

England are where all generations meet. You might see us in a pub in the lunchtime crowd, but in the evenings you wouldn't go to a pub, an older person, you just wouldn't be part of the crowd in a pub now. But no, I do see myself as Canadian, but I have a warm spot for England.... I remember England as it was, and when we go there, we go there a lot...we stay with [my brother's] widow and we have a great time. And we have relations in Lymington in England and up in London so we always have a good time, but we're always in the south part of England.... It's not as pleasant in middle England and northern England, the towns are totally run [sic] by the Pakistan population and so on which I guess is not my idea of what England is or was. And I read horrific things about, you know, skin heads and things like that going on in England, but...we go to the nicest parts.

Memories of how England was and perceptions of how England is, even though these are sometimes misinformed, are an important component in national identity assessment. As we have seen, it is common for individuals to feel some affinity toward both Canada and England. This leads us to the final section of this chapter: exploring dual and multiple identities. Best-selling novelist, Peter Robinson articulated—not without a degree of contradiction—the ambiguity of being Canadian and English. He took out Canadian citizenship in 1986; this was not a big decision because he could keep his British citizenship. He emphasized that he clings to his Englishness. He was not sure what being English meant, but while mediating between the past and present, he suggested it involved things like history, landscape, Elgar, the Brontës, Nick Drake, The Who, and Steel Eye Span. He says he is seen as a Yorkshireman living abroad, and Americans see him as a British crime writer.

Dual and multiple identities

Matryoshka dolls are an appropriate metaphor for identity, as noted by T.C. Smout, the Historiographer Royal in Scotland[35] and an English immigrant living there. In considering his own identity he wrote, "I am not Scottish because that is a matter of roots and upbringing, so I cannot be, but I like being here. I am an Englishman who no longer wishes to live in England: again roots and upbringing make me English. I am British: both Scotsmen and

Englishmen can claim British nationality, just as all Brits can claim European identity and all Europeans human identity. It is a nest of Russian dolls."[36]

In Louise Penny's detective novel *Bury Your Dead,* her fictional hero Gamache, the head of the famed homicide department of the Sûreté du Quebec, is reminded of a nesting doll when he thinks about the English community in Quebec City: "the most public face was North America and huddled inside that was Canada and huddled inside Canada was Quebec. And inside Quebec? An even smaller presence, the tiny English community."[37] As we saw at the beginning of the chapter, the formation of identities is a complex process; identities change over time and in different contexts, and can be modified by their reception. This was certainly the case for most of our interviewees.

Jeremy Plunkett said he felt Canadian "as soon as I'd put my foot down here." His testimony demonstrates, however, that the way he deconstructed and reconstructed his identity was considerably more complex:

My mother was a child born out of wedlock after the First World War. And my father finally found out who her mother had been...and my poor maternal grandmother had an affair with a passing soldier, became pregnant. Her husband... probably said, "I'll keep thee but not thy bastard." So my mother was put up for adoption and was adopted by a nice righteous couple...John and Eliza Thomas, whence my middle name, and so I've never known who my [grand]father is. He was definitely Lancastrian...probably the result of the Vikings when they passed through there...[laughs] a long time ago, but I've never known what the other half of my genetic side is. So I have great fun whenever anyone gets anti-Semitic; I say, "Well, I'm Jewish"—at least I could be, or anything else. And there were an awful lot of Canadian soldiers around at that time in Britain, brought through for the [war], so I could be half Canadian. And so this lovely unknown 50 percent of my ancestry leaves me free to be anyone I want. And I'm pretty sure it must have been Canadian simply because when I landed, oh immediately, I just felt totally at home, like I'd been born here.

At this point in his life story Jeremy talked about meeting his wife, a Pole, who along with her family had been chased out of Poland and France by the Nazis during the war. He then talked about going back to France with his wife on holiday, before returning to his thoughts on identity: "I feel very European; perhaps that's the better thing, I feel very Canadian and very European in that I'm certainly not North American in the same way that anyone from the United States is. That's one of the things I like about Canada, because I abhor the ignorance and the stupidity that's so prevalent in the United States, so I'm European and I'm Canadian. I'm a Euro-Canadian." When asked to define what being Canadian meant Jeremy replied:

> Er, saying thank you to a cash dispenser, [laughs] easy going, polite, deferential, very proud of the vastness of the country, very proud of the social achievements of the country as compared, to our cousins or whatever they call it, our neighbours to the south, sad about some of the stupidity of politics but still extremely proud. It's a very gentle nationalism. I've been everywhere in Canada, you know, BC, the Northwest Territories, the Maritimes, the Prairies, sometimes part of work, and sometimes just for the hell of it. And, as my wife says, "the one thing that unifies the whole of Canada is not the flag, the language, it's the mall [laughs], the shopping mall." No it's a very easygoing country, and it's vast; I don't feel claustrophobic. [By contrast,] we drive around France every couple of years or so and we're forever setting out from Paris on the A12 or something like that heading out towards Angers or Normandy or Brittany…and then looking at my map and saying, "Oh shit, we're a hundred kilometers past where we're going" because you glance at the map and you're always thinking in terms of Canadian scale… In the nineteenth century an English journalist travelling across on the train said, "It's a wonderful country but it's greatly in need of editing." You know, that's being Canadian to me, okay?

In these testimony extracts Jeremy articulated many of the themes and issues covered earlier in this chapter. He also used the concept of "other" when he observed that for Canadians, "it's like the mouse in bed with the elephant but…the United States is a wonderful country that has just fallen on hard times morally." One could argue that he provides near perfect reflection of the matryoshka doll image.

Jeremy was far from being the only interviewee with a sense of more than one identity. Roger MacKay considered he had a dual identity: "I'm a Canadian citizen, I'm a British subject. I suppose I'm a bit of both. I've lived as long in both places. I really think that I'm a bit of both. I mean I can't say I'm totally Canadian; two of my children were born in England, I happened to be over there on assignment when they were born, the younger two, so they physically were born in England...but no, I don't consider myself as any one or the other, I just consider that I'm lucky to be both."

John Steven also had a schizophrenic attitude to identity, but he expressed it in a different way. He felt he was "stranded in mid Atlantic somewhere" making him a "world citizen." Like some other interviewees, John was aware of the temporal changes surrounding ideas of what it meant to be Canadian. When he arrived in 1969, he found Canada to be "quite English":

It gradually changed, particularly when Trudeau was in power. It all gradually changed over a period of five or ten years, slowly so that you didn't quite notice, but then, you know, bilingualism came in, and a lot of the socialism measures that I had actually left the U.K. to get away from were brought in, and it all kind of gradually evolved away from this sort of environment and focus that I was quite familiar with, and it gradually evolved away into something which I wasn't so familiar with. So as I say it was driven mainly by the Trudeau administration.

In spite of, or perhaps because of, his political reservations, John went on to define his sense of national identity:

I don't see myself as being a hundred percent Canadian, although I am a Canadian citizen and I have a Canadian passport and so on. I don't sound Canadian...people always think I sound English, but on the other hand I don't think of myself as being English...I find somewhat strangely that, again this is unusual for me coming from England where people do regard themselves as English, we have these hyphenated Canadians, which was always a surprise to me. Ontarians regard themselves as Canadians first and Ontarians second, and [people from] most other provinces... regard themselves as Newfoundlanders or Quebecers or Albertans first and Canadians second. I've found this extraordinary. How the heck can you have a country where loyalties are so divided? But then Canada is kind of, in my opinion, quite loosely held together because of, well, there's been nothing to glue it really when you get down to it, apart from the railway.

Some of John's observations were endorsed by other interviewees. Peter Semple described his identity as being "mid-Atlantic." James Roland noted, "It seems to me that Ontarians tend to think of themselves as Canadians, whereas most of the rest think of themselves as belonging to the province." Intriguingly, given the patent confusion between Englishness and Britishness, he added "I think of England and Britain as kind of synonymous." The conflation of local and national identities expressed in John Steven's testimony is a relatively common phenomenon. Minorities sometimes see their identity as distinct when compared with a larger whole. This form of identity construction is not unique to Canada, as in the cases identified by John above. Many people living in the North of England will see themselves as Lancastrians or Yorkshire men and women first, and English second. While John Steven and James Roland both made perceptive comments about the dual nature of provincial and national Canadian identities, none of our interviewees talked about personal feelings of provincial identity. Most saw themselves, to one degree or another, as part-Canadian and part-English or British.

We have employed the tools and concepts discussed earlier in this chapter in our attempt to assess perceptions of national identity. The aforementioned identity scholars, however, have in our experience given insufficient prominence to the role of home and family in identity formation. Nearly all of our interviewees who had children and grandchildren saw Canada as their home with their offspring being the magnet to hold them to Canada. The immigrants' children were brought up as Canadians, went to school in Canada, and quickly acquired Canadian accents. Those who were born in Canada were automatically Canadian citizens. Most of the children enjoyed further education, pursued careers, and married in Canada. Few of the first-generation immigrants were willing to leave their children behind to retire to England or elsewhere. An exception was Mary Irvine, who retired to England to be close to her daughter. She left two sons and grandchildren behind in Canada. More typical was May Bell. "This is my home," she explained. "I'm Canadian. I'm Canadian first and English second. I mean my roots are there, but my children are born [here]. I mean, how could I leave three children and eight grandchildren to go and live there?" When she retired, May's sister, who lived in "gorgeous" Qualicum Beach on Vancouver Island, tried to persuade her to move there. Another friend tried to persuade her to move to Saskatoon. May turned down both invitations saying, "My family is all in Ottawa and apart from family, lots of friends. I've been in Ottawa, what, forty-five years and you know a lot of people in that time." May often returns to England on holiday but is adamant that she does not want to live there again. Confirming her attachment to Canada, and using the concept of "other," she moans that when in England people confuse the Canadian intonations in her accent: "[They say] 'You're an American,' and I say, 'Yes, I'm a North American, but I'm a Canadian. I don't live in the United States.' They seem to lump it all as one, you know. I said, 'There are three countries in North America; there's Mexico, the United States, and Canada, and we're all North American, but I am Canadian.'"

Conclusions

While matters relating to national identity were not generally foremost in the interviewees' testimonies, it is possible to conclude, by drilling down in the immigrants' narratives, that they generally felt deep levels of affection toward, and affiliation with, Canada. Most postwar English immigrants undoubtedly felt, to a greater or lesser degree, Canadian, usually mixed with some feelings of Englishness or Britishness. We did not interview return immigrants, however, and it is likely that many of these had negative feelings about Canada. There were also people like Pat Connor, who after thirty-eight years in Canada, said, "I don't identify myself as a Canadian. Not because I don't think Canada isn't a wonderful country, because it is, and it's been great to me. But you know, I was born in England, and it's my country and it's my Queen, and it's my roots, you know." Others, like Sue Jones, who spent most of her life in Canada, caring for her Down's syndrome son, confessed that she had not really thought about her national identity. But she went on to say, "I was not proud of being British, and I travelled on a Canadian passport...because I knew in a lot of countries, when we were travelling, a British passport was not accepted as well as a Canadian passport. We definitely think of ourselves as Canadian. Obviously we have been here all our lives, both my husband and myself. And my kids are Canadian and they think of themselves as Canadian, but they do value their British heritage, I think." The interview forced Sue to consider an issue that she rarely thought about. Her comments understandably display hesitation and uncertainty, which is even more apparent when you listen to the recording.

For those who had thought about their national identity, there were also elements of uncertainty and contradiction, often arising from a sense of confusion about what national identity actually means. Our interviewees provided many different and varied examples of what it meant to be Canadian or English. Their thoughts ranged from open spaces, to shopping malls, respectful Canadian attitudes, flags, cheering Canada or England at the Olympics, brash Americans, their Canadian children and grandchildren, opportunity, and much more. Perhaps our interviewees' reactions can best be summed up by amending the epigrammatic observation of Sarah Walsh's Polish friend: "I love Canada as I love my wife and I love England as I love my mother."

Finally, it is interesting to compare Canada's postwar English immigrants with those who settled in Scotland and Australia. In his Scottish study, Watson found that over a third of English migrants considered that they became wholly Scottish; one in ten felt they were British or English, with the majority holding multiple or dual identities.[38] That most English migrants in Scotland simultaneously held more than one national identity mirrors what we found in Canada. Hammerton and Thomson, in their study, were more hesitant in generalizing about the degree to which Poms ended up feeling British or Australian or both. They did observe, however, that there were many diverse ways in which these immigrants sought to make sense of their identities.[39] In this respect this group of Australian immigrants also mirrors the experiences of their Canadian compatriots.

AFTERWORD

Since the sixteenth century, emigration from England has formed one of the most significant population movements in history. Yet, compared with what has been written about the Scots, Irish, Jewish, Italian, German, Polish, Black, and other diasporas, little has been written about the English. Why should this be the case? "Did the English simply disappear into the host population? Or were they so fundamental, and foundational, to the Anglophone, Protestant cultures of the evolving British World that they could not be distinguished in the way Catholic Irish or continental Europeans were?"[1] On the whole, scholars have failed to explain why there are so few studies of English immigration. What is clear is that continuing interest in their place in their host societies is an important area of enquiry and study.

Our study concentrates on English immigration to Canada in the postwar era, the last period in which the English came to Canada in significant numbers. The English also migrated in large numbers to other parts of the world during these years. Our understanding of English migration to Canada is enhanced through comparison with similar studies in Australia, New Zealand, and Scotland.[2] Strictly speaking, the Australasian studies were about British migration, but both differentiate between the English, Scots, Welsh, and Northern Irish. The postwar English immigrants in these countries displayed similar characteristics, a number of which distinguished them from other groups of immigrants. Al Thomson observed that "most migration and oral history recognizes the complex interconnections between migration and the formation and development of migrant communities and ethnic identities."[3]

The testimonies of our English immigrant interviewees displayed complex interconnections, but they tended not to form and develop English ethnic communities and identities. Postwar English immigrants to Canada came from all social classes. Australia, however, attracted a larger proportion from the working class and Canada proportionately more from the professional and middle classes. The postwar English also tended to emigrate as nuclear families or as single people. There is little evidence of chain migration or migration in larger family groups. As a result, the English settled among the host society. They did not live in ethnic enclaves as did many other immigrants, say, in Chinatowns or Little Italies. This pattern of settlement helps to explain English invisibility.

The dispersion of English immigrants also contributed toward their relative ease of absorption into the host society; other factors were also influential, including home-making, children, grandchildren, success in employment, community involvement, leisure, socializing, and a general perception of a better standard of living and quality of life. All, or a mix, of these factors combined to contribute to the immigrants' perceptions of their national identity. Many began to see themselves as Canadians, Australians, New Zealanders, or Scots, or some form of dual identity combining English and/or British with that of their new country. This sense of national identity differentiated the English from other immigrant groups such as the Scots, Italians, and Chinese, who tended to cling to their original sense of national identity with greater tenacity, often into subsequent generations.

Our life-story approach to gathering oral evidence emphasized the importance of viewing the migration experience as a lifetime process, from pre-migration motivation through the excitement and trepidation of arrival to building, developing, and sustaining a new life. Understanding this personal and complex process is not easy, but the thoughtful reflections of our interviewees provided revealing insights that can often only be gained from oral history. It is important to understand the individual experiences and how they vary; inevitably, there are many differences in social backgrounds, personal aspirations, and responses to life's trials and opportunities. Making generalizations and drawing conclusions is potentially problematic. Nonetheless, a number of distinct patterns emerged from our close scrutiny of the testimonies.

The aftermath of World War II, particularly in the years up to and including the Suez crisis, witnessed high levels of emigration from England. Rationing, austerity, a housing shortage, and difficult economic conditions led many to consider emigration. At the same time, a number of Commonwealth countries, including Canada, needed immigrants and actively promoted the benefits of migration. As the British economy improved, then declined, then improved again, the flow of English emigrants continued until the 1970s. Beyond these external influences, aspiring migrants—whether single, couples, or nuclear families—had their own uniquely personal reasons for wanting to escape, to seek adventure, or to improve their quality of life. Testimony after testimony demonstrated there was usually a mix of reasons for wanting to emigrate. Vicky Williams shrewdly observed that "happenstance" was a significant factor. Happenstance was evidently the case for a number of our interviewees, who responded to unexpected opportunities. For example, John Steven got an unexpected telephone call from Canada offering him a job following a chance conversation with a work colleague in the U.K. Noel Taylor was persuaded that Canada was the land of opportunity through acquaintance with Morley Safer, the Canadian broadcaster who was studying in England when Taylor was a journalist on the *Oxford Mail*.

Having decided to emigrate, many then had to choose their destination. Some of our interviewees always wanted to go to Canada, but others considered different locations, with Australia being a popular alternative. The issue of distance and separation from families and friends in England was a critical consideration. All of our interviewees' testimonies emphasized the stresses of family separation, an issue that continued throughout the immigrants' lives in Canada. We noted how, in the early years, communication was restricted to regular air letters. The introduction of passenger jet aircraft in the 1960s enabled regular travel back to England as well as visits to Canada by family members left behind. In recent years the Internet, particularly the use of e-mail, social networking, and video conferencing has further revolutionized the immigration experience.

Our narrative in the early chapters was essentially chronological. Once we had considered the immigrants' arrival in Canada, we adopted a thematic approach to reflect the complex, multi-faceted, and overlapping nature of the testimonies' content. Settling in and building a life in Canada was related to homemaking, employment, socializing, engaging in community life, bringing up families, and much more. How people adapted to life in Canada was a complex process and differed from individual to individual, and from family to family. There were further differences arising from year of arrival, age, life stage, gender, and social class. Bearing in mind our earlier caution about the problematic nature of making generalizations, it would, nevertheless, be reasonable to assert that the majority of our interviewees perceived that their move to Canada had brought personal happiness and a sense of fulfillment. Most had achieved career success, often overcoming difficulties along the way. Most, even those experiencing family breakdowns, had successfully brought up families as Canadians. Most were actively engaged in a wide range of community pursuits, some of which were distinctly Canadian. The majority, to a greater or lesser degree, saw themselves as Canadian or part-Canadian. One measure of their commitment to their new lives in Canada was the near-universal desire to remain in Canada and not return to England in retirement. The desire to be near their Canadian children and grandchildren was a strong motive, but not the only one, in this context.

In concluding, we would like to suggest that it is regrettable that one of the most common words in titles of academic works about English immigrants is *invisible*.[4] The English, in Canada and throughout the rest of the world, represent too large and too significant a diaspora to remain under-studied. Much work remains to be done. A number of potentially productive areas for future research have emerged from this study. These include: English return migration, the Quiet Revolution and English-born immigrants in Quebec, the role of sensory perception in immigrant adaptation, transnationalism, and the impact of the Internet on the dynamics of immigrant family relationships, among others.

Throughout this book, our prime source has been the recorded testimonies of our English immigrant interviewees. We thought it appropriate to end with the final words from five of the testimonies:

Vicky Williams—landed 1956
I feel how extraordinarily fortunate that that chuckle-headed child
[laughs] came here. I mean, I think most people's lives are much more
a collection of happenstance, which they had the sense to exploit,
than plan. But I just think how fortunate I was to become Canadian.

Roger MacKay— landed 1968
One of the things that will keep me in Canada is the outdoor life. It's
always been great, you know, to get outside. We've got our mosquitoes
to worry about here, but you know what, after a while they don't really
bother you that much, blackflies a little bit in the spring, but other
than that no, not really, so that's probably why I like it so much here.

Noel Taylor—landed 1956
I'm a bit sorry there aren't more English immigrants still coming
in, 'cause I think in a way they're the best, and I don't mean that in
a chauvinistic way; they are the most desirable because they're very
well behaved and they're very well off [laughs] and they, you know,
they absorb themselves, they just fit into society that much easier. It's
much easier for me than it is for an immigrant from Lebanon or the
Philippines, or wherever. They have a problem with language; that
must be awful. That's why they have these little groups in town.

Robert Bateman—landed 1966
We have no real estate between us in the U.K. anymore. Anything
that came to us from our parents has been sold off, so we have
nowhere to put down a root. So long as the kids stay here and the
grandkids stay here, then this is where we are going to stay.

Pat Connor—landed 1968
I hope I haven't bored you too much.

ACKNOWLEDGEMENTS

This book owes an enormous debt to many people. At the top of the list are all the English immigrants who were interviewed or contributed in other ways. We appreciate the help and encouragement we have received from other members of the history department at Carleton University, especially Bruce Elliott, Del Muise, John Walsh, Carter Elwood, and Brian McKillop. We are grateful to Jim Hammerton of La Trobe University in Australia for his advice, helpful criticism, and permission to use transcripts of interviews he conducted with English immigrants in Canada. Thanks go to Patricia Roy of the University of Victoria, who provided insightful and much appreciated comments. Similarly, we are indebted to the work carried out by a number of graduate students studying oral history as part of their master's degrees. Those who conducted interviews included: Sharon Arsenault, Stacey Campbell, Adriana Gouvêa, Michael Hartmann, Kristy Martin, Erika Reinhardt, Pascale Salah, Mary-Ann Shantz Lingwood, Andréa Ventimiglia, Lorna Chisholm, Emilie Lonie, Christine McGuire, Kate Talarico, Lauren Wheeler, Jennifer Wilhelm, and Ashley Wright.

We owe a debt to a number of librarians and archivists, all of whom have been unfailingly helpful and patient. These include personnel at: Library and Archives Canada, the Archives of Ontario, Ottawa Public Libraries, Pier 21 in Halifax, the MacOdrum Library at Carleton University, and the library at the University of Dundee. Various members of the British Association of Canadian Studies, the Canadian Historical Association, and the TransAtlantic Studies Association also provided welcome guidance during the early stages of our research.

A number of organizations provided invaluable help, especially in sourcing and finding interviewees. These included: CBC Radio, the British Isles Family History Society of Greater Ottawa, the Ontario Jaguar Owners Association, the OSCAR newspaper, Alternative Old Pocklingtonians, and the Ottawa English Country Dance Club, who also attempted, unsuccessfully, it must be said, to teach one of the authors English country dancing. We are also grateful to Rosemary Sloan for allowing us to reproduce photos from her family albums.

Guy Goodman and Maggie Watson merit special thanks. Guy, an English immigrant, worked enthusiastically in helping identify and find interviewees and painstakingly proofread and commented on early drafts. Maggie, Murray Watson's long-suffering wife, spent hundreds of hours transcribing recorded interviews; it took about seven hours of typing for each hour of recording. Thanks are also owed for her persnickety proofreading of the draft text. Any mistakes in this book are ours.

Research for this book was largely self-funded by the authors, but invaluable financial support was provided by the Carleton Centre for the History of Migration, the Shannon Fund, and The Foundation for Canadian Studies in the United Kingdom.

Finally, we would like to thank Skype. You will have read in Chapter 6 how the Internet enhanced extended family communications and helped to revolutionize the immigrant experience. For us, Skype facilitated hours of transatlantic video conferencing, enabling the authors to discuss and debate the content of this book.

MB and MW

NOTES

Introduction

1   Beak, *We Came to Canada*, 9. The author landed in Toronto in 1955.

2   Oral history interview with Peter Whilesmith (pseud.). He landed in Montreal in 1952.

3   See Dunae, *Gentlemen Immigrants*; Lower, *Canadians in the Making*; and three essays in Messamore, *Canadian Migration Patterns* (Buckner, "English Canada— The Founding Generations"; Elliott, "Regional Patterns of English Immigration and Settlement in Upper Canada"; and Harper, "Crossing the Atlantic: Snapshots from the Migration Album"). There is nevertheless a small number of publications that are about English immigrants. In addition to a few diaries and biographies, the most common are about English child migrants and war brides; the latter were considered to be Canadian, having married Canadian military personnel.

4   Elliott, "The Genealogist and the Migration Historian."

5   Pooley and Whyte, *Migrants, Emigrants and Immigrants*, 4.

6   *The Times*, "Mr. Churchill's Warning, Choice Before the Nation, Call to Emigrants," Monday, 18 August 1947, 2.

7   Childs, *Britain Since 1945*, 80.

8   U.K. Data Archive, *SN 6099* – "'Brain Drain' Debate in the United Kingdom."

9   See Chapter 1.

10   Foucault, "Nietzsche, Genealogy, History" in Rabinow, *The Foucault Reader*, 89.

11   Hammerton and Thomson, *Ten pound Poms*, 16.

12   Caunce, *Oral History and the Local Historian*, 8.

13   Thompson, *The Voice of the Past*, First Edition, Chapters 1–3.

14   Thomson, Frisch, and Hamilton, "The Memory and History Debates," 34.

15   High, Graduate Student Lecture Series, Carleton University, Winter 2010.

16   Portelli, "What Makes Oral History Different," in Perks and Thomson, eds., *The Oral History Reader*, 2nd Edition (London, 1998), 36.

17   Summerfield, *Reconstructing Women's Wartime Lives*, 2.

18   Thompson, *The Voice of the Past*, First Edition, 229–31.

19   Thompson, "Life Histories and the Analysis of Social Change," in Bertaux, ed., *Biography and Society,* 290.

Chapter 1: Migration and Society in the Postwar Years

1   Pooley and Whyte, *Migrants, Emigrants and Immigrants,* 4.

2   *The Times,* "Mr. Churchill's Warning," 18 August 1947, 2.

3   *Daily Express,* 10 April 1946, 3.

4   *Ottawa Citizen,* "U.K. immigrant's concern," 13 February 1967, 7.

5   One of the best-known examples came from the Irish-born "English" general, the Duke of Wellington, who famously proclaimed, "Not everything born in a stable is a horse."

6   *Profiles United Kingdom,* 3–4. Note that these are British and U.K. statistics, of which the English will be only a part, albeit the largest part.

7   Anderson and Frideres, *Ethnicity in Canada,* 140–55.

8   Ravenstein, "The Laws of Migration," *Journal of the Statistical Society of London,* 167–235, and "The Laws of Migration," *Journal of the Royal Statistical Society,* 241–305.

9   Arango, J., D., Massey, G. Hugo, A. Kouaouci, and J. Taylor, "An Evaluation of International Migration Theory," *Population and Development Review* 20 (1994).

10   Howe and Jackson, "Immigration: A Survey of Current State of Practice and Theory," 19–23.

11   Ibid., 19.

12   See, among others, Devine, *The Scottish Nation, 1700–2000,* 486–500.

13   Barlow, Review of Elliott, "Regional Patterns of English Immigration and Settlement in Upper Canada," in Messamore, ed., *Canadian Patterns of Migration,* http://www.hnet.org/reviews/showrev.cgi?path=172751117651365 (accessed 31 May 2006).

14   Ibid.

15   Hammerton and Thomson, *Ten pound Poms*; Hammerton, "Migrants, Mobility and Modernity"; Watson, *Being English in Scotland.*

16   Anderson, *Imagined Communities*; Gellner, *Nations and Nationalism*; and Smith, *Nationalism.*

17   Richmond, *Post-War Immigrants in Canada,* 252. The point that we make here largely refers to the late twentieth century. From the nineteenth century, the Canada-U.S. border was permeable, and migrants as well as Canadians crossed it often.

18   Portes, Haller, and Guarnizo, "Transnational Entrepreneurs: The Emergence of an Alternative Form of Immigrant Adaptation," 278–294.

19   Hammerton and Thomson, *Ten pound Poms,* 9.

20   See Boyle and Halfacree, *Migration and Gender.*

21   Massey et al., "Theories of International Migration: A Review and Appraisal," 432.

22   Arango et al., "An Evaluation of International Migration Theory," 463.

23   Eurostat, *Analysis and Forecasting of International Migration,* 100.

24   National Archives, Cabinet Minute 0051, 18.

25   Ibid.

26   The East End was the heavily bombed docklands area to the east of the City of London.

27   National Archives, http://www.nationalarchives.gov.uk/documents/education/canada.pdf (accessed 10 February 2012). Also see Bilson, *The Guest Children*.

28   *Weather Magazine*, "In the Extreme," Spring 2011, 28.

29   Marwick, *British Society since 1945*, 4.

30   *The Times*, "More Production 'The Only Answer' to Inflation," 22 July 1957, 4.

31   Quoted in *Independent*, "The Austerity Issue: Don't Panic," 2 November 2008.

32   See Zelwiger-Bargielowska, *Austerity in Britain: Controls and Consumption*, 99.

33   United States Department of Agriculture War Food Administration, *Food Consumption Levels*, 121.

34   Bumsted, *The Peoples of Canada*, 314.

35   Richmond, *Post-War Immigration in Canada*, 3.

36   Canada, *House of Commons, Debates*, 1955, 1254.

37   Hawkins, *Canada and Immigration*, 238–62.

38   Ibid., 410.

39   *The Times*, "Take the crowds at the last six Wembley cup finals...And that's the number of Britons who have settled in Canada since the end of the Second World War," 21 November 1960, 5.

40   *The Times*, "Why not Canada?" 25 February 1963, 2.

41   *The Times*, "In Canada you have a wide choice of location and occupation," 29 February 1964, 4.

42   *The Times*, "There is opportunity for you in young dynamic Canada," 25 October 1967, 10.

43   Hawkins, *Canada and Immigration*, 272. Freda Hawkins, a distinguished academic scholar with an interest in Canadian immigration, emigrated to Canada from England with her husband and daughter in 1955.

44   Ibid.

45   Gaumont British News, *Canada Greets Immigrants from Britain*, Newsreel issue 1419.

46   Igartua, *The Other Quiet Revolution*, 1.

47   See, among others, Hawkins, *Canada and Immigration*.

48   Ibid., 405.

49   "Pom" or "Pommy" is Australian slang for an English person.

50   Hammerton and Thomson, *Ten pound Poms*, 28–31.

51   Hutching, *Long Journey for Sevenpence*, 9–11.

52   Hawkins, *Canada and Immigration*, 438.

53   Hammerton and Thomson, *Ten pound Poms*, 29.

54   National Archives, Cabinet Minute 0051, 2–3.

55   Ibid., 3.

56   The heading of this section owes its origins to the approach adopted by Norman Longmate in his book *How We Lived Then: A History of Everyday life During the Second World War*.

57   Marwick, *British Society since 1945*, vii.

58   Seymour and Gardner, *Lynn*, 22–30.

59   Marwick, *British Society Since 1945*, 136.

60   *Evening Argus* (Brighton), 3 November 1951.

61   CSO, *Annual Abstract of Statistics* (1980), Table 2.8.

62   See, among others, Roberts, *Women and Families*; Natalie Higgins, "The Changing Expectations and Realities of Marriage" (PhD diss.) in Szreter and Fisher, *Sex Before the Sexual Revolution*, 42; and Kynaston, *Family Britain*, 583–96.

63   Kynaston, *Family Britain*, 572–3.

64   Ibid., 571–2.

65   See, among others, Young, and Willmott, *Family and Kinship in East London*; Stacey, *Tradition and Change*; Glass, ed., *Social Mobility in Britain*; and Blythe, *Akenfield*.

66   Zweig, *The British Worker*, 204.

67   Mugglestone, *"Talking Proper,"* 1.

68   *Television Heaven: The Frost Report*, http://www.televisionheaven.co.uk/frostreport.htm.

69   *Coventry Evening Telegraph*, 28 April 1952, quoted in Kynaston, *Family Britain*, 239.

70   *New Statesman*, 7 April 1956, quoted in Kynaston, *Family Britain*, 648.

71   Marwick, *British Society since 1945*, 28.

72   National Archives, www.nationalarchives.gov.uk/pathways/citizenship/brave_new_world/welfare.htm (accessed 21 February 2012).

73   Bumsted, *The Peoples of Canada*, 353–9.

74   National Archives, CAB 195/11/1, 3 February 1954.

75   Kynaston, *Family Britain*, 448–9.

76   *Daily Telegraph*, http://www.telegraph.co.uk/comment/3643823/Enoch-Powells-Rivers-of-Blood-speech.html (accessed 27 February 2012).

77   Kynaston, *Family Britain*, 256.

78   Green, *Them*, 90–91.

79   Mitchell and Jones, *Second Abstract of British Historical Statistics*, 106.

80   Leibling, *RAC Foundation for Motoring: Car Ownership in Great Britain*, 3.

81   Marwick, *British Society since 1945*, 91.

82   Johns, *St Ann's, Nottingham*, 54.

83   Marwick, *British Society since 1945*, 91.

84   See, among others, Jay, *Calder Hall*.

85   Krenz, *Deep Waters*, 135.

86   See Economic and Social Data Service, *SN 6099 –'Brain Drain' Debate*.

87   Savage, *Teenage*, iii.

88   Kynaston, *Family Britain*, 538.

89   Harper and Constantine, *Migration and Empire*, 38.

Chapter 2: Why Emigrate? Why Canada?

1   Agnes Butcher (pseud.).

2   May Preston (pseud.).

3   Richard and Heather Nash (pseuds.).

4   Robertson Davies (1913–1995) is one of Canada's best-known and distinguished novelists. His eighteen books include *Tempest-Tost* (1951) and *Fifth Business* (1970).

5   Charles Hall interviewed by A.J. Hammerton, Montreal, QC, 29 October 2000.

6   Richard Nash interviewed by A.J. Hammerton, Nanaimo, BC, 16 October 2000.

7   Kynaston, *Austerity Britain 1945–51*, 510–11.

8   Marwick, *British Society Since 1945*, 48.

9   Hammerton and Thomson, *Ten pound Poms*, 84–7. Hammerton and Thomson examine teenagers' mixed emotions regarding family migration and provide examples of resistance.

10   Pamela Austin interviewed by A.J. Hammerton, Lachine, Quebec, 13 July 2000.

11   Childs, *Britain Since 1945*, 127.

12   See Barber, *Immigrant Domestic Servants in Canada*, 14–19; Barber, "Hearing Women's Voices," 68–76.

13   Hammerton and Thomson, *Ten pound Poms*, 66–67.

14   Clarke, *Hope and Glory*, 290–93.

15   See Barber, "Sunny Ontario for British Girls, 1900–30," in Burnet, ed., *Looking into My Sister's Eyes*, 55–73.

16   Hammerton and Thomson, *Ten pound Poms*, 29–34.

17   Anne Graves interviewed by A.J. Hammerton, Nanaimo, BC, 30 July 2000.

18   Malcolmson, *Nella Last's Peace*, 175. The collection of Nella Last's diaries also include *Nella Last's War* and *Nella Last in the 1950s*. The original of Nella Last's diary is held in the Mass Observation Archive at the University of Sussex.

Chapter 3: Crossing the Atlantic

1   According to the *Ottawa Citizen*, 13 February 1967, these words of Winston Churchill, spoken in 1952, were used on a poster outside the office of H.L. Voisey, Canada's immigration director.

2   Anne Graves interviewed by A.J. Hammerton, Nanaimo, BC, 30 July 2000.

3   Ibid.

4   Ibid.

5   Ibid.

6   Ibid.

7   Ibid.

8   Ibid.

9   Toronto *Financial Post*, 14 March 1964. Cited by Hawkins, *Canada and Immigration*, 448.

10   Both Drew and Bell were Conservatives who supported immigration from Britain.

11   Hawkins, *Canada and Immigration*, 63.

12 Ibid., 237–87.

13 Ibid.

14 See Chapter 1.

15 Hawkins, *Canada and Immigration*, 262–3.

16 This is an error in James Roland's memory. He really meant passage loan scheme, as the Canadian government did not offer an assisted passage package.

17 Charles Hall interviewed by A.J. Hammerton, Montreal, QC, 19 June 2001.

18 Florence Foster interviewed by A. Coleman and S. Schwinghame, Lawrencetown, NS, 17 July 2001.

19 See Chapter 1 for further comment about wartime child evacuation.

20 Maisie Lugar and Stanley Goat interviewed by A. Coleman, Pier 21, Halifax, NS, 2 August 2005.

21 Ibid.

22 Hawkins, *Canada and Immigration*, 335.

23 National Fish was a harvester, procurer, processor, and marketer of fish and seafood.

24 Gerrard Lodge was a rooming house and is now a registered heritage property.

25 Florence Foster interviewed by A. Coleman and S. Schwinghame, Lawrencetown, NS, 17 July 2001.

26 Unnamed senior civil servant, interviewed by F. Hawkins, Ottawa, ON, 16 June 1966; Hawkins, *Canada and Immigration*, 337.

27 Steinbeck, *Travels with Charley*.

28 Ron Inch interviewed by A.J. Hammerton, Etobicoke, ON, 30 June 2000.

29 See Hammerton and Thomson, *Ten pound Poms*; and Hutching, *Long Journey for Sevenpence*.

Chapter 4: Adaptation

1 Interview with Sarah Walsh (pseud.).

2 Knowles, *Strangers at Our Gates*, 177. Knowles notes that it was the urbanized and industrialized provinces—Ontario, Quebec, Alberta, and British Columbia—that benefited most from postwar immigration.

3 Francis, Jones, and Smith, *Destinies: Canadian History Since Confederation*, Chapter 17, "The Making of Modern Quebec," 396–420, provides one of many textbook accounts of the Quiet Revolution.

4 Palmer, "Reluctant Hosts," 297–98.

5 Richard Nash interviewed by A.J. Hammerton, Nanaimo, BC, 17–18 June 2001.

6 Pamela Austin interviewed by A.J. Hammerton, Lachine, QC, 13 July 2000.

7 See Behiels, *Quebec and the Question of Immigration*; and Francis, Jones, and Smith, *Destinies: Canadian History Since Confederation* (Chapter 17, "The Making of Modern Quebec").

8 Finkel and Conrad, *History of the Canadian Peoples, 1867 to the Present*, 408. The authors state that in Montreal, church attendance dropped by half in the 1960s. In 1946 there were 2,000 new priests in Quebec; in 1970 only 100.

9 Watson, *Being English in Scotland*, 96–98.

10   Hammerton and Thomson, *Ten pound Poms*, 147–153 ("What's a Pommie bastard, mum?").

11   Jackel, *A Flannel Shirt and Liberty*, xx. See also, Dunae, *Gentlemen Emigrants*. Jackel suggests that English gentlewomen may have been less subject to suspicion than the gentlemen emigrants.

12   Godfrey, *No Englishman Need Apply*, 17.

13   Ibid., 53.

14   Ibid., 77.

15   Ron Inch interviewed by A.J. Hammerton, Etobicoke, ON, 30 June 2000.

16   Broadfoot, *The Immigrant Years*, 192.

17   Norma Inch interviewed by A.J. Hammerton, Etobicoke, ON, 30 June 2000.

18   Iacovetta and Korinek, "Jell-O Salads, One-Stop Shopping, and Maria the Homemaker: The Gender Politics of Food," in Epp et al., eds., *Sisters or Strangers?* 190–230. See also Iacovetta, *Gatekeepers*, Chapter 6, "Culinary Containment? Cooking for the Family, Democracy, and Nation," 137–69; and Iacovetta, Korinek, and Epp, *Edible Histories*.

19   Iacovetta and Korinek, "Jell-O Salads," in Epp, Iacovetta, and Swyripa, eds., *Sisters or Strangers?*, 197–98.

20   Bully beef was corned beef imported from Argentina.

21   Charles Hall interviewed by A.J. Hammerton, Montreal, QC, 19 June 2001.

22   Ron Inch interviewed by A.J. Hammerton, Etobicoke, ON, 30 June 2000.

23   For a social history of alcohol in Canada see Heron, *Booze: A Distilled History*.

24   Norma Inch interviewed by A.J. Hammerton, Etobicoke, ON, 30 June 2000.

25   The importance of the senses in understanding the past is now receiving considerable attention in historical studies. See, for example, Classen, *Worlds of Senses: Exploring the Senses in History and across Cultures*; Langfield and Maclean's chapter, "'But Pineapple I'm Still Wary Of'": Sensory Memories of Jewish Women Who Migrated to Australia as Children, 1938–39," in Hammerton and Richards, *Speaking to Immigrants*, 83–109, is one interesting study of the significance of the senses in migrant memories.

26   Hammerton and Thomson, *Ten pound Poms*, 133.

27   You may find it instructive to look at similar use of this type of language in other testimony extracts.

28   Charles Hall interviewed by A.J. Hammerton, Montreal, QC, 19 June 2001.

29   Broadfoot, *The Immigrant Years*, 53. "War bride" was a misnomer, as Broadfoot and others have pointed out. These women had often been married for a few years when they migrated to Canada. Calling them "war brides" highlighted romance rather than the realities of some of their lives.

30   Norma Inch interviewed by A.J. Hammerton, Etobicoke, ON, 30 June 2000.

Chapter 5: Earning a Living

1   Massey, "How Immigration Could Revitalise Scotland," *Scotsman*, 7 July 2012, 27.

2   "Work and Occupations" in Borgatta and Montgomery, *Encyclopedia of Sociology*, 3261–3269.

3   See, http://wall.oise.utoronto.ca/.

4   "'Labour Force: Definitions and Measurement,'" in *International Encyclopedia of the Social Sciences* 8 (1972), 469–474.

5   Strong-Boag, "Canada's Wage-Earning Wives and the Construction of the Middle Class, 1945–60," 14.

6   Lunn, *Star Weekly Magazine*, "Men, let's get tough," 20 Feb. 1960, 12.

7   Bettelheim, *Star Weekly Magazine*, "Fathers Shouldn't Be Mothers," 9 Aug. 1958, 6.

8   Strong-Boag, "Canada's Wage-Earning Wives," 16.

9   See Chapter 2.

10   Bertaux-Wiame, "The Life History Approach to the Study of Internal Migration."

11   *The Times*, "Canada Department of Citizenship and Immigration," 30 November 1959, iii.

12   National Archives, Cabinet Minute 0051, 2.

13   Ibid., 4.

14   Ibid., 5.

15   Li, "Immigrants' Propensity to Self-Employment," 1106–28.

16   Schwarz et al., eds., *Chambers English Dictionary*, 7th ed.

17   Kenneth Cecil went on to comment that, "Level 5 is reserved for people who were born speaking French."

18   *The Montreal Protocol on Substances that Deplete the Ozone Layer*, signed in 1987, is an international treaty designed to protect the ozone layer by phasing out the production of numerous substances believed to be responsible for ozone depletion.

19   This meteorological event was particularly severe in Quebec and Ontario, where many farmers did not have electricity for four weeks or more and many lost their herds.

20   Clark, *Growth and Governance of Canadian Universities*, 19–25.

21   Ibid., 24.

22   See Brouwer, *Immigrants Need Not Apply*.

23   See Chapter 1.

24   In addition to being a famous pioneering nurse, Florence Nightingale was one of the first people to make a recording. Her voice can be heard online in the Oral History collection at the British Library at http://www.bl.uk/oralhistory/.

25   Flynn, "Race, the State, and Caribbean Nurses, 1950–1962," in Feldburgh, Ladd-Taylor, and Li, eds., *Women, Health and Nation*, 251.

26   Ibid., 249–60.

27   Francis, Jones, and Smith, *Journeys: A History of Canada*, 293.

28   Hanson, *Will You Walk a Little Faster*, 135.

29   See Hammerton and Thomson, *Ten pound Poms*.

30   See among others, Strong-Boag, "Canada's Wage-Earning Wives"; Armstrong, *Labour Pains: Women's Work in Crisis*; Strong-Boag, "Independent Women, Problematic Men"; and Gairdner, *The Trouble with Canada*.

31   Strong-Boag, "Canada's Wage-Earning Wives," 11.

32   See among others, Pringle, "How I Broke Out of Solitary Confinement," *Chatelaine*, May 1948, 34; and Clarke, "Stop Pitying the Underworked Housewife," *Maclean's*, 19 July 1958, 37–38.

33   See among others, Hardyment, *From Mangle to Microwave*; Davidson, *A Woman's Work Is Never Done*; and Cowan, *More Work for Mother*.

34 *Planning to Work in Canada? An Essential Workbook for Newcomers*, http://www. credentials.gc.ca/immigrants/workbook/index.asp (accessed 8 June 2012).

Chapter 6: Home, Family, Community

1 George Santayana, 1863–1952, philosopher, poet, essayist, and novelist.

2 The Pointe Claire Yacht Club, now an important community landmark, dates its origin to 1879.

3 Clark, *The Suburban Society*, 98.

4 Ibid., 37.

5 See Strong-Boag, "Home Dreams," for one analysis.

6 See Owran, *Born at the Right Time*, especially Chapter 3, "Safe in the Hands of Mother Suburbia: Home and Community, 1950–1965," in which Owran discusses the significance of suburbia for the baby-boom generation.

7 Hugh Morris Woods, interviewed by A.J. Hammerton, Mississauga, ON, 24 October 2000.

8 As well as offering mortgage refinancing, Household Finance provides personal loans.

9 See Korinek, *Roughing It in the Suburbs*; and Fraser, *Chatelaine: A Woman's Place*, especially Chapter 3, "Her Home, Her Castle."

10 Parr, *Domestic Goods*, 143–64. Parr addresses the significance of maple furniture in Canadian consumer culture.

11 Ed Broadbent graduated from Trinity College, University of Toronto, in 1959, and went on to obtain a PhD at the University of Toronto in 1966. First elected to the House of Commons in 1968, Broadbent was leader of the federal New Democratic Party from 1975 to 1989.

12 Norma Inch (Levy) interviewed by A.J. Hammerton, Etobicoke, ON, 30 June 2000.

13 Ron Inch interviewed by A.J. Hammerton, Etobicoke, ON, 30 June 2000.

14 Norma Inch (Levy) interviewed by A.J. Hammerton, Etobicoke, ON, 30 June 2000.

15 Elizabeth Anne Graves (Parker) interviewed by A.J. Hammerton, Nanaimo, BC, 30 July 2000.

16 See Conrad, "'Sundays Always Make Me Think of Home': Time and Place in Canadian Women's History," in Latham and Pazdro, eds., *Not Just Pin Money*, 3–4.

17 Hammerton and Thomson, *Ten pound Poms*, 276.

18 Family responsibilities would also have led to return migration from Canada.

19 Harper, *Adventurers and Exiles: The Great Scottish Exodus*, 238.

20 Cameron, Haines, and McDougall Maude, *English Immigrant Voices*, xxx–xxxiv.

21 Gautier, "Letter Sheets of Canada and Newfoundland."

22 Cameron, Haines, and McDougall Maude, *English Immigrant Voices*, xxx.

23 See Table 2, Chapter 3.

24 Hammerton and Thomson, *Ten pound Poms*, 13.

25 Clark, *The Suburban Society*, 139.

26 Walsh and High, "Rethinking the Concept of Community," explore Canadian scholarship dealing with the concept of community. See also Bender, *Community and Social Change in America*; Stanger-Ross, "An Inviting Parish." Bender examines the expansion of the Toronto Italian community across territorial

boundaries in the postwar era. See also Loewen and Friesen, *Immigrants in Prairie Cities*. Their Chapter 6, "Gender and Family in Hybrid Households," shows how professional migrants of various ethnic backgrounds in the latter twentieth century tended to disperse in the suburbs but maintain ethnic ties through technology and associations.

27 See Chapter 7 for more on this topic.

28 Strong-Boag, "Home Dreams," 491; Clark, *Suburban Society*, 121.

29 Strong-Boag, "Home Dreams," 490.

30 Ibid., 495–503.

31 Collin, "A Housing Model for Lower- and Middle-class Wage Earners in a Montreal Suburb," 4. Collin highlights some of the diversities in suburban development while discussing the Montreal suburb of Saint-Leonard.

32 Richard Nash interviewed by A.J. Hammerton, Nanaimo, BC, 16 October 2000.

33 Davidoff and Hall, *Family Fortunes*, 370–75.

34 See http://www.viu.ca/milnergardens. Princess Diana and Prince Charles visited the house in 1986, and the Queen and Prince Philip stayed at the house for three days in October 1987.

35 Jennifer Short interviewed by A.J. Hammerton, Nanaimo, BC, 15 October 2000.

36 Charles Hall interviewed by A.J. Hammerton, Town of Mount Royal, QC, 29 October 2000.

37 Elliott, "English," in Magocsi, ed., *Encyclopedia of Canada's Peoples*, 474–83.

38 Storey, *The St. George's Society of Toronto 1834–1967*, 11.

39 Gail Rayment (Acland) interviewed by A.J. Hammerton, Toronto, ON, 2 July 2000.

40 Richard Nash interviewed by A.J. Hammerton, Nanaimo, BC, 16 October 2000.

41 Elizabeth Anne Graves (Parker) interviewed by A.J. Hammerton, Nanaimo, BC, 30 July 2000.

42 Taylor, *Multiculturalism and "The Politics of Recognition*," 25–31.

43 Burnet, "Multiculturalism, Immigration and Racism," 35–39. Burnet argues that newer immigrant groups who are most concerned about economic discrimination and racism are more likely to value human rights rather than the collective group rights promoted by more established immigrants and their descendants, such as the Ukrainian-Canadian proponents of multiculturalism.

44 Jennifer Short interviewed by A.J. Hammerton, Nanaimo, B.C., 15 October 2000.

Chapter 7: National Identity

1 This joke appeared in a number of guises on various Internet sites. This one was accessed on http://www.rantnroll.com/html/canadian (accessed 22 September 2012).

2 Prior to 1947 there was no such thing in law as a Canadian citizen. Canadian nationals were legally defined as British subjects. However, citizenship was already up for discussion. As Liberal cabinet minister Paul J.J. Martin stated, it was important that "all of us are able to say with pride and say with meaning 'I am a Canadian citizen'" (*House of Commons Debates*, 28 Oct 1945). A new citizenship act was passed in 1977, which is still in force today.

3 Habermas, "The Public Sphere," in Seideman, ed., *Jurgen Habermas on Society and Politics*, 231.

4   Bechhofer et al., "Constructing National Identity," 527.

5   Smith, *National Identity.*

6   Anderson, *Imagined Communities,* 141–2.

7   Ibid., 145.

8   Resnick, *Thinking English Canada,* 25–34.

9   Ayres, "National No More: Defining English Canada," *American Review of Canadian Studies* 25, 2/3 (1995).

10   See Colley, "Britishness and Otherness: An Argument," 309–29; and Said, *Orientalism: Western Representations of the Orient.*

11   Colley, "Britishness and Otherness," 309–29.

12   Watson, *Being English in Scotland,* 169.

13   Our thanks for this observation, which was made in an Australian context, to Curthoys, "Identity Crisis," 167.

14   Igartua, *The Other Quiet Revolution,* 221.

15   See Ayres, "National No More: Defining English Canada," 181–201; Ayres, "Political Process and Popular Protest: The Mobilization Against Free Trade in Canada," *American Journal of Economics and Sociology* 55 (1996): 473–88; and Ayres, "Political Process and Popular Protest: The Mobilization Against Free Trade in Canada," *American Journal of Economics and Sociology* 55 (1996): 107–23.

16   Ayres, "National No More," 181–201.

17   Ibid.

18   See, among others, Colls, *Identity of England*; Paxman, *The English: A Portrait of a People*; and Marr, *The Day Britain Died.*

19   Paxman, *The English,* 1.

20   Marr, *The Day Britain Died.*

21   Strictly speaking, these British passports were European Union (EU) passports. The old blue British passports ceased to exist after Britain joined the EU, which was known at the time of joining as the European Economic Community (ECC). A number of the interviewees used these terms interchangeably. The red EU passport is technically British with a clear statement within saying, "Her Britannic Majesty's Secretary of State requests and requires in the Name of Her Majesty all those who it may concern to allow the bearer to pass freely without let or hindrance, and to afford the bearer such assistance and protection as may be necessary."

22   We appreciate that Pembrokeshire is in Wales, but Robin flew to England, where he stayed in the Union Jack Club, of which he was a member, in London.

23   Howell, *Blood, Sweat, Cheers: Sport and the Making of Modern Canada,* 7.

24   The Six Nations tournament is an annual competition involving national rugby teams from England, France, Ireland, Italy, Scotland, and Wales. On international weekends the Heart and Crown is usually heaving with expats wearing the favours of their national team.

25   Hutching, *Long Journey for Sevenpence,* 168.

26   Watson, *The Invisible Diaspora: The English in Scotland, 1945–2000,* 239.

27   Anne Graves interviewed by A.J. Hammerton, Nanaimo, BC, 15–18 June 2001.

28   Hugh Woods interviewed by A.J. Hammerton, Mississauga, ON, 2–3 April 2001.

29   See, among others, Trudeau, *Federalism and the French Canadians.*

30   Bumsted, *The Peoples of Canada,* 372.

31 Ibid.

32 Historian John Saywell has argued that the October Crisis was a turning point in Canadian history. See Saywell, *Quebec 70: A Documentary Narrative*, 152.

33 Charles Hall interviewed by A.J. Hammerton, Montreal, QC, 29 October 2000.

34 Act II, Scene II in John Osborne's *Look Back in Anger*, first performed in London in 1956.

35 The Historiographer Royal is an unpaid member of the Royal Household, with responsibilities for advising the Monarch on matters relating to Scottish history.

36 Correspondence with T.C. Smout, 10 December 2002.

37 Penny, *Bury Your Dead*, 24.

38 Watson, *Being English in Scotland*, 173.

39 Hammerton and Thomson, *Ten pound Poms*, 325. This book was about British—that is English, Welsh, Scottish, and Northern Irish—immigrants. It is generally accepted that the word *Pom* refers to English people. In other words, a Scot would not be considered a Pom.

Afterword

1 Locating the Hidden Diaspora conference promotional information, http://www.northumbria.ac.uk/sd/academic/sass/about/humanities/history/research/projects/englishdiaspora/ web site accessed 21/November 2012.

2 See Hammerton and Thomson, *Ten pound Poms*; Hutching, *Long Journey for Sevenpence*; and Watson, *Being English in Scotland*.

3 Thomson, "Moving Stories," 25.

4 See Erickson, *Invisible Immigrants*; Hammerton and Thomson, *Ten pound Poms*; and Watson, *The Invisible Diaspora*.

BIBLIOGRAPHY

Interviews

1. Oral and written testimonies gathered by the authors and Carleton University graduate students. All names are pseudonyms, except those marked with an asterisk (*).

Allen, Reggie
Andrews, Abbi
Baldwin, Margaret
Baldwin, Robert
Bell, Margaret
Billington, Nigel
Bulmer, Emma
Bulmer, Gordon
Butcher, Agnes
Butcher, Frank
Carter, Jenny
Cecil, Janet
Cecil, Kenneth
Charles, Jeremy
Charles, Mary
Connor, Pat
Cranston, Avril
Derbyshire, John
Eliot, Nora
Flower, Maggie

Hinton, Charlotte
Irvine, Mary
Jones, Sue
King, John
Knight, Tom
Lanson, Robin
Leonard, James
MacKay, Roger
Maltby, Tony
Marriot, Hannah
Martin, Joan
Martin, Tom
Minto, James
Plunkett, Jeremy
Preston, May
Rankin, Tom
Robinson, Peter*
Roland, James
Semple, Peter

Sinclair-Chang, Isobel
Smith, David
Steven, John
Stone, Alastair
Summers, Elizabeth
Taylor, Noel*
Thoms, Alan
Trueman, Barbara
Trueman, Roy
Turner, Christine
Turner, Les
Walsh, Sarah
Walsh, Tom
Watson, Rob
Whilesmith, Peter
Whilesmith, Rosemary
Williams, Vicky
Wood, Arthur
Wood, Doreen

2. Oral testimonies recorded by A.J. Hammerton. None are pseudonyms.

Austin, Pamela
Graves, Anne
Hall, Charles

Inch, Norma
Inch, Ron
Nash, Richard

Rayment, Gail
Short, Jennifer
Woods, Hugh

3. Oral testimonies recorded by A. Coleman and S. Schwinghame. None are pseudonyms.

Foster, Florence

Goat, Stanley

Lugar, Maisie

Books

Anderson, A.B., and J. Frideres. *Ethnicity in Canada: Theoretical Perspectives*. Toronto: Butterworths, 1981.

Anderson, B. *Imagined Communities: Reflections on the Origins and Spread of Nationalism*. London: Verso, 1992.

Armstrong, P. *Labour Pains: Women's Work in Crisis*. Toronto: Women's Press, 1984.

Barber, M. *Immigrant Domestic Servants in Canada*, Canada's Ethnic Groups booklet no. 16. Ottawa: Canadian Historical Association, 1991.

Beak, T.W. *We Came to Canada: Facts and Figures about Canadian Life by a Family which Emigrated from Britain*. Montreal: Burton, 1960.

Behiels, M.D. *Quebec and the Question of Immigration: From Ethnocentrism to Ethnic Pluralism, 1900–1985*, Canada's Ethnic Groups booklet no. 18. Ottawa: Canadian Historical Association, 1998.

Bender, T. *Community and Social Change in America*. Baltimore: Johns Hopkins University Press, 1978.

Bertaux, D., ed. *Biography and Society*. Beverly Hills: Sage, 1981.

Bilson, G. *The Guest Children: The Story of the British Child Evacuees Sent to Canada During World War II*. Saskatoon: Fifth House, 1988.

Bissoondath, N. *Selling Illusions: the Cult of Multiculturalism in Canada*. Toronto: Penguin Books, 2002.

Blythe, R. *Akenfield: Portrait of an English Village*. London: Penguin Books, 1969.

Borgatta, E.F., and M.L. Montgomery, eds. *Encyclopedia of Sociology*. New York: Macmillan Reference USA, 2000.

Boyle, P., and K. Halfacree. *Migration and Gender in the Developed World*. London: Routledge, 1999.

Broadfoot, B. *The Immigrant Years: From Europe to Canada 1945–1969*. Vancouver: Douglas and McIntyre, 1986.

Brouwer, A. *Immigrants Need Not Apply*. Ottawa: Caledon Institute of Social Policy, 1999.

Bueltman, T., D.T. Gleeson, and D.M. Macraild, eds. *Locating the English Diaspora, 1500–2010*. Liverpool: Liverpool University Press, 2012.

Bumsted, J.M. *The Peoples of Canada: A Post-Confederation History*. Don Mills: Oxford University Press, 2004.

Burnet, J.R., ed. *Looking into My Sister's Eyes*. Toronto: Multicultural History Society of Ontario, 1986.

Cameron, E. *Multiculturalism and Immigration in Canada*. Toronto: Canadian Scholars' Press, 2004.

Cameron, W., S. Haines, and M. McDougall Maude. *English Immigrant Voices: Labourers' Letters from Upper Canada*. Montreal: McGill-Queen's University Press, 2000.

Caunce, S. *Oral History and the Local Historian*. Harlow: Longman, 1994.

Childs, D. *Britain Since 1945: A Political History*. London: Routledge, 2000.

Clark, H.C. *Growth and Governance of Canadian Universities: an Insider's View*. Vancouver: UBC Press, 2000.

Clark, S.D. *The Suburban Society*. Toronto: University of Toronto Press, 1966.

Clarke, P. *Hope and Glory: Britain 1900–1990*. London: Penguin, 1996.

Classen, C. *Worlds of Senses: Exploring the Senses in History and across Cultures*. London: Routledge, 1993.

Colls, R. *Identity of England*. Oxford: Oxford University Press, 2002.

Cowan, R.S. *More Work for Mother*. New York: Basic Books, 1983.

Davidoff, L. and C. Hall. *Family Fortunes*. London and Chicago: Routledge, 1987.

Davidson, C. *A Woman's Work Is Never Done*. London: Chatto and Windus, 1982.

Devine, T.M. *The Scottish Nation, 1700–2000*. London: Allen Lane, 1999.

Dunae, P.A. *Gentlemen Emigrants: From the British Public Schools to the Canadian Frontier*. Vancouver: Douglas and McIntyre, 1981.

Epp, M., F. Iacovetta, and F. Swyripa. *Sisters or Strangers? Immigrant, Ethnic, and Racialized Women in Canadian History*. Toronto: University of Toronto Press, 2004.

Erickson, C. *Invisible Immigrants: The Adaptation of English and Scottish Immigrants in Nineteenth-Century America*. London: London School of Economics, 1990.

Feldburgh, G., M. Ladd-Taylor, and A. Li, eds. *Women, Health and Nation: Canada and the United States since 1945*. Montreal: McGill-Queen's University Press, 2003.

Finkel, A. and M. Conrad. *History of the Canadian Peoples, 1867 to the Present*. Toronto: Pearson Education Canada, 2002.

Francis, R.D., R. Jones, and D.B. Smith. *Journeys: A History of Canada*. Independence, KY: Cengage Learning, 2009.

——. *Destinies: Canadian History Since Confederation*, 3rd ed. Toronto: Harcourt Brace Canada, 1996.

Fraser, S., ed. *Chatelaine: A Woman's Place*. Toronto: Key Porter, 1997.

Gairdner, W.D. *The Trouble with Canada*. Toronto: BPS Books, 1991.

Gellner, E. *Nations and Nationalism*. London: John Wiley, 1998.

Glass, D.V., ed. *Social Mobility in Britain*. London: Routledge and Keegan Paul, 1967.

Godfrey, D. *No Englishman Need Apply*. Toronto: Macmillan of Canada, 1965.

Green, J. *Them: Voices from the Immigrant Community in Contemporary Britain*. London: Martin Secker and Warburg, 1990.

Greenhill, P. *Ethnicity in the Mainstream: Three Studies of English Canadian Culture in Ontario*. Montreal: McGill-Queen's University Press, 1994.

Hammerton, A.J. and A. Thomson. *Ten pound Poms: Australia's Invisible Immigrants*. Manchester: Manchester University Press, 2005.

Hammerton, A.J. and E. Richards. *Speaking to Immigrants: Oral Testimony and the History of Australian Migration*. Canberra: History Program and Centre for Immigration and Multicultural Studies, Research School of Social Sciences, The Australian National University, 2002.

Hanson, P. *Will You Walk a Little Faster*. Bloomington, IN.: Trafford Publishing, 2004.

Hardyment, C. *From Mangle to Microwave: The Mechanisation of Housework*. Oxford: Polity Press, 1988.

Harper, M. *Adventurers and Exiles: The Great Scottish Exodus*. London: Profile Books, 2003.

——. *Scotland No More? The Scots Who Left Scotland in the Twentieth Century*. Edinburgh: Luath Press, 2012.

Harper, M., and S. Constantine. *Migration and Empire*. Oxford: Oxford University Press, 2010.

Hawkins, F. *Canada and Immigration: Public Policy and Public Concern*. Montreal: McGill-Queen's University Press, 1988.

Heron, C. *Booze: A Distilled History*. Toronto: Between the Lines, 2003.

Howell, C. *Blood, Sweat, Cheers: Sport and the Making of Modern Canada*. Toronto: University of Toronto Press, 2004.

Hutching, M. *Long Journey for Sevenpence: Assisted Immigration to New Zealand from the United Kingdom 1947–1975*. Victoria, New Zealand: Victoria University Press, 1999.

Iacovetta, F. *Gatekeepers: Reshaping Immigrant Lives in Cold War Canada*. Toronto: Between the Lines, 2006.

Iacovetta, F., V.J. Korinek, and M. Epp, eds. *Edible Histories, Cultural Products: Towards a Canadian Food History*. Toronto: University of Toronto Press, 2012.

Igartua, J. *The Other Quiet Revolution: National Identities in English Canada 1945–71*. Vancouver: UBC Press, 2006.

Jackel, S. *A Flannel Shirt and Liberty; British Emigrant Gentlewomen in the Canadian West, 1880–1914*. Vancouver: UBC Press, 1982.

Jay, K. *Calder Hall: The Story of Britain's First Nuclear Power Station*. London: Methuen, 1956.

Johns, R. *St Ann's, Nottingham: Inner-city Voices*. Warwick: Plowright Press, 2002.

Knowles, V. *Strangers At Our Gates: Canadian Immigration and Immigration Policy, 1540–2006*. Toronto: Dundurn, 2007.

Korinek, V.J. *Roughing It in the Suburbs: Reading Chatelaine Magazine in the Fifties and Sixties*. Toronto: University of Toronto Press, 2000.

Krenz, K. *Deep Waters: The Ottawa River and Canada's Nuclear Adventure*. Montreal: McGill-Queen's University Press, 2004.

Kynaston, D., *Austerity Britain 1945–51*. London: Bloomsbury Publishing, 2007.

———. *Family Britain 1951–57*. London: Bloomsbury Publishing, 2009.

Latham, K., and R.J. Pazdro, eds. *Not Just Pin Money*. Victoria, BC: Camosun College, 1984.

Leibling, D. *RAC Foundation for Motoring: Car Ownership in Great Britain*. London: RAC Foundation, 2008.

Lerda, V.G., ed. *From Melting Pot to Multiculturalism: The Evolution of Ethnic Relations in the United States and Canada*. Rome: Bulzoni, 1990.

Loewen, R., and G. Friesen. *Immigrants in Prairie Cities*. Toronto: University of Toronto Press, 2009.

Longmate, N. *How We Lived Then: A History of Everyday Life During the Second World War*. London: Pimlico, 1971.

Lower, A. *Canadians in the Making: A Social History of Canada*. Toronto: Longmans, 1958.

Magocsi, P.R., ed. *Encyclopedia of Canada's Peoples*. Toronto: Buffalo, 1999.

Malcolmson, P. and R., eds. *Nella Last in the 1950s*. London: Profile Books, 2010.

———. *Nella Last's Peace*. London: Profile Books, 2008.

Marr, A. *The Day Britain Died*. London: Profile Books, 2000.

Marwick, A. *British Society since 1945*. London: Penguin, 2003.

Messamore, B., ed. *Canadian Migration Patterns: From Britain and North America*. Ottawa: University of Ottawa Press, 2004.

Mitchell, B.R., and H.G. Jones. *Second Abstract of British Historical Statistics.* Cambridge: Cambridge University Press, 1971.

Mugglestone, L. *"Talking Proper": The Rise of Accent as a Social Symbol.* Oxford: Clarendon Press, 1995.

Osborne, J. *Look Back in Anger.* London: Faber and Faber, 1956.

Owran, D. *Born at the Right Time: A History of the Baby Boom Generation.* Toronto: University of Toronto Press, 1996.

Parr, J. *Domestic Goods: The Material, the Moral, and the Economic in the Postwar Years.* Toronto: University of Toronto Press, 1999.

Paxman, J. *The English: A Portrait of a People.* London: Penguin, 1999.

Penny, L. *Bury Your Dead.* London: Minotaur Books, 2010.

Perks, R., and A. Thomson, eds. *The Oral History Reader,* 2nd edition. London: Routledge, 1998.

Pooley, C.G., and I. Whyte. *Migrants, Emigrants and Immigrants: A Social History of Migration.* London: UCL Press, 1991.

Rabinow, P. *The Foucault Reader: An Introduction to Foucault.* London: Pantheon, 1991.

Resnick, P. *Thinking English Canada.* Toronto: Stoddart Publishing, 1994.

Richmond, A.H. *Post-war Immigrants in Canada.* Toronto: University of Toronto Press, 1967.

Roberts, E. *Women and Families: An Oral History 1940–1970.* London: Wiley-Blackwell, 1995.

Said, E. *Orientalism: Western Representations of the Orient.* London: Routledge and Kegan Paul, 1978.

Savage, J. *Teenage: The Creation of Youth 1875–1945.* London: Pimlico, 2007.

Saywell, J.T. *Quebec 70: A Documentary Narrative.* Toronto: University of Toronto Press, 1971.

Schwarz, C. et al., eds. *Chambers English Dictionary,* 7th ed. Edinburgh: Chambers, 1991.

Seideman, S. ed. *Jurgen Habermas on Society and Politics: A Reader.* Boston: Beacon Press, 1989.

Seymour, L., and P. Gardner. *Lynn.* London: HarperCollins, 1984.

Smith, A.D. *Nationalism.* London: Polity, 1991.

Stacey, M. *Tradition and Change: A Study of Banbury.* Oxford: Oxford University Press, 1960.

Steinbeck, J. *Travels with Charley.* New York: Curtis Publishing, 1961.

Storey, A. *The St. George's Society of Toronto 1834–1967.* Agincourt, ON: Generation Press, 1987.

Summerfield, P. *Reconstructing Women's Wartime Lives.* Manchester: Manchester University Press, 1998.

Szreter, S., and K. Fisher. *Sex Before the Sexual Revolution: Intimate Life in England 1918–1963.* Cambridge: Cambridge University Press, 2010.

Taylor, C. *Multiculturalism and The Politics of Recognition.* Princeton: Princeton University Press, 1992.

Thompson, P. *The Voice of the Past: Oral History.* Oxford: Oxford University Press, 1988.

Trudeau, P. *Federalism and the French Canadians.* Toronto: Macmillan of Canada, 1980.

Tulchinsky, G. *Immigration in Canada: Historical Perspectives.* Mississauga, ON: Copp Clark Longman, 1994.

Watson, M. *Being English in Scotland.* Edinburgh: Edinburgh University Press, 2003.

Young, M., and P. Willmott. *Family and Kinship in East London.* London: Routledge, 1957.

Zelwiger-Bargielowska, I. *Austerity in Britain: Controls and Consumption.* Oxford: Oxford University Press, 2000.

Zweig, F. *The British Worker.* London: Penguin, 1952.

Academic Articles and Papers

Arango, J., D.S. Massey, G.Hugo, and A. Kouaouci. "An Evaluation of International Migration Theory: The North American Case." *Population and Development Review* 20 (1994).

Ayres, J.M. "Political Process and Popular Protest: The Mobilization Against Free Trade in Canada." *American Journal of Economics and Sociology* 55 (1996).

———. "National No More: Defining English Canada." *The American Review of Canadian Studies* 25, 2/3 (1995).

Badgley, K. "'As Long as He is an Immigrant from the United Kingdom': Deception, Ethnic Bias and Milestone Commemoration in the Department of Citizenship and Immigration, 1953–1965." *Journal of Canadian Studies* 34, 3 (1998).

Barber, M. "Hearing Women's Voices: Female Migration to Canada in the Early Twentieth Century." *Oral History* 33, 1 (2005).

Bechhofer, F., et al. "Constructing National Identity: Arts and Landlord Elites in Scotland." *Sociology* 33, 3 (1999).

Bertaux-Wiame, I. "The Life History Approach to the Study of Internal Migration." *Oral History* 7, 1 (1979).

Buckner, P. "English Canada—The Founding Generations: British Migration to North America 1815–1865," Canada House Lecture Series, No. 54 (London, 1993).

Burnet, J. "Multiculturalism, Immigration and Racism." *Canadian Ethnic Studies* 8, 1 (1975).

Colley, L. "Britishness and Otherness: An Argument." *Journal of British Studies* 31 (1992).

Collin, J.-P. "A Housing Model for Lower- and Middle-class Wage Earners in a Montreal Suburb: Saint-Leonard, 1955–1967." *Journal of Urban History* 24, 4 (1998).

Curthoys, A. "Identity Crisis: Nation and Gender in Australian History." *Gender and History* 5, 2 (1993).

Elliott, B. "The Genealogist and the Migration Historian." The J. Houston Memorial Lecture to Ontario Genealogical Society Seminar, 2000.

Foucault, M. "Nietzsche, Genealogy, History," in Rabinow, P., ed., *The Foucault Reader: An Introduction to Foucault's Thought* (London, 1991).

Hammerton, A.J. "Migrants, Mobility and Modernity: Understanding the Life Stories of English Emigrants to Canada, 1945–1971." *British Journal of Canadian Studies* 6, 1 (2003).

Howe, N., and R. Jackson. "Immigration: A Survey of Current State of Practice and Theory." Centre for Retirement Research Working Papers (Boston, 2004).

Li, P. "Immigrants Propensity to Self-Employment: Evidence from Canada." *International Migration Review* 35, 4 (2001)

Massey, D.S., J. Arango, G. Hugo, A. Kouaouci, A. Pellegrino, and J.E. Taylor. "Theories of International Migration: A Review and Appraisal." *Population and Development Review* 19, 3 (1993).

Palmer, H. "Reluctant Hosts: Anglo-Canadian Views of Multiculturalism in the Twentieth Century," in Tulchinsky, G., ed., *Immigration in Canada: Historical Perspectives*. Mississauga, ON: Copp Clark Longman, 1994.

Portes, A., W. Haller, and L.E. Guarnizo. "Transnational Entrepreneurs: The Emergence of an Alternative Form of Immigrant Adaptation." *American Sociological Review* 67, 2 (2002).

Ravenstein, E. "The Laws of Migration." *Journal of the Royal Statistical Society* 52, 2 (June 1889).

———. "The Laws of Migration." *Journal of the Statistical Society of London* 48, 2 (June 1885).

Stanger-Ross, J. "An Inviting Parish: Community without Locality in Postwar Italian Toronto." *Canadian Historical Review* 87, 3 (September 2006) .

Strong-Boag, V. "Canada's Wage-Earning Wives" in Armstrong, P., *Labour Pains: Women's Work in Crisis*, Toronto: Womens' Educational Press, 1984.

———. "Home Dreams: Women and the Suburban Experiment in Canada, 1945–60." *Canadian Historical Review* 72, 4 (1991).

———. "Independent Women, Problematic Men: First and Second-Wave Anti-Feminism in Canada from Goldwin Smith to Betty Steele." *Occasional Working Papers* 2, 2 (1993). Centre for Research in Women's Studies and Gender Relations, University of British Columbia.

Thompson, P. "Life Histories and the Analysis of Social Change," in Bertaux, D., ed., *Biography and Society*. London: Sage, 1982.

———. "Moving Stories: Oral History and Migration Studies." *Oral History* 27, 1 (1999).

Thomson, A., M. Frisch, and P. Hamilton. "The Memory and History Debates: Some International Perspectives." *Oral History* 22, 2 (1994).

Walsh, J.C., and S. High. "Rethinking the Concept of Community." *Histoire Sociale / Social History* 32, 64 (1999).

Newspapers and Magazines

Chatelaine
Coventry Evening Telegraph
Daily Express
Daily Telegraph
Evening Argus (Brighton)
Independent
Maclean's
New Statesman
Ottawa Citizen
Scotsman

Star Weekly Magazine
The Times
Toronto Financial Post
Weather Magazine

Websites, Film, and Miscellaneous Documents

Canada, *House of Commons, Debates*, 1955, 1254.

CSO, *Annual Abstract of Statistics* (1980).

Economic and Social Data Service, *SN 6099, "Brain Drain" Debate in the United Kingdom, c. 1950–1970.*

Eurostat, *Analysis and Forecasting of International Migration by Gender, Age and Major Groups (Part 2)*, Eurostat Working Paper 3/1999/E/no. 9 (Luxembourg, 2002).

Gaumont British News, *Canada Greets Immigrants from Britain*, Newsreel issue 1419, 11 August 1947.

Gautier, P. "Letter Sheets of Canada and Newfoundland: Forerunners and Unstamped Forms," *BNA Topics*, July–Aug–Sep, 3.

Locating the Hidden Diaspora, conference promotional information, http://www.northumbria.ac.uk/sd/academic/sass/about/humanities/history/research/projects/englishdiaspora/ web site accessed 21/November 2012.

National Archives (U.K.), CAB (Cabinet Secretary's notebooks), 195/11/1.

National Archives (U.K.), Cabinet Minute, 0051.

National Archives (U.K.), http://www.nationalarchives.gov.uk/pathways/citizenship/brave_new_world/welfare.htm.

National Archives, www.nationalarchives.gov.uk/documents/education/canada.pdf.

Planning to Work in Canada? An Essential Workbook for Newcomers, http://www.credentials.gc.ca/immigrants/workbook/index.asp.

Profiles United Kingdom. Immigration Research Series, Government of Canada, (Ottawa, 1996).

Television Heaven: The Frost Report, http://www.televisionheaven.co.uk/frostreport.htm.

U.K. Data Archive, *SN 6099—"Brain Drain" Debate in the United Kingdom, C1950–1970*, web site, http://www.data-archive.ac.uk/findingData/snDescription.asp?sn=6099.

United States Department of Agriculture War Food Administration, *Food Consumption Levels in the United States, Canada and the United Kingdom*. Washington, 1944.

Watson, M. "The Invisible Diaspora: The English in Scotland, 1945–2000." PhD thesis, University of Dundee, 2003.

Mass Observation, www.massobs.org.uk/index.htm.

Work and Lifelong Learning Research Network, http://wall.oise.utoronto.ca.

INDEX

Teacher's Guide to

Kids Today,
Parents Tomorrow

Mona Loy Klein

NEW HARBINGER
PUBLICATIONS, INC.

Distributed in the U.S.A. by Publishers Group West; in Canada by Raincoast Books; in Great Britain by Airlift Book Company, Ltd.; in South Africa by Real Books, Ltd.; in Australia by Boobook; and in New Zealand by Tandem Press.

Cover design © 1999 by Lightbourne Images
Edited by Kayla Sussell
Text design by Tracy Marie Powell
Text drawings by Atiba Azikiwe Andrews

We would like to acknowledge the following high school classroom teachers for their valuable input as peer reviewers for *Kids Today, Parents Tomorrow* and the *Teacher's Guide*: Joy Aiello of Discovery Bay; Janet Crocker of Newark; Joyce Hammond of Yuba City; Jennie Harris of Pico Rivera; Janica Paustian of Pleasant Hill; Lynn Thurston of Clovis; Linda Triplett of Fairfield; and Gelene Welch-Woods of Harbor City.

ISBN 1-57224-180-2

New Harbinger Publications' Website address: www.newharbinger.com

01   00   99

10   9   8   7   6   5   4   3   2   1

First printing

This book is dedicated to Janice De Benedetti for her commitment to the teachers and students of Home Economics Careers and Technology in California. This book is also dedicated to all Home Economics teachers who prepare the parents and professionals of tomorrow.